Florence R. Sanders

News-y Puget Sound

D0722002

CANNIBALS, WITCHES, AND DIVORCE

Selected Papers from the English Institute
New Series

Cannibals, Witches, and Divorce
ESTRANGING THE RENAISSANCE

 Selected Papers from the English Institute, 1985

New Series, no. 11

Edited by Marjorie Garber

THE JOHNS HOPKINS UNIVERSITY PRESS
BALTIMORE AND LONDON

The Johns Hopkins University Press, 701 West 40th Street, Baltimore, Maryland 21211
The Johns Hopkins Press Ltd., London

The paper used in this publication meets the minimum requirements of American National Standard for Information Sciences—Permanence of Paper for Printed Library Materials, ANSI Z39.48-1984.

∞

Library of Congress Cataloging-in-Publication Data

Cannibals, witches, and divorce.

  (Selected papers from the English Institute; 1985, new ser., no. 11)
  Bibliography, p.
  Contents: Spenser's Undersong/John Hollander—Suspended instruments/Patricia Parker—Shakespeare and the cannibals/Stephen Orgel—[etc.]
   1. English literature—Early modern, 1500–1700—History and criticism.   2. Shakespeare, William, 1564–1616—Criticism and interpretation.   3. Spenser, Edmund, 1552?–1599—Criticism and interpretation.   4. Milton, John, 1608–1674. Paradise lost. I. Garber, Marjorie B.   II. Series: Selected papers from the English Institute; new ser., no. 11.
PR413.C3   1987   820'.9'003   86-45472
ISBN 0-8018-3405-8 (alk. paper)

Contents

.

Introduction

The concept of a "Renaissance" implies both a priority and a belatedness. Indeed, the use of the term *Renaissance* is itself belated with respect to the phenomenon it purports to name. In order for a culture retrospectively to canonize a part of its historical production as a rebirth or a reconception, it must present the period in question as a repetition or return of something previously experienced and known. Whenever the term *Renaissance* is used, it therefore implies three distinct historical moments: the moment of naming, the moment of the phenomenon named, and the moment that phenomenon is said to repeat. Yet scholars of the English Renaissance today are increasingly viewing the moment of naming as a moment of appropriation, and the repetition as the return of the repressed. In their view, the moment of naming involves the telling of a story that suppresses or obscures, in the very process of its elaboration, other stories implicit in—and in some cases complicit with—its myth of etiology, its hypothetical recovering of lost origins. What is recognized (or re-cognized) in the Renaissance is then itself a construction, projected from and by the wishes and fears—as well as the presuppositions—of critics and scholars inevitably reading its cultural codes in relation to their own.

What do we recognize in the Renaissance? What, precisely, is being brought to birth? Or, to put the question somewhat differently, how do we conceive the other within the self? In recent years poststructuralist critics with a variety of theoretical interests—New Historicists, Marxists, cultural materialists, feminists, deconstructors—have given particular attention to the construction of the self in the period we know as the English Renaissance, and to what Michel Foucault has called "the techniques of the subject." The general term *cultural production,* used by New Historicist scholars to describe the complex interaction of Renaissance literary, historical, economic, and aesthetic or artistic texts, is likewise appropriated as a description of the production of a "self" as boundary, territory defined and demarcated by a contiguous, potentially invasive series of "others"—women, bar-barians, cannibals, witches, the French, the New World, death, and the world beyond the grave.

Recent theorists have argued that apparently subversive gestures on the part of a text or a culture are actually moves by the dominant ideology to appropriate the activity of subversion and to contain it. Likewise, encounters with the other, through the gaze or visual spec-tacle, as well as through more institutionalized cultural interventions like marriage or colonization, establish a pattern of dominance and marginalization that is available for exploitation. Estrangement as a strategy—the identification of an other against which the self may be not only measured but defined and demarcated—is found over and over again in the works of English Renaissance authors and, not sur-prisingly, with special frequency in the three most canonized figures of the English Renaissance, Spenser, Shakespeare, and Milton. Like Desdemona devouring up Othello's discourse of cannibals and An-thropaphagi with a "greedy ear," like Miranda sitting spellbound at the feet of her father, Prospero, while he instructs her in the niceties of the Elizabethan world picture and prepares her for a suitable Euro-pean marriage, readers, critics, and audiences of Renaissance cultural history and literature have exoticized certain tales of adventure and exploration, while establishing them as securely "other." When Othello kills himself by taking by the throat the Turk who is insep-arable from his persona as "civilized Venetian," these distinctions col-lapse. When Prospero says of Caliban, "This thing of darkness I ac-knowledge mine," a concomitant mirroring occurs. Yet in both instances the presence of an onstage audience distances even these recognitions, containing them through narrative encapsulation and control. Such a recognition becomes the story of someone else.

The essays in this collection all undertake, in different ways, to de-familiarize the familiar image of the Renaissance and to reconceive it to permit the repressed to return, to acknowledge the presence of the unassimilable ghost, the mark of difference of an age that is at once self and other.

The two essays on Spenser, by John Hollander and Patricia Parker, were delivered in the context of a 1984 English Institute panel on "The Lyric Spenser," which sought to approach Spenser not through *The Faerie Queene,* as is so often done by critics and readers, but through the specificity of his lyric achievement, and his discourse *on* and *about* as well as through the lyric mode. John Hollander's subtle intertextual audition of "Spenser's Undersong" traces that Spenserian coinage through its romantic revision, to make a compelling argument about the notion of a poetic source. Hollander charts the influence of Spenser's river song and notes the recurrence of the Spenserian signature trope of "tuning" a poetic voice or instrument "to the water's fall."

In "Suspended Instruments: Lyric and Power in the Bower of Bliss," Patricia Parker examines lyric as the poet's response to the monarch, exploring in her richly textured study of Guyon and Acrasia the question of feminine dominance and male resistance, the constitution of the gendered subject, and the representation of the dynamics of patronage and subjectivity in psychological and sociopolitical terms. Her reading of this famous episode draws on mythological and mythographic iconographies to elicit some of the problematics of a poet writing about, and for, a female monarch of disabling—and enabling—power.

The 1985 panel on "New Perspectives in Shakespeare" was arranged to offer some examples of the vital and productive work being done in poststructuralist Shakespeare studies: feminist, New Historicist, deconstructive. Janet Adelman's essay, "'Born of Woman': Fantasies of Maternal Power in *Macbeth,*" presents a fascinating reading of the play as encoding the fantasy of an absolute and destructive maternal power and, concurrently, the fantasy of escape from this power. Adelman sees Duncan, King of Scotland, as an ideal androgynous parent, whose murder leads to acute anxiety and psychological distress. The malign presence of the witches or of the "unsexed" Lady Macbeth threatens the male order and leads to a desire for a man not "born of woman." "The play," she suggests, "portrays the failure of the androgynous parent to protect his son, that son's consequent fall into the dominion of the bad mothers, and the final victory of a masculine order in which mothers no longer threaten because they no longer exist." The problem of being "a man" encountered by Macbeth and others in the play is "solved" by eliminating the female as a locus of power.

Both Steven Mullaney and Stephen Orgel use New Historicist concerns—with subversion and containment, power and patronage, the construction of the self and its defense against an alien (and often internalized) other—as ways to open up new readings of Shakespeare's plays. In "Brothers and Others, or the Art of Alienation," Steven Mullaney discusses *The Merchant of Venice* in the context of a consideration of New World voyages and encounters. Mullaney points out that what he calls "the commodity of strangers" has a symbolic as well as a commercial valency, and that not only dramatic but also historical characters are cultural constructions, theatrically conceived in both psychological and political terms. Investigating the relationships between Shylock and the case of Dr. Lopez, the Queen's Jewish physician, and between Portia and Elizabeth, he argues for the play as a staging area for cultural construction through difference—and, in his conclusion, for the social construction of the self as the foundation not only of Elizabethan and Jacobean theatricalization, but also for the modern subject.

Stephen Orgel's essay, "Shakespeare and the Cannibals," discusses the problem of the other in *The Tempest,* showing that the construction of the self is a commutative relation: Europeans figure themselves as Indians, Indians as Europeans. Commenting that "Shakespeare has taken everything from Montaigne except the point" of Montaigne's famous essay "Of Cannibals," Orgel persuasively reads Caliban's attack on Miranda as an imperial rape, dismaying not so much for its personal affront as for its political and dynastic consequences. Successful imperial rapes, he points out, like the rape of the Sabine women, have become sources of national pride. Miranda's value to her father lies in her virginity, which assures the legitimacy of her potential offspring. Orgel, like Mullaney, draws tantalizingly on details from New World narratives, and also on informed readings of the mythological subtext; his discussion of the famous crux about "widow Dido" is both enlightening and suggestive, and his essay includes a number of startling visual representations of the New World as it encodes and replicates the Old.

In my own essay, "Shakespeare's Ghost Writers," I attempt to take on the notorious authorship controversy and to present it as evidence for the implicit, internally subversive uncanniness of the play texts themselves. Rather than championing the cause of "the man from Stratford" or one of his celebrated rivals, Francis Bacon, the Earl of Oxford, Christopher Marlowe, even Queen Elizabeth herself—all suggested at one time or another as the true author of the Shakespeare plays—I ask what is at stake in the question of authorship and examine the ways in which the absence of documented Shakespearean biography has led poets and critics—as well as dedicated amateurs—to fashion a Shakespeare of their own. The authorship controversy, I suggest, is present *in* the plays, in the dissemination of authority and the preoccupation with written texts and handwriting evidence—the very "ocular proofs" offered by Stratfordians and anti-Stratfordians to demonstrate the legitimacy of their claims.

Mary Nyquist's long and closely argued discussion of Milton's Eve, his divorce tracts, and the exegetical tradition as recently examined by feminist Biblical scholars, "Gynesis, Genesis, Exegesis, and the Formation of Milton's Eve," was originally presented in a panel on "The Bible: Text and Ideology" at the 1985 meeting. Drawing on traditional and revisionist accounts of the creation of woman in Genesis 1 and 2, Nyquist explores the ideological ramifications of Milton's masculinist privileging of the Yahwist or "J" text over the Priestly or "P" text, and its consequences for the theory of marriage encoded in both the divorce tracts and *Paradise Lost*. By means of an analysis of the narrative distribution of the Genesis creation accounts, Nyquist argues that gendered subjectivity is given a historically specific bourgeois construction in *Paradise Lost*.

Taken together, these essays, critically situated at points of marginality made newly central in Renaissance studies, offer a lively overview of the range of work now being undertaken in the field.

And now, as Mary Shelley wrote of *Frankenstein,* her own project of estrangement, I have only to bid our hideous progeny go forth and prosper.

Marjorie Garber
Harvard University

CANNIBALS, WITCHES, AND DIVORCE

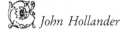

John Hollander

Spenser's Undersong

The undersong I shall consider is the refrain of *Prothalamion*, that magnificent spousal verse that Spenser wrote on the occasion of the announced marriage of the two daughters of the Earl of Somerset in the fall of 1596. It is a poem that descants upon itself obliquely, but with a sad power that not even Spenser's earlier *Epithalamion,* sung by the bridegroom and addressing itself as a text and as a trope for a masque or pageant, at the very end, could summon up. *Prothalamion* sings, you will remember, of these incipient paired marriages in an account of a walk along a river—*the* river—and an encounter first with nymphs gathering flowers on the bank as if for their own wedding day, then with a pair of swans swimming along the river, and a continued procession of swans, nymphs, and narrator along the river to Essex House, where the two bridegrooms receive their two "faire Brides," the two allegorical "faire birdes" having shed their figuration by metathesis of the letters *r* and *i* (of such words as "river" and "rival"). But the poem broods throughout over the poet's own "sullein care" and "freindlesse case" and "long fruitlesse stay/In princes court."

The poem's celebrated refrain is called an "undersong" at only one point. One of the nymphs sings what is in fact a monostrophic epithalamion embedded in the larger poem, occupying the sixth of its ten strophes (of eighteen lines each, a number Alastair Fowler has associated with Gemini, the twins of the swan and Leda, and hence with the geminations and doublings throughout the poem). The daughter of the flood—one of the group whom the poet, in the second strophe, encounters as they gather flowers, all looking themselves bridelike—sings this:

Ye gentle Birdes, the worlds faire ornament,
And heavens glorie, whom this hapie hower
Doth leade unto your lovers blisfull bower,

Joy may you have and gentle hearts content
Of your loves couplement:
And let faire *Venus,* that is Queene of love,
With her heart-quelling Sonne upon you smile,
Whose smile they say, hath vertue to remove
All Loves dislike, and friendships faultie guile
For ever to assoile.
Let endlesse Peace your steadfast hearts accord,
And blessed Plentie wait upon your bord,
And let your bed with pleasures chast abound,
That fruitfull issue may to you afford,
Which may your foes confound,
And make your joyes redound,
Upon your Brydale day, which is not long:
    Sweet *Themmes* run softlie, till I end my Song.

[91–108]

Five previous occurrences of the great refrain have already made it
resonant: the "not long" of the bridal day has been both "not far off,
not long in coming," and "not long, certainly not as long as the long
midsummer day of my own marriage poem." And the possessive pro-
noun of "my song" has been, until the nymph in either fictional in-
nocence or a sort of neoclassical allusiveness made it her own, purely
Spenser's, in as *propria persona* as he gets. But then, starting the next
strophe, the poet calls attention to the refrain. The other nymphs take
it up chorally and reinterpret the coming bridal day as their own. The
river bank affirms and authenticates the wording. And the whole
account resounds with consciousness of the degree to which the
refrain itself is an unwitting echo, both for the nymph and to the
degree that every refrain per se echoes its first occurrence.[1] This is
how he does so:

[Sweete *Themmes,* runne softlie, till I end my Song.]

So ended she; and all the rest around
To her redoubled that her undersong,
Which said, their brydale daye should not be long.
And gentle Eccho from the neighbour ground,
Their accents did resound.

[109–13]

—And then, speaking of the pair of swans he has encountered, the Somerset sisters both literally and figuratively "bred of Somers-heat"—

> So forth these joyous Birdes did passe along,
> Adowne the Lee, that to them murmured low,
> As he would speake, but that he lackt a tong
> Yet did by signes his glad affection show,
> Making his streame run slow.

[114–18]

The "Lee" down which the swans are swimming—and they are designated as doing so at their first appearance in the opening lines of the third strophe—is remarkably problematic throughout the poem; current scholarship is in debate about whether it means a lee-ward shore, the lea or meadow through which the river runs and in which the nymphs are first encountered gathering flowers, or, as here, the river Lee itself, which runs into the Thames at Greenwich. As Angus Fletcher has pointed out,[2] the complicated geography of the poem's itinerary implies that the Spenser who walked forth to ease his pain "along the shoare of silver streaming Themmes" would be walking upstream in the course of the ode, starting from Greenwich, following the procession of attendant swans who have joined the first two after they have somehow turned into the course of the Thames. Upstream, past the Temple, whose towers once housed the chivalric Templars and now remain emblems of how "they decay'd through pride," as well as houses "Where now the studious lawyers have their bowers." Upstream past these to Leicester House, built by Spenser's patron ("Where oft I gayned giftes and goodly grace / Of that great lord which therein wont to dwell, / Whose want too well now feeles my freendles case" [138–40]), now belonging to the Earl of Essex, the victor of the Battle of Cadiz, the Devereux whose name puns on "endless happinesse," but who, and whose head, would fall two years after he had had to pay for Spenser's funeral. Upstream with time, encountering on the banks the souvenirs of decayed hopes, expectations, tropes (Artegall replaced by the tribe of Coke and Bacon!). Upstream, and yet, the Thames being a tidal estuary, with the tide (which in Middle English means "time" and "season" as well), which forms its own countercurrent.

Consciousness of the current, the flow of the river, keeps breaking through the account of the poetic walk in the intermittent refrain. In considering it, one wants to listen for a moment to the earlier refrain of *Epithalamion,* the great "song made in lieu of many ornaments" for his own wedding, the transcendental epithalamium that he figuratively sang as poet-bridegroom, and into which he imported a mythological pageant. In place of the conventional "io Hymen Hymenaee" of Catullus' epithalamium, we hear the characteristic Spenserian alexandrine of closure, always rhyming with the word "sing" in the penultimate short line of the long, complex stanzas: "So I unto myself alone shall sing:/The woods shall to me answer and their echo ring" (17–18). This refrain refigures an echo of affirmation (which comes from Theocritus and Virgil–not an Ovidian, mocking echo) in two ways. First, it adds an answer *to* the echo (rather than going, say, "The woods shall to me answer, by their echoing"); and it schematically embodies echoing (1) in the way in which the rhyme-word "sing" is answered by "ring," and (2) in the bipartite, reciprocal patterning of clauses across the caesura as a figure of echo itself.

But the echo-refrain of this earlier poem, despite its role in the marking out of the hours of the day, and (as A. K. Hieatt showed some time ago) specifically those of daylight on the midsummer occasion of the wedding, is largely unconcerned with time outside the poem (save for the last line of the poem, about being "for short Time an endlesse moniment," the one terminal beyond refrain). The mellower, yet more anxious concerns of the *Prothalamion* undersong, however, point to its own demarcation of period. The whole sui generis song of the therapeutic walk upstream is a forerunner of romantic crisis lyrics: I can think of no earlier nor more momentous source of the notion that a poet might take a walk "to ease my payne" (and surely not in the "*Natureingang*" of medieval German lyrics, which is another matter entirely). The timing effect of the later undersong is deeper, and more figurative. It is as if the cheerful numerology in the hermetic subplot of *Epithalamion* were being remembered in a late sadness, and being caused to yield up the suppressed consequences of what Harold Bloom called, à la Nietzsche, "lying against time." The earlier refrain's introductory verb, "sing," rhymes chorically with everything; but "undersong," or any kind of song, rhymes with "belong," "long," "wrong," and—strangely—"strong," and yet we never find a "strong"-ly rhymed "undersong" in Spenser or any later writer using the word.

The earlier refrain is, as was observed, an alexandrine; the song by the Thames exhibits a recurrent pentameter, although T. S. Eliot, ironically quoting the refrain in "The Fire Sermon" part of *The Waste Land*, reechoes it in an oddly poignant, interpretively augmented alexandrine: "Sweet Thames run softly, for I speak not loud nor long"—as if this were the way it should have gone all the time. "Sweete Themmes runne softly, till I end my song"—surely one of the sets of resonances struck by the line in subsequent poetry comes from the overtone "sweet theme," which later on in the seventeenth century, Sir John Denham, with neoclassical tact, would merely predicate ("O could I flow like thee! and make thy stream/My great example, as it is my theme"), and safely rhyme with the name of a synecdoche, rather than more powerfully and Spenserianly punning on the name of the river itself. But Donald Cheney, a modern scholar with a fine Spenserian ear, hears "Sweet Time" lurking in the epithet. We might adduce here the brooding ambiguity of the refrain's first half-line running throughout, the "wedding day which was [is] not long": not long in coming, and not as long in duration as the great midsummer of the poet's own wedding day, celebrated in the earlier poem.

But the Thames, unlike the woods, does not echo the poet's song. Moreover, the refrain is of the sort whose grammar is an imperative, exemplified by those of Theocritus and Virgil, and by Catullus' Parcae, as they sing their chant, *perfidiae quod post nulla arguet aetas* ("which no tract of time shall belie"), for the wedding of Peleus and Thetis. That refrain, *currite ducentes subtegmina, currite, fusi* ("run, drawing the thread out, spindles, run") is an undersong that urges the completion of the song itself. The fatal spindles have replaced the Muses of pastoral as the empowering deity to be invoked, and the yarn they spin, the story they tell, is not only the stuff of fable, but, we must always remember, the stuff of life itself. In Spenser, the Thames is commanded, not to generate the song, not manifestly to aid its production, nor even, in direct opposition to that, to desist while the poet sings. Rather, it is asked to lower its voice, in order to provide what we should today call an accompaniment to the voice of the singer, whether in the frame song or the inset epithalamium sung by the nymph. Such a modern notion of accompaniment—the piano part of "Wohin?" with its brook noises, in Schubert's setting of *Die schöne Müllerin*, as it were—was not a musical actuality in Spenser's day, although a notion of companionship is represented everywhere in *The Faerie Queene*. In this case, we are not told what the Thames might have been implying in the sounds of its motion. But mythologically, it surely derives (in all senses) from the common source of all poetic rivers, whether Petrarch's Rhône, Milton's revised Alpheus in *Lycidas,* or all of the rivers discussed so eloquently by David Quint.[3]

The undersong also affirms, then, the Thames as the flow of English poetic eloquence, the Thames with whose marriage to the Medway Spenser had concerned himself probably from 1580 on. Drawing not only on an old trope of flowing water for discourse (as opposed to standing pond and reflective pool, with their silent surfaces and depths, for thought), the Thames here replaces earlier poetic rivers, even those that had been intimately associated with the scene of writing for him (the "*Mulla* mine, whose waves I whilome taught to weepe").[4] But it also replaces in a different way the central poetic river of Greek mythology, by repeated allusion: first by likening the whiteness of the swans to that of the snow on Mount Pindus in Thessaly whence it springs, then to Peneus itself, flowing through the plain of Tempe (in connection with the nymphs gathering flowers), the river of the father of the nymph Daphne, and hence father as well of all the poetic consequences of Apollo's loss. (Petrarch had also invoked

Peneus in just such a context. In *Canzoniere* 23 he juxtaposes the white feathers of Cygnus—associated in Ovid with the Po—with Peneus and the Rhône, as Spenser does with the Thames.)

But if these poetic rivers are tributary in a figurative sense, the literal influx of the river Lee, "The wanton Lee, that oft doth loose his way" (*FQ* 6.11.29), is also significant. Regardless of the primary meaning of the phrases "downe along the Lee" (and perhaps there is an overlay of the down of swans here?) and "adowne the Lee," the minor river flows into the poem from one of its precursor texts. *A Tale of Two Swans* by William Vallans, published in 1590 overflows with awareness of its own precurrent text in Spenser's unpublished *Epithalamium Thamesis,* the work he contemplated writing in quantitative meters in 1580. Vallans' blank-verse itinerary of the course of the river Lee from its sources until it runs into (and in his Spenserian fable, marries) the Thames starts with an etiological myth of the swans in England: Venus, seeing the beauty of the river "and the meades thereof/Fit for to breed her birdes of greatest prise" (15–16), sends Mercury to get two cygnets of the best from "Cayster, silver streame," a Boeotian river that Ovid associates twice with crowds of singing swans. There is indeed a "commodious vicus of recirculation" in Vallans' stream feeding on and later back into Spenser's, as there is indeed a rearrival, in *Prothalamion,* of the figurative flow of life, when the whole procession comes to what the poet calls "mery London, my most kyndly nurse,/That gave to me this lifes first native sourse" (127–28). The river, then, like the flow of poetic life, gliding by its rival banks that are set with emblems first of poetry and love and beauty, then of the objects of "expectation vayne/Of idle hopes" (7–8) must inevitably sing out for a while under each strophe, invoked in, and seeming to become, its undersong.

But here I should like to dwell on the word itself. *Undersong* is one of those Spenserian coinages that, reechoed and redoubled by subsequent poets from Drayton and Browne through Wordsworth, Coleridge, Keats, and Emerson, emerges from a private life in the poetic ear into the more general air.[5] At its first occurrence in English, it means nothing but "refrain," a refrain specifically linked to the tradition of pastoral refrain stemming from Theocritus and Virgil. In the "August" eclogue of *The Shepheardes Calender,* a "delectable controversie"—as Spenser refers to the subgenre of amoebaean or alternating song—between Perigot and Willye. The two shepherds compete, as you will remember, in a singing contest for a prize to be awarded by a cowherd, Cuddie, and at the completion of their bout, Cuddie himself sings a sestina, "a dolefull verse/Of Rosalend (who knows not Rosalend?)" (140–41) composed by Colin Clout, or Spenser himself. What is unusual about their contest is that they do not, unlike their classical precursors, compete in kind, as in Virgil's seventh and eighth eclogues, where quatrains, or whole songs, alternate (in this latter case, each song has its own refrain). Instead, Willye sings the first and third lines of a balladlike song, and Perigot sings a refrainlike second and fourth, always starting up with an unvarying "hey ho," and always picking up a phrase or notion from Perigot's first line and playing with it. Here, for example, are a few exchanges from the beginning of their joint effort:

Perigot.	It fell upon a holly eve,
Willye.	hey ho hollidaye,
Per.	When holly fathers wont to shrieve:
Wil.	now gynneth this roundelay.
Per.	Sitting upon a hill so hye
Wil.	hey ho the high hyll,
Per.	The while my flocke did feede thereby,
Wil.	the while the shepheard selfe did spill:
Per.	I saw the bouncing Bellibone,
Wil.	hey ho Bonibell,
Per.	Tripping over the dale alone,
Wil.	she can trippe it very well:
Per.	Well decked in a frocke of gray,
Wil.	hey ho gray is greete,
Per.	And in a Kirtle of greene saye,
Wil.	the greene is for maydens meete:

["August," 53–68]

The competition here is between the powers of the primary and the antithetical, the phraser and the echoing, mocking paraphraser;[6] in the improvisatory tradition of jazz, it is like what is called a "cutting session" between two soloists. Moreover, Willye's opening pair of lines invoke the clocking, pacing function of the classical pastoral refrain, the signaling effected by modulating the refrains not from positive to negative, as in *Epithalamion,* but by Theocritus' refrain in his first idyll, which changes from "Start up the pastoral music, Muses" to "Continue the pastoral music" to "Finish up the pastoral music" during the course of the idyll. The measuring quality of this sort of refrain, particularly when the recurring line is an imperative sentence allegorically addressed to the poem being uttered itself, is most important, and I shall return to it later on. At this point, I shall only observe that in the radically experimental revisionary uses of schemes and subgenres that mark *The Shepheardes Calender,* the contention of verses and refrains, while seemingly an elegantly technical matter merely, is instead a very deep one, a testing out of a dialectic of paradigms of the sort that will, in *The Faerie Queene,* involve vast patterns, patrons, presences, and forms. And it is here to be observed that Colin, and thus Spenser himself, outdoes this "delectable controversie" with an exemplar—and a unique variation on the canonical form, at that—of that most intricately arrayed set of one-word refrains, the sestina. In a sense, he resolves the dialectic at a level higher than that of mere contention, first splitting the prize between the two contestants, and then incorporating refrain and main text in a form whose every new line is in fact a refrain.

It is in bestowing his split award that Cuddie remarks, "Little lacketh Perigot of the best, / And Willye is not greatly overgone, / So weren his undersongs well addrest" (127–28). The word is remarkable here, as elsewhere, because of its paired meanings. [Spenser has no other word for *refrain* throughout his works: the very word *refrain* is used in our modern verbal sense of "desist" or more literally "rein in" (from *refréner*) throughout Spenser, and the word *burden* only to mean "lead" (as derived from OE *byrthen* and ultimately from the same root as the verb one bears it with).] E. K. in his gloss remarks that "Willy answereth every under verse," in the sense that, in writing, a line that follows another comes under it; but Willye's continuing stream of refrain is also like a sort of drone, not a returning *ostinato,* but a continuous sound of the kind invoked by the other etymology of the other meaning of *burden* (from *bourdon,* "drone pipe"). The two senses are clearly different, in that one must wander away from something in order to return to it: the river I walk beside, perhaps singing as I go, can provide a drone or *bourdon,* but only the fountains placed at measured intervals along the paved walk I take can assent to my sung blues with refrains of their own. But Willye's undersongs have been both refrainlike and dronelike, and the resonance of the word, the interrelations of its meanings, and the reinterpretations of those in later poems all help us to hear some of the remarkable resonances of the undersong of *Prothalamion.* Intermittence can be a trope of bouts of strife, but it can also become the alternations of task, of assistance in work and in love. So, at any rate, does it become in a very different version of pastoral alternation in *Colin Clout's Come Home Again,* for example, where Colin's chiasmic formulation represents his relation to The Shepherd of the Ocean (and, therewith, Spenser's relation to Ralegh): "He pip'd, I sung, and when he sung, I pip'd,/By chaunge of turnes, each making other mery" (76–77). The piping here becomes the returning, purely melodic, less densely textual utterance; but it is also something else, an accompaniment, our word for which is not used in a musical sense before the middle of the eighteenth century. (Some of the consequences of this for Spenser will reemerge a bit later on, when we must glance at the possible parsing of the phrase "tune his pipe unto the water's fall.") In *Colin Clout's Come Home Again,* Colin describes a poem by that same mariner shepherd, a "lamentable lay . . . Of Cynthia, the Ladie of the Sea," and observes that

> And ever and anon, with singults rife
> He cryed out to make his undersong
> Ah my loves queene, and goddesse of my life
> Who shall my pittie, when thou doest me wrong?

[168–71]

Here the primary sense is "refrain"; and yet there is a tinge of that figurative sense that "the burden of his song" began to take on in the seventeenth century, that rhetorical sense of a continuous point, apparently being returned to but, for the listener, continually droning on, beneath the surface of apparent argument and exemplification. This reductive sense of a burden is implictly directed against eloquence itself, implying that it always has holes through which a continuous drone breaks out in what appears to be a mere recurring refrain, and it is this reductive relation between the senses of drone and fragmentary recurrence that has always been most common.

Spenser's most significant invocation of refrain as an undersong is in the very refrain that so designates itself. The complaint of Alcyon, the allusively Chaucerian man in black, for the dead Daphne in Spenser's 1591 *Daphnaïda* is composed of seven sections of seven stanzas of seven lines; each section ends with a stanza that concludes with the refrain, as in the case of the first of these.

> She fell away in her first ages spring,
> Whil'st yet her leafe was greene, and fresh her rinde,
> And whilst her braunch faire blossoms foorth did bring,
> She fell away against all course of kinde:
> For age to dye is right, but youth is wrong;
> She fel away like fruit blowne downe with winde:
> Weepe Shephearde weepe to make my undersong.

> [11.239–45]

This beautiful and highly architectonic stanza shifts the position of one line in the traditional rhyme-royal to produce a pair of *terza rime* tercets with a concluding extra line (as in the last seven lines of the *Paradiso*). In this instance, the refrain line, "Weepe Shepheardes weepe to make my undersong," seems at first to refer to the anaphora of "she fell away." It is only as the dirge unfolds that it is seen to be self-invocatory; rhyming in alternate sections with "wrong" and "long" and once with the verb "prolong," its last occurrence is in the modulated form familiar to readers of Virgil's eighth eclogue: "Cease Shepheard cease and end thy undersong." The "Shepheard" in question has been the pastoral narrator whose account of meeting Alcyon frames the elegy; the shift from "my undersong" to "thy undersong," at the end, avows that the audient attendant accompanist—who in Spenser's modernist modulation of Theocritus takes the place of the pastoral Muses themselves—implicitly reclaims the responsive refrain when the song itself is done.

Moreover, the undersong is "made" of weeping, that is, of Colin Clout's "singults" or sobs, and the flow of tears. Together they make up the essential Spenserian occasion of eloquence, music "tuned to" the sound of water. Colin's "laye" in the "April" eclogue was so composed, we are told: he "tunèd it unto the waters fall," in a phrase so resonant that every Spenserian for the next seventy years or so would work it into a poem of his, sometimes more than once, the phrase having become a covert Spenserian trademark even as the alexandrine would always be. (That the first occurrence of the phrase in Spenser is to be found in his earliest known writing, the verse translations for the *Theatre for Worldlings* of 1569, is remarkable; that it emerges in the first alexandrine in all of Spenser's poetry, itself occurring as an apparent *lapsus metricae* among nothing but pentameters, is spooky, and I have discussed this whole matter at length elsewhere.[7])

That the undersong of *Daphnaïda* should be literally a refrain, and figuratively both the command to the poem itself to get itself written, which all imperative refrains seem to be enacting, and the association of intermittent sobs with the continuous drone of falling or flowing water is, I think, important. The word used here seems to be a confluence of some of the streams of meaning that have come up: accompaniment, but then again, principal theme; periodic point, but then again, drone. In addition, the *under* part of the word suggests that, at bottom, the sound of moving water is the ground—musically as a bass, epistemologically primary, mythologically as an *Urgeräusch* or primal sound of poetic discourse. (I find it interesting and puzzling that the scheme of *epizeuxis*—e.g., Tennyson's "The woods decay, the woods decay and fall"—a repetition rather like that of refrain, Puttenham calls "the underlay or cuckoo-spell.") A sound going on *underneath* discourse implies a lower polyphonic part, at a metaphorically "lower" pitch, and placed spatially below others in staff notation, and/or one that is "lower" in volume and goes on at a lower level, as it were, of audibility. The introduction of the technical acoustical term *overtone* by Helmholtz in the nineteenth century led soon to figurative uses of both that word and an analogous *undertone* (but Keats in *Lamia* 2.291: "'Fool!' said the sophist, in an under-tone/Gruff with contempt," where it means simply "sotto voce"). *Undertone* begins to take on implications of implication itself, of a latent meaning or purpose or intent flowing along "below" (in an incipient layering of structures of consciousness) the manifest, and it reflects an earlier Renaissance sense of the most important matters being necessarily half-hidden. That excellent Spenserian, James Russell Lowell (a better poet, perhaps, when he discoursed on allegory in prose than ever in verse), spoke of great poetic allegory as "not embodying metaphysical abstractions, but giving us ideal abstracted from life itself, suggesting an under-meaning everywhere, forcing it upon us nowhere" (this rare word is also used by Ruskin, in *Sesame and Lilies* 2, par. 93). Even the common use of *undercurrent* in an extended sense to invoke a layer of significance is pointedly post-Spenserian, I think (an early *OED* citation is from Coleridge, *Biographia Literaria:* "Our genuine admiration of a great poet is a continuous under-current of feeling" [1.1.23]). Other post-Spenserian undersongs resonate with some of these implications. Although some poets merely dutifully employ the word in a pastoral context, alluding to Willye's refrain in "August" (thus Drayton, Eclogue 9 G.3b: "When now at last . . . Was pointed who the roundelaye should singe/And who againe the undersong should beare"; or Dryden, translating Virgil's third eclogue's *incipe Damoeta; tu deinde sequere Menalca,* "The challenge to Damoetas shall belong:/Menalcas shall sustain the under-song"; or, following directly in this line, Ambrose Phillips: "As eldest, Hobbinol, begin:/And Lanquet's Under-Song by Turns come in" [Pastoral 6.7–8]), others trope Spenser's later implicit senses of the word in *Daphnaïda* and *Prothalamion.* Wordsworth, at the end of the first sonnet of "Personal Talk," turns off the switch, as it were, of social noise to provide a scene of meditation:

Better than such discourse doth silence long,
Long, barren silence, square with my desire;
To sit without emotion, hope, or aim,
In the loved presence of my cottage-fire,
And listen to the flapping of the flame,
Or kettle whispering its faint under-song.

[9–14]

On the other hand, it is just the sound of conversation forsaken by Wordsworth that Keats incorporates into the concerted music at the banquet in *Lamia.*

Soft went the music the soft air along
While fluent Greek a vowelled undersong
Kept up among the guests, discoursing low
At first, for scarcely was the wine at flow.

[2.199–202]

In "Isabella," Lorenzo's ghost appears speaking with a strange voice, "And Isabella on its music hung":

Languour there was in it, and tremulous shake,
    As in a palsied Druid's harp unstrung,
And through it moaned a ghostly under-song,
Like hoarse night-gusts sepulchral briars among.

[st. 36]

(And here the untuned, abandoned instrument in the Gothicized version of the harp of Psalm 137 in the process of becoming Aeolian, produces not instrumental or vocal music, but poetic "under-song.")

Nevertheless, the most significant extended uses of the word seem always to occur in the presence of moving water. William Browne's river in *Britannia's Pastorals* praises his love, "his hasty waves among/ The frothied rocks, bearing his undersong" points specifically to the literal "refrain" with its verb "bearing" (2.3.1028), and the water-as-swain is really less Spenserian than the swain undersung by water. Coleridge's Spenserian stanzas to Joseph Cottle map out a poetic landscape, with a Parnassian-Heliconian-Acidalian hill, a poisonous Lethean stream, and, above that but still on the lower slopes, a meadow with another sort of brook:

Nor there the Pine-grove to the midnight blast
Makes solemn music! But th'unceasing rill
To the soft Wren or Lark's descending trill
Murmurs sweet undersong mid jasmine bowers.[8]

But most significantly for this discussion, Coleridge blends the voice of the river Greta, in the later "Recollections of Love," with that of a putative beloved and of personified Love itself. Hearing, after an absence of eight years, "quiet sounds from hidden rills / Float here and there, like things astray," he half-remembers a presence; and in lines that themselves, with their striking anacolouthon, replace a person with a river, calls that very memory into deep question.

You stood before me like a thought,
    A dream remembered in a dream,
    But when those meek eyes first did seem
To tell me, Love within you wrought—
    O Greta, dear domestic stream![9]

It is the sound of that "dear domestic stream," a voice quite other than that of the Spenserian lyric water-muse, or even that of the Thames of poetic tradition, that is addressed in the final stanza.

Has not, since then, Love's prompture deep,
    Has not Love's whisper evermore
    Been ceaseless, as thy gentle roar?
Sole voice, when other voices sleep,
    Dear under-song in clamor's hour.

The "ceaseless" essence of the undersong here is no longer a matter of a droning bourdon; for only the desire for death would hear the hum of life, or sounds of its tributary streams of love and memory, as oppressive drone, and one of the secondary undersongs of the Thames in *Prothalamion* has occasioned a new and revised audition.

Emerson carries the romantic revision of the Spenserian undersong one stage further; in "Woodnotes II," the pine tree, singing the song of "the genesis of things," of how

The rushing metamorphosis
Dissolving all that fixture is

Melts things that be to things that seem,
And solid nature to a dream.
O, listen to the undersong,
The ever old, the ever young;
And, far within those cadent pauses,
The chorus of the ancient Causes!

[112–19]

If Coleridge's Greta sang her undersong to the listening of loss, Emerson's undersong is that of no particular river, no local or national voice, but that of flux itself. It does reecho the "sweet Time" that Cheney hears in Spenser ("The ever old, the ever young"), and it seems remarkably attentive to the notion of continuous drone intermittently making itself heard as periodic refrain: "And far within those cadent pauses,/The chorus...." The "cadent pauses," each rumoring, but only falsely, of final, cadent closure, each marking pace and time, each falling into place with the water's fall, allow the united choral voices of the conditions of Creation to arise as repeated chorus after the unrolling of each successive epochal strophe. (Emerson uses "undersong" once again, more trivially, in the Concord "Ode" of 1857: "United States! the ages plead,–/Present and Past in undersong" [17–18]. But even here, the stream of time is clearly the source of the Spenserian undersinging.)

A final transumptive elicitation of one of the undersongs of sense in Spenser's word appears in Robert Frost's etiological fable—post-Ovidian, post-Spenserian, post-Miltonic all in different ways—of the institution of meaning in natural noise. "Never Again Would Birds' Song Be the Same" does an end run around Virgil's Tityrus teaching the woods to echo the name of Amaryllis, but like all such preposterous etiologies, it resounds with the Spenser who has come between: Frost's sonnet tells of how Adam

would declare and could himself believe
That the birds there in all the garden round
From having heard the daylong voice of Eve
Had added to their own an oversound,
Her tone of meaning but without the words.

[1–5]

Here, I cannot help but feel, the "oversound," playing against the modern figurative sense of "overtone," is returning "undersong" in a strangely inverted way.[10]

The song of the river—the sound of water generally—outlasts all others and, in narrative and descriptive accounts, frequently concludes catalogues of harmonizing natural noises by being placed below them. So with the sounds at the beginning of Wordsworth's "Resolution and Independence"—

> The birds are singing in the distant woods;
> Over his own sweet voice the stock-dove broods;
> The Jay makes answer as the Magpie chatters;
> And all the air is filled with pleasant noise of waters.
>
> [4–7]

—where the water sound underlies and underscores the others in a Spenserian alexandrine. No more than a month or so later, Wordsworth recalled the stock-dove's consciousness of its "own sweet voice" (perhaps *its* undersong was some dove-talk version of "So I unto myself alone shall sing") and finally brought it down into the bottom line, in the Westminster Bridge sonnet's "The river murmurs at its own sweet will," Spenser's prothalamic Thames, taking its own sweet time. To varying extents, all of Wordsworth's discursive rivers partake of Spenser's Thames. From the Derwent in book 1 of *The Prelude*, the voice that flowed along his dreams, that made

> ceaseless music through the night and day
> Which with its steady cadence, tempering
> Our human waywardness, composed my thoughts
> To more than infant softness, giving me
> Among the fretful dwellings of mankind
> A knowledge, a dim earnest of the calm
> That nature breathes among the hills and groves.
>
> [1805, 1.276–285]

to the Duddon, which Wordsworth twenty-five years or so later diverts into being a master-trope for a series of sonnets variously composed, the Thames' undersong is never far away. The "After-

Thought" sonnet to the river Duddon sequence refigures the river not
as Heraclitean time, but as the history of consciousness:

> For backward Duddon! as I cast my eyes,
> I see what was, and is, and will abide;
> Still glides the stream, and shall for ever glide;
> The Form remains, the Function never dies.
>
> [3–6]

And here the silence of the water ("Still glides the stream") cannot
help but entail, through an inevitable and unwitty pun, the ceaseless-
ness of its current, the eternity of the form and function, as contrasted
with the feeble mortality of the mere substance, of discourse.

I mentioned earlier both the Spenserian signature trope of "tuning"
a poetic voice or instrument "to the water's fall" and Vallans' *Tale of
Two Swans*. They converge here most significantly. Vallans' poem
sought to make restitution for a missing Spenserian river-poem (even
as it was itself followed by a very great one), and at the crucial
moment toward its beginning, when Venus receives the pair of swans,
she

> like the Goddesse of great Love,
> Sate lovely by the running river side,
> Tuning her Lute unto the waters fall.

The trope of singing to the water, attuning or according with it, also
involves addressing it. The figure constitutes a hidden undersong for
Spenser's actual and remembered oeuvre. It is exemplified most
audibly in *Prothalamion,* a poem that tunes its own utterance to the
water's fall, although always in full cognizance of the greater power
of the river: its audible volume, physical force, and long, long duration, both backward, preexisting Spenser's poem as an almost natural
trope of poetic discourse (the books in the running brooks are the
oldest ones) and forward, outlasting any human voice that, like
Spenser's, could speak to, or of, or for it.

Moving water is in the Spenserian undersong, at least as the deep,
private scholarship of poets seems to have perceived it. And so is
poetic self-reference. Hart Crane's reposing river, now turned into a

meditative pool by having run into the sea, remembers not its own voice but the "slow sound" carried by the willows on its banks, "A sarabande the wind mowed on the mead." But had the poet not become the river, in order, so late in the poetic day, to join it rather than to succumb to it, it should itself have spoken. Like the raving of Shelley's Arve in its "dizzy ravine"; like the river Duddon, playing in Wordsworth's sonnet the role of the wide water of *Il Penseroso* for the poet for whom "the summits hoar/Of distant moon-lit mountains faintly shine,/Soothed by the unseen River's gentle roar." Or the sound of water with which, when conjoined with the sound of the wind in the pines, all pastoral is initiated (in Theocritus I); the plaintive mythological streams of Spenser's early pastoral, whose "song" rhymes with lamented "wrong"; his local Irish river, which he loved both in actuality and in trope ("Mulla whom I whilome taught to weepe"); the everlasting universe of things running through the mind, the trope of that flow in the actual river that runs on "with a sound but half its own"; the schoolbook lesson of Spenser-for-the-young in the undersong of Tennyson's brook ("O men may come and men may go/But I go on forever"); the underground sacred Alphs that break out from time to time for all of us, an accompaniment breaking out into refrain between strophes, a refrain becoming the argument it was measuring out, an ancillary sound that recurrently rises into mastery, as it does for Mrs. Ramsay in *To the Lighthouse,* reading the story to James, "reading and thinking, quite easily, both at the same time; for the story of the Fisherman and his wife was like the bass gently accompanying a tune, which now and then ran up unexpectedly into the melody." Only Stevens' river of rivers "that flows nowhere, like a sea" can be so silent, refusing to follow the course of the old trope, but the sound of the flowing rises again into refrain, one of the only natural refrains, even after the song of its unsinging has been ended.

NOTES

1. There may be further allusion in the resonance of "blisfull bower" early in the strophe. See my *The Figure of Echo* (Berkeley & Los Angeles: University of California Press, 1981), 83–84.

2. In conversation and in an unpublished lecture. I should acknowledge his assistance on Spenserian matters generally; I should also like to express gratitude to Harry Berger, Kenneth Gross, and Joseph Loewenstein for what they have written about *Prothalamion*. Lawrence Manley reminded me, in his beautiful essay "Spenser and the City: The Minor Poems" (*MLQ* 43, no. 3 [1984]: 223–27) that "the Orphic Poet who civilized with his song, it was said, possessed as well the power to halt the flow of rivers."

3. David Quint, *Origins and Originality in Renaissance Literature* (New Haven: Yale University Press, 1983), esp. 133–66.

4. *FQ* 4.11.41.

5. Indeed, a Spenserian scholar of the older school – H. S. V. Jones, in *A Spenser Handbook* ([New York, 1930], 18) – remarks of a particular stanza of *Daphnaïda*, which I consider later, that it is "suggestive of Elizabethan music with its counterpoint and undersong," no doubt believing *undersong* to be a technical musical term, which it is not. Jones can only have misunderstood Spenser's own refrain in that stanza.

6. The "green" is hardly "for maydens meete": this sarcasm is only one of Willye's many cutting moves.

7. For a full discussion of this topos in Spenser, see my "Footing of His Feet: On a Line of Milton's," in *On Poetry and Poetics*, ed. Richard Waswo (Tübingen: Gunter Nan Verlag, 1985), 22–28.

8. Samuel Taylor Coleridge, "To the Author of Poems Published Anonymously at Bristol in September 1795." I note with interest the allusively Spenserian use of "tune to" – as in tuning one's playing or singing to the fall of water – as here adapted in the opening addressing the bard "whose verse concise yet clear/Tunes to smooth melody unconquer'd sense."

9. Lines 21–25. How very problematic this interruption is may depend upon whether "wrought" is transitive or, most uncommonly, intransitive here.

10. Further Spenserian allusion in later occurrences of *undersong* and its derivatives remain interesting, and I wish I had time here to go into D. G. Rossetti's "while Love breathed in sighs and silences/Through two blent souls one rapturous undersong" (*The House of Life*, 13) and William Morris' lines from "August" on the leaves on the apple bough: "In the mute August afternoon? They trembled to some undertune/Of music in the silver air."

Patricia Parker

Suspended Instruments

LYRIC AND POWER IN THE BOWER OF BLISS

In the midst of the Bower of Bliss, the culminating episode of Guyon's quest in book 2 of *The Faerie Queene,* the Elfin knight and his Palmer guide gain a sight of the Bower's reigning Enchantress and Verdant, her male victim.

> His warlike armes, the idle instruments
>   Of sleeping praise, were hong upon a tree,
>   And his brave shield, full of old moniments,
>   Was fowly ra'st, that none the signes might see;
>   Ne for them, ne for honour cared hee,
>   Ne ought, that did to his advauncement tend,
>   But in lewd loves, and wastfull luxuree,
>   His dayes, his goods, his bodie he did spend:
> O horrible enchantment, that him so did blend.
>
> [2.12.80][1]

The immediate resonance of these "idle instruments/Of sleeping praise," suspended or "hong" upon a tree, is the iconography of Venus and Mars—with Verdant lying like the disarmed warrior in the lap of his paramour before Vulcan, the formerly impotent voyeur husband, rushes in upon them with his crafty "net." The suspension or hanging of these instruments reiterates the suspensions of the Bower itself, and the hovering of Acrasia as she cannibalistically "pastures" her eyes upon her powerless subject. But the instruments hung upon a tree also recall a very different and specifically lyric context—one that will lead us toward the various strains of lyricism that cross in this crucial Spenserian scene. This context is the suspended song and suspended lyric instruments of the haunting Psalm 137.

> By the rivers of Babel we sate, and there we wept, when we remembered Zion.
> We hanged our harpes upon the willowes in the middes thereof.
> When thei that led us captives required of us songs and mirth, when we

had hanged up our harpes, saying, Sing us one of the songs of Zion.
How shall we sing, said we, a song of the Lord in a strange land?
If I forget thee, O Ierusalem, may my right hand forget to play.
If I do not remember thee, let my tongue cleve to the rofe of my
    mouth . . .
O daughter of Babel, worthie to be destroied, blessed shal he be [who]
    rewardeth thee, as thou hast served us.
Blessed shal be he that taketh and dasheth thy children against the
    stones.[2]

That this biblical lyric of lament should sound in the midst of the
otherwise euphonious and *carpe diem* lyricism of the Bower of Bliss—
filled with songs and lyric traditions of its own—should not, on reflection, be surprising. The psalm sings of abandoned instruments in Babylonian exile and captivity: Verdant's instruments are suspended on
the tree of a "Witch" only too easily assimilated to Babylon and its
famous Whore. Calvin, in his gloss on the psalm, speaks of its Babylon as a *locus amoenus* very much like the Bower of Bliss—as a "fair
and fertile" place "with charms which could corrupt effeminate
minds" and "tempt them to forget their native inheritance." Augustine speaks of its "Babylon" as the pleasures of this world and of the
"willows" on which its lyric instruments are hung as ultimately barren rather than fruitful trees—an emblem of barrenness in the midst
of apparent fertility that repeats the biblical dynamic of Spenser's
principal subtext, the Garden of Armida in Tasso which stands upon
a Dead Sea.[3] The invocation of the psalm not to forget—or to be punished with speechlessness and forcibly suspended song as a result—
thus joins the Homeric, lotos-eating resonances of this Spenserian
scene, and both figure the necessity of the withheld and vigilant mind,
the reversal of Verdant's suspended instruments, which themselves
provide a sign not of song refused but, more ominously, of song as
in some other sense suspended.

The psalm behind Verdant's suspended instruments, however, also
imports into this private and enclosed erotic scene the powerful
political dimension this psalm has always had for singers conscious of
the wider context of their singing, a resonance that might make it a

powerful subtext for lyric poets in the era of Spenser, subject to a queen who very much demanded their voices. Hanging up one's instrument stands here as a sign of resistance, a refusal to hire out one's voice on the part of a people who otherwise sure can sing and dance. The specifically political force of this psalm continues in a contemporary reggae version of the impossibility of singing in Babylon, a version that chillingly suppresses the psalm's own violent ending— "Blessed shal he be that taketh and dasheth the children of Babylon against the stones"—and ambiguously substitutes for it another very different psalm text, "May the words of our mouths and the meditations of our hearts be *acceptable* in thy sight" (emphasis mine).

The echo of this psalm's suspended instruments introduces if only elliptically into Spenser's scene the threat of the silencing, controlling, or compromising of song, one that is biblical in its immediate reference but also, in Acrasia's leafy retreat, inevitably evokes a particularly pastoral lyric tension between power and song—that tension that opens Virgil's *Eclogues* with an allusion to the "god" who has given the singer his "ease." Indeed, the other lyric context recalled in the stanza of Verdant's suspended instruments is this specifically pastoral one, hanging up one's instruments being not just the gesture of a Mars-like warrior abandoning the instruments of war, the hanging up of trophies as signs of victory, or the lament of a Dido-like abandoned lover (as in Spenser's "Willow worne of forlorne Paramours" or "Hang my harp on a weeping willow tree"), but also the suspending of instruments on trees in pastoral lyric, a suspension of song that may reflect the suspension Paul Alpers and others find characteristic of pastoral lyric itself.[4] In Sannazaro's *Arcadia,* one of the principal subtexts for Spenser's *Shepheardes Calender,* the hanging of the instrument of Pan upon a tree generates an entire history of pastoral lyric from Theocritus to Virgil and, by implication, to the poet-persona of the *Arcadia* itself.[5] The suspending of Pan's instrument there—in a way suggestive for a Spenserian episode that signals its debts to multiple predecessors—is an emblem of the interval before a new poet takes up these temporarily "idle instruments" and turns them into the instruments of his own potency.

Within this specifically pastoral lyric context, Verdant's suspended instruments summon up a Spenserian echo as well, and one intimately bound up with the tensions within Spenser's lyric vocation. Readers of *The Shepheardes Calender* will remember that it opens with Colin Clout, Spenser's own pastoral persona, not just suspending but breaking his pastoral instrument. And it ends with Colin hanging his pipe upon a tree, in a gesture that more than one commentator has linked with a sense of the impotence of song, or of the necessary compromising of lyric voice in a political context which would make only too appropriate a conflation of a recall of Psalm 137 with a reminder of Colin's own suspended instrument.[6] *Otium,* or idleness, is traditionally the attraction of pastoral, as it is also of the fatal Bower of Bliss; but the "idleness" of the suspended instruments of Verdant suggests in their echo of Colin's gesture the potential impotence of poetry itself in a state in which it was scorned as a form of effeminacy, or idle "toye," in contrast to more active, imperial pursuits,[7] in which it was highly problematic whether there was any alternative to the opposed temptations of the idle Phaedria and the industrious Mammon of book 2—an opposition that Blake might later ridicule as a "cloven fiction," but one that continued to dominate a whole post-Spenserian tradition of the potential impotence or irrelevance of lyric. The Romantics' Aeolian harp, we may remember, is one of the descendants of this suspended instrument.

There is, however, yet another aspect of Verdant's suspended instruments that needs to be explored and, though it will emerge only after a brief excursus, another specifically lyric dimension of this episode and the defeat of its reigning queen. The pervasive phallic symbolism of Guyon's Odyssean journey to the Bower of Bliss makes it impossible to miss the fact that these suspended "instruments" are also clearly *male* instruments and that the impotence their suspension betokens is an impotence that is sexual as well as martial or lyric.[8] A link between the instruments of war and the instruments of virility is, of course, part of the visual cliché of the iconography of Mars and Venus: we think of Botticelli's painting with its wreathed phallic lance, clearly no longer ready for immediate use as an instrument of war, though still serviceable as an instrument of a different kind.

The sense not just of lyric but of sexual contest within the stanza of Verdant's suspended instruments evokes a recall not only of Mars and Venus but of a whole series of subject males and dominating female figures, from Hercules and Omphale to Samson reclining in the lap of that Delilah who deprives him of his strength, a figure of the man dedicated to higher things who cannot, however, ultimately escape the power of women, an emblem whose link with Spenser's pair is made even stronger by the fact that Samson in sixteenth-century depictions was also represented as laying aside his warlike instruments. Spenser's scene manages to evoke the iconography of both Virgin Mother with her sleeping infant and the more sinister Pietà, a dead Adonis in the lap of a powerful maternal Venus. And the emblem of Samson made impotent in Delilah's lap also shares with the tableau of Verdant and Acrasia anxieties of a particularly oral kind, the reduction of the male subject to an infant, or *infans*. Acrasia, like Delilah throughout much of her pictorial history, is not just a temptress but an overpowering mother; and it is in this respect worth citing at least one Renaissance representation of that overpowering. Madlyn Millner Kahr, in *Feminism and Art History,* cites a late sixteenth-century drawing entitled "Allegory of the Power of Woman," which shows in the foreground a woman nursing an infant in one arm and holding a royal scepter and golden chain in the other, and standing on the broken instruments—shield and sword—of male power: in the background are the women who tempted Solomon to idolatry (and hence, ultimately, into Babylon) and Delilah cutting off the hair, and strength, of Samson in her lap.[9]

The underlying threat of the story of Samson's abandoned instruments is, of course, the threat of castration. The only hair mentioned in the case of Verdant is the just beginning hair on his boyish face: if Acrasia is a Delilah, she has only a symbolic need for scissors. But the sense of castration pervades the entire scene, and the unavoidably phallic overtones of Verdant's removed and now useless "instruments" bring to the scene an echo of the severed instruments of yet another boy—Attis, who after transgressing the demand of the Great

Mother Cybele that he remain forever a boy, in a frenzy castrates himself, thus becoming not just an impotent Adonis to Cybele's Venus but also the prototype of the Magna Mater's Galli or eunuch servants. Attis is traditionally represented as an effeminate youth, wearing the distinctive Phrygian cap whose droop, as Neil Hertz has recently reminded us,[10] conveys an equivocal sense of both the possession and the lack of phallic power, as indeed the effeminately dressed porter of the Bower of Bliss wields his "staff" for "more [we may hear "mere"] formalitee" (48.9), and reminds us of the Attis-like Aeneas at the court of another powerful female, his forgetfulness of outside world and higher task the Virgilian counterpart of the dangers of oblivion in Babylon.

The evocation of these pairs of dominant female and subject, even castrated, male in the episode of Verdant's suspended instruments works with other elements of the description to establish the Bower as a predominantly female space—whose enclosures suggest the *hortus conclusus* of the female body—and a place that might excite the knight to forget his own higher purpose, an act of submission that would suspend his "instruments." But the motif of male subjection within at least some of the plots suggested here—the case of Hercules, for example—is one in which the moment of male subjection is only one moment in a larger narrative progression. Though Guyon, unlike his prototype Odysseus, does not use his sword to overcome the Bower's Witch, the culminating or phallic narrative "point" (1.7) of his Odyssean journey substitutes, for homecoming to Penelope, the overpowering of a threatening Circe through the potent "vertue" (41.5) of the Palmer's simultaneously phallic and Mosaic staff, which, like the staff of Mercury to which it is kin, is able both to recall souls from the symbolic Hades of subjection to female power and also to "rule the *Furyes*, when they most do rage" (41.5), a hint perhaps of the relation between the establishment of civilization and the taming of the female from the story of yet another dangerously powerful queen.

But the echo of Cybele in particular gives a further dimension to this episode's suspended—and (in the case of Guyon) potentially suspended—instruments, both lyric and virile, one that involves not just the episode's narrative progression but a specific form of lyric tradition adumbrated within it. Cybele, the Magna Mater of imperial Rome, is one of *The Faerie Queene*'s most ubiquitous figures for the presiding patroness of "Troynovaunt" and hence for Elizabeth, the poem's allegorically shadowed Queen, who was repeatedly represented (and self-represented) as the great "Mother," and even nursing mother, of her subjects. Virgil's Roman version of the Magna Mater carefully removes the more oriental and threatening female aspects of her cult—including the castration of Attis and her subject males. But Spenser's allusions to Cybele include this more ambivalent complex, Cybele's "franticke rites" (1.6.15) as well as her maternal embodiment of order and civilization.[11] The Cybele-Attis iconography of the Isis Church episode of book 5 of *The Faerie Queene*, with its Galli-like priests who "on their mother Earths deare lap did lie" (5.7.9), links the pair of Great Mother and castrated boy emblematically with the posture of the mother-Queen of the Bower of Bliss and the reclining youth who has surrendered his "instruments." But interestingly enough, the vision at Isis Church also comes within the larger story of the powerful Amazon Radigund's subjection of Artegall, who comes under her control by abandoning his sword (5.5.17), which she then breaks, causing his "warlike armes" to be "hang'd on high," suspended so that they "mote his shame bewray," and forcing him to dress in "womans weedes" (20–22). The echoes of the Verdant-Acrasia scene in Artegall's humiliating subjection to a woman also, however, contain a stanza that makes explicit reference to *Spenser*'s ruling Queen, the exceptional powerful female dominant over her male subjects.

> Such is the crueltie of womenkynd,
>   When they have shaken off the shamefast band,
>   With which wise Nature did them strongly bynd,
>   T'obay the heasts of mans well ruling hand,
>   That then all rule and reason they withstand,
>   To purchase a licentious libertie.

But vertuous women wisely understand,
That they were borne to base humilitie,
Unlesse the heavens them lift to lawful soveraintie.

[25]

Elizabeth here is so belatedly made an exception to the rule—indeed,
only in a single concluding alexandrine—that what emerges in the picture of the monstrosity of the subjection of male to female power
makes one wonder whether, reading back from this episode to the
hints of Attis's severed instruments in the Bower of Bliss, Elizabeth
herself is not also "shadowed" in the scene of suspended instruments,
evocative both of male "vertue" and of instruments of a more lyric
kind.

Recent Spenser criticism has increasingly drawn attention to the relation between the combination of eroticized Virgin and dominating
mother in the figure of Acrasia and the typical self-presentation of
Spenser's ruling Queen.[12] Certainly, the *otium* and debased lyric
"toyes" of Acrasia's Bower echo the debased social situation of which
Cuddie complains in lamenting the impotence of his own lyric instruments in the *October* eclogue, implying that, at least in part, the pre-
dicament of the poet in the age of Elizabeth—his potentially impotent, or suspended, instrument—is that he is subject to powers that
necessarily compromise his song. Cuddie's complaint resembles the
lyric lament of the Muses themselves in another Spenserian intertext
for Verdant's suspended instruments, *The Teares of the Muses,* whose
complaint of internal exile (341) and of the "idleness" and brute sloth
(99, 335) of the contemporary English context recall at once the language of the Bower of Bliss and the lament of suspended song in Psalm
137, which might indeed provide its most appropriate lyric epigraph.
The episode of Guyon in the Bower has long been interpreted, following Milton, as the drama of an individual trial. But the affinities
of its language with a lament published only a year later imports into
the Bower itself a suggestion of that contemporary "Babylon" in
which the Muses' "sweete instruments" (20) can no longer be heard
and are finally broken, replaced instead by vain idle "toyes" (325), a
place where it is difficult to distinguish between "Poets" and "Syco-

phants" (471–72), or to save one's own lyric instruments from a subject's use.[13] Once again, Elizabeth is in this lament made explicitly an exception, but in a fashion reserved until the end, and in a praise so exceptional that it, too, seems a second thought (571ff.)

The iconography of subject male and dominant female in the scene of Verdant's suspended instruments brings us, then, to our last of the lyric traditions figured in this scene—not just the suspended lyricism of Psalm 137 or the pastoral topos of pipes hung on trees, but also the polarized structure of Petrarchan lyric, itself dependent on the polarity of male subject and elevated female figure, a polarity of which the suspended dyad of the subjected Verdant and dominant Acrasia offers an almost parodic visual emblem. This context for these suspended instruments necessarily returns us to our first—the suspension of song in an alien political context—for in both, as so much of recent Spenser criticism suggests, the relationship of lyric to society, in the terms of Adorno's famous essay, is one that cannot be simply overlooked.

It has long been recognized that the vogue for Petrarchan lyric in the era of Elizabeth was inseparable from the structure of a politics in which political and erotic codes interpenetrated to a remarkable degree, in which Elizabeth's courtiers related to their queen as Petrarchs to an often cruel mistress, and in which the male poet was "subject" in both the political and in the Petrarchan lyric sense. Petrarchism was not just a lyric but also a dominant cultural form, a politicized lyric structure inscribed within the complex sexual politics of the exceptional rule of a woman in an otherwise overwhelmingly patriarchal culture. Stephen Greenblatt and others have noted the antagonism—or implicit contest of wills—always present within this Petrarchan politics of courtier-lover and tantalizing, dominant, and even cruel mistress.[14] Greenblatt cites the example of Ralegh's playing a frenzied Orlando to Elizabeth's disdainful beloved; and Elizabeth figured as Ariosto's already highly Petrarchanized Angelica, who drives her courtier-knights mad, might also easily be shadowed as a dominating Acrasia artfully orchestrating both her own rival romance and her own Petrarchan poetics. The Bower of Bliss is a threatening female space not just because of its enervating *carmina* and etymologically related "charms" but also in part because, while it arouses hopes of gratification, it does not clearly fulfill them or fulfills them only in an illusory or compromising way; in the stanza of Verdant's suspended instruments, the knight's slumber seems postcoital, but it is not at all clear from the syntax what his share has been in these delights ("There she had him now layd a slombering,/In secret shade, after long wanton ioyes" [72.5.6]). And Bacon, for one, could easily assimilate Elizabeth's Petrarchan politics to the arts of "the Queen in the blessed islands . . . who allows of amorous admiration but prohibits desire."[15]

The antagonism within this politicized lyric structure, however, also left the way open for a male remastering of its dominant Petrarchan mistress. As Sir John Harington observed, the queen's male, Petrarch-like subjects could and would themselves make "matter" out of their *Magna Mater,* her subjects (both in the political and in the erotic sense) make the queen in turn the "subject" of their verse,[16] just as in the emblem of suspended pastoral instruments, which Spenser echoes from Sannazaro, the origin of those instruments is in the death of Syrinx, in the transformed body of that female figure who becomes literally the enabling instrument of pastoral song.

The dynamics of this threatening female dominance and male remastery—the narrative dynamism of the overpowering of the Bower's Queen—is, however, already part of the sexual politics of Petrarchan lyric itself. Nancy Vickers, in *Writing and Sexual Difference,* describes the threat of dissolution or dismemberment that haunts the subject-object structure of the Petrarchan poetry of praise, in which the male subject is always potentially an Actaeon, torn apart after his vision of an unattainable Diana.[17] The canto of the Bower of Bliss bears a hint of this potential dismemberment as well as the castration of the male poet-lover in its reference both to Ida (2.12.52)—sacred to Cybele and her Phrygian rites—and to Rhodope, where Orpheus, the male lyric poet par excellence, not only sang but was undone by women. Its suspended instruments obliquely recall the lyric contests not just between shepherd-singers hanging their pipes upon a tree or between sacred and secular lyric traditions (as is suggested in the echo of Psalm 137 in the midst of the Bower's very different lyricism) but also between male poet and female object of desire in Petrarchan lyric, a relationship of power potentially translatable into both psychological and sociopolitical terms.

The vulnerable, subject status of the male lover within this Petrarchan lyric structure is countered by the mastery of the poet. In Petrarch himself, as Vickers suggests, the poet reverses the dangers of subjection and dismemberment by scattering the body of his mistress across his own *rime sparse* or scattered rhymes. In Spenser, the same stanza as evokes Ida and Rhodope in the Bower of Bliss makes reference to "Thessalian *Tempe,* where of yore / Faire *Daphne Phoebus* hart with love did gore" (52.4–5), a reference to the first, or lover, moment of the myth—the victimage of the male subject before a cruel and unattainable mistress—but one that inevitably provokes consciousness of its second moment—the transformation of the body of Daphne into a laurel, the triumphant sign of Phoebus' poetic power, the *lauro* that in Petrarchan lyric punningly assimilates the body of *Laura,* just as Syrinx becomes in her death (an event that, though it means a loss for her lover, also removes her threat) quite literally the instrument of Pan.

The Diana-Actaeon structure of Petrarchan lyric and its underlying dyadic antagonism were clearly part of the Petrarchan politics of a reign in which Elizabeth herself was represented as an unobtainable Diana and in which the Ovidian story had already been assimilated to relationships of power through a play on the Latin words *cervus/servus* ("stag" and "slave") and a comparison of the fate of Actaeon to the perils of life at court.[18] Like the myth of Attis' permanently suspended instruments, the threat of the Actaeon persona of the Petrarchan lyric poet is, once again, castration—a threat that Spenser recalls in the "Some would have gelt him" (7.6.50.3) of the story of the Actaeon-like Faunus in the *Cantos of Mutabilitie.* The same threat enters euphemistically into the Bower of Bliss when Guyon's quaintly named "courage cold" (2.12.68) begins to rise up at the sight of the naked bathing nymphs. The Actaeon-Diana story has been thought to be one of the many myths relating to the incest prohibition, the consequence of a forbidden view of the body of the mother; and certainly Guyon and the Palmer creep somewhat pruriently through the female brush (76) to gaze upon the simultaneously erotic and maternal "Witch" of this scene before they destroy it. The infant posture of the sleeping Verdant, together with the echo of the silencing of song from Psalm 137, reflects as well the threat of speechlessness in this Petrarchan structure, as in the Circean metamorphosis of her male victims. Petrarch, the threatened poetic Actaeon of his own canzone 23, can utter his lyrics only because he has an Orpheus-like respite between a forbidden seeing and dismemberment, and through his respite is able to silence rather than be silenced, to scatter the body of Laura rather than be dismembered himself. In Spenser's episode, Verdant's suspended instruments—signs of his status as what Mariann Sanders Regan suggestively calls "Lover *infans*"[19]—may figure a threat in which the potentially suspended instrument is poetic voice itself.

The split within the male subject of lyric that Regan represents as the split between Lover and Poet is matched in the episode of the Bower of Bliss by the splitting of the male figures of the scene between the subjected and symbolically castrated Verdant—his instruments hung like a sign of victory on Acrasia's tree—and the mastering Guyon, who by implication releases them. Ralegh presented the whole of *The Faerie Queene* not as the more usually cited outdoing of the narrative Ariosto but as an overgoing of the lyric Petrarch, written by a subject of a queen greater than Laura. But to become merely a Petrarch-like lyricist in praise of Elizabeth would be in some sense to become an imitative subject of the queen herself, held within a structure already appropriated as an instrument of power and presented elsewhere in *The Faerie Queene* as both paralyzed and paralyzing. In overgoing Petrarch in a poem that seems to repeat the Petrarchan lyric structure at a higher level, Spenser may also be subtly reversing the relation dictated by his own subject status, a position in which a gentleman by education only, himself dependent on the patronage system manipulated by the queen, might well conflate a visual icon reminiscent of a Petrarchan cruel mistress and her paralyzed male subject with echoes of the psalm of suspended instruments and potentially captive as well as captivating song. But like Petrarch, the poet subject to his mistress is also capable of creating—or decreating—her, and Spenser at the end of book 2 gives us an episode whose pervasive echoes of Aeneas at the court of Dido already evoke a text in which this moment of potential suspension is left behind by the narrative itself, and a female ruler is both surpassed and overruled.

The Belphoebe who shadows Elizabeth in her aspect as unattainable virgin or Petrarchan cruel mistress is, in the simile that describes her in book 2, compared (in a fashion that anticipates the Amazon Radigund who suspends the warlike instruments of Artegall) to "that famous Queene/Of *Amazons* whom *Pyrrus* did destroye" (2.3.31), thus, as Louis Montrose reminds us,[20] in a single line suggesting not just an exceptional female power but its remastery and destruction. Certainly the destruction of the Bower of Bliss is as violent as the prophesied ending of Psalm 137, with its captive and suspended instruments. Paradoxically, as Stephen Greenblatt and others have observed,[21] the final act of the Knight of Temperance is an act of intemperate violence, destruction of the Bower as a place of dangerous female dominance as well as of a suspect and seductive lyricism. Though the Cave of Mammon in this book is left standing and Verdant is let go with a mere lecture, Acrasia herself is led away in triumph. As with the dyadic antagonism of Petrarchan lyric, there seems to be here, ironically, no temperate middle way, no alternative to the polarity of subject or be subjected.

Regan, in *Love Words,* offers a psychologized theory of amorous or Petrarchan lyric in which the "charm" or "spell" that holds the lover resembles the Lacanian Imaginary or Melanie Klein's primal dyad of mother and child. We do not need object-relations theory or Lacanian psychoanalysis to catch the spellbound or oral fix of Verdant in the arms of a maternal Acrasia: indeed, the attempt to apply such contemporary theories to Renaissance texts often simply reveals the bluntness of our own instruments. And yet the simultaneous use and critique of Lacan in a famous essay by Laura Mulvey on the male gaze (in cinema)[22] might provide a suggestive supplement for students of this particular Spenserian episode, undergraduates and overgraduates alike. Mulvey describes the mediatory function of the female—and the threat of castration she represents—in the movement from the mother-child dyad, which Lacan terms the Imaginary, to the realm of the Symbolic, the name of the Father and the Law. The narrative of the overpowering and surpassing of Acrasia uncannily resembles the narrative progression of this Lacanian family romance, the raised and potent Mosaic "staffe" of the Palmer (which makes possible a detour out of this enclosure) managing to recall both the Law and the Father at once and rescuing Guyon as potential second Verdant or arrested boy from the fate of the latter's suspended instruments, from the posture of the speechless *infans* caught within a spellbinding female space. What Mulvey goes on to say of the voyeuristic *scopophilia* of the male gaze recalls much of the striking voyeurism of the visitants who come to destroy the Bower of Bliss, and her description of the two ways of overcoming the threat of castration figured by the female has interesting resonances both for the defeat of Acrasia and for the representation of Elizabeth, Spenser's Petrarchan mistress-queen. The first way, writes Mulvey, involves turning the dangerous female figure into an image entirely outside the narrative—as, for example, in the cult of the female star, a strategy that might shed some light on the cult of Elizabeth as Astraea, or quite literally a "star," transcendent embodiment of all the idealized Stella figures of Petrarchan lyric, outside the sublunar system as Gloriana is figured as outside *The Faerie Queene* or Elizabeth presented repeatedly as transcendent exception to the threatening dominant females within it.

The other means of escape from female power and the anxiety of castration, however, is a specifically narrative one, an overcoming through narrative of the "extra-diegetic tendencies" of woman as spectacle, whose "visual presence tends to . . . freeze the flow of action in moments of erotic contemplation"—a visual freeze that resembles the moments of paralysis, astonishment, or stonification in Petrarchan lyric as well as the potentially suspending moments of centripetal gaze that A. Bartlett Giamatti and others have described within *The Faerie Queene*.[23] It is, in Mulvey's description, the active male protagonist, the gazer rather than the gazed upon, who neutralizes this dangerous suspension by specifically narrative means, by a reenactment that repeats both the original trauma of the castrating female and the process of her overcoming. This sense both of resolute narrative movement and of reenactment as a form of control is conveyed in the canto of Acrasia by the resolutely "forward" movement (2.12.76.5) of Guyon's quest and by the aura of repetition and even déjà vu in its imitation of earlier literary scenes, which suggest that the victory over its threatening female is in a sense already won: certainly Guyon's almost ritual reenactment of Odysseus' resistance to the Sirens suggests that they are by no means as threatening the second time around. In Mulvey's account, in a way reminiscent of Guyon's destruction of the Bower, this narrative process of overcoming is not only voyeuristic but sadistic, its violence a sign both of the form of the threat and of the imperative of asserting control.[24] In Spenser, the "suspended instruments" of Acrasia's male captives are recovered as the Bower itself is overcome, and as Guyon and his Mosaic guide move forward to the narrative "point" or end of a Book of the Governor in which both a threatening female ruler and her suspect lyricism are finally mastered and surpassed.

Perhaps because of the notorious difficulty of defining it, lyric is frequently described in oppositional terms, by its relation or tension with something else—lyric cynosure as distinct from outside world, lyric as opposed to epic or narrative, and so on. *The Faerie Queene* seems to be exploring the implications of this opposition in its very form—narrative in its forward, linear quest and yet composed out of lyric stanzas that, like the enchantresses within it, potentially suspend or retard. It would be crude simply to transcode genre into gender here, though much of the history of lyric associates it with the female or the effeminate, and though Spenser's episode contains that confrontation which Horkheimer and Adorno saw as part of a revealing "dialectic of enlightenment" between a questing Odysseus and those Sirens evocative of both lyric and threatening female "charm." But Guyon's defeat of Acrasia seems both to involve and to suggest something more than one of the poem's many narrative defeats of a potentially suspended, centripetal, "lyric" space, to be not just, as Green-blatt suggests, a repression of pleasure for the sake of an empire ruled by Elizabeth (who in this reading would be simply *opposed* to Acrasia) but more complexly an overgoing of the potentially paralyzing suspensions—unpleasure as well as pleasure—of a lyric form adapted to the domination of a woman.

Whatever is at stake in this episode, it manages to suggest a sense not only of contest but of hierarchy—of the Sirens defeated by female Muses, who are in turn subject to Apollo, of the Virgilian epic surpassing of the female, of *eros,* and of the lyric genre of Spenser's own simultaneously pastoral and Petrarchan *Shepheardes Calender* and its suspended instruments, or of the traditional subordination, in Renaissance lyric theory, of secular lyric to the higher lyricism of the Psalms (as Spenser's *Fowre Hymnes* reconverts Petrarchan lyric into the higher sacred form). The Palmer's power to defeat all "charmes" gives to this episode a sense, ultimately, of something suspect about all *carmina,* something Protestant as well as male about its anxieties, though the defeat of Acrasia's "subtile web" (77) by the Vulcan-like Palmer's "subtile net" (81) suggests a strategy more complex than simple straightforward "enlightenment," a sense, as Keats put it, that only the poet's fine "spell of words" can rescue from a "dumb" and paralyzing "charm" and, perhaps, from an enchantress. A poem, finally, as dedicated as Spenser's is to the polysemous perverse might well comprehend the psychological dynamic of the overpowering of a potentially castrating female, the covert political allegory of the overgoing of a lyricism associated with Elizabeth, and a simultaneously aesthetic and moral uneasiness about the seductiveness of lyric "charm," even if that charm is an inseparable part of the attraction of his own poetry, its own tantalizingly suspending instrument.

NOTES

1. The edition used for this and all subsequent quotations from Spenser is *Poetical Works,* ed. J. C. Smith and E. de Selincourt (London: Oxford University Press, 1912).
2. Geneva Bible (1560) version. I am indebted to John Hollander's valuable discussion

of the different versions and pervasive poetic influence of this psalm in *The Oxford Anthology of English Literature,* ed. Frank Kermode et al. (New York: Oxford University Press, 1973), 1: 534–42. For the influence of the psalms themselves on Renaissance lyric and lyric theory, see, inter alia, O. B. Hardison, Jr., *The Enduring Monument: A Study of the Idea of Praise in Renaissance Literary Theory and Practice* (Chapel Hill: University of North Carolina Press, 1962), 95–102, and Barbara Kiefer Lewalski, *Donne's Anniversaries and the Poetry of Praise* (Princeton: Princeton University Press, 1973), 11–41.

3. See Calvin, *Commentaries on the Book of Psalms,* trans. James Anderson, 5 vols. (Grand Rapids, Mich.: William B. Eerdman's, 1949), 189–90, and Augustine, *Expositions on the Book of Psalms,* trans. J. Tweed et al., 6 vols. (Oxford: John Henry Parker, 1847–57), 163. Armida's garden appears in Tasso's *Gerusalemme liberata,* 16. Calvin's commentary doubles "hanged our harpes" with singers themselves held "in suspense," and this paralleling of the suspended instruments with a more properly psychological or spiritual "suspension" in the singer is continued in the versions of Thomas Campion, Thomas Carew, and Sir John Denham cited by Hollander in *The Oxford Anthology.*

4. See, for example, the analyses in Paul Alpers, *The Singer of the "Eclogues": A Study of Virgilian Pastoral* (Berkeley & Los Angeles: University of California Press, 1979), 97ff., 102, 134.

5. Jacopo Sannazaro, *Arcadia,* chap. 10, prose.

6. See, for example, the discussion in Richard Helgerson, *Self-crowned Laureates* (Berkeley & Los Angeles: University of California Press, 1983), 65–82; and Louis Adrian Montrose, "'The perfecte paterne of a Poete': The Poetics of Courtship in *The Shepheardes Calender,*" *Texas Studies in Language and Literature* 21 (1979): 34–67.

7. The Bower of Bliss episode twice uses "toyes" for "trifles" or "trifling." Thomas Watson, *Hekatompathia or Passionate Centurie of Love,* ed. S. K. Heninger, Jr. (Gainesville, Fla.: Scholars' Facsimiles, 1964), 5, speaks of poems themselves as "idle toyes proceeding from a youngling [i.e., prodigal, errant] frenzy." Sir John Harington, Elizabeth's godson and translator of Ariosto, feared that in becoming "a translator of Italian toys," he was wasting his education and later bade farewell to his "sweet wanton Muse." See Ludovico Ariosto, *Orlando furioso,* ed. Robert McNulty, trans. Sir John Harington (Oxford: Clarendon Press, 1972), 14–15; Sir John Harington, *Nugae Antiquae,* ed. Henry Harington (London, 1804), 1:333; and Helgerson's seminal discussion of these and other texts in relation to the profession of poetry, in *Self-crowned Laureates.*

8. The crossing of phallic with lyric instruments is of course not an exclusively Spenserian one, "instruments" being itself a fertile source of sexual double entendre. Cloten in *Cymbeline* (2.3.13–14), setting up with his musicians to woo Imogen, arranges his lyric entertainment in the hope that it will "penetrate" ("Come on, tune: if you can penetrate her with your fingering, so: we'll try with tongue too").

9. See Madlyn Millner Kahr, "Delilah," in *Feminism and Art History,* ed. Norma Broude and Mary D. Garrard (New York: Harper & Row, 1982), 137, an essay first brought to my attention by my colleague Mary Nyquist. That the evocation of Samson

and Delilah would not be inappropriate within a Renaissance *locus amoenus* such as the Bower of Bliss is suggested as well by Kahr's citation of the reclining Samson in the *Small Garden of Love*. Kahr's entire discussion of the oral and maternal aspects of this iconography is useful in juxtapostion with Spenser's scene. In one representation (c. 1508) by the great Dutch graphic artist Lucas van Leyden, Samson has laid his shield and halberd on the ground beside him, stressing his defenselessness as he sleeps in Delilah's lap; in another by the same artist (c. 1517–18), the abandoned weapon is a spiked club, perhaps a reference to the club of Hercules.

10. See Neil Hertz, "Medusa's Head: Male Hysteria under Political Pressure," *Representations* 1, no. 4 (1983): 40–50.

11. See Peter Hawkins, "From Mythography to Myth-making: Spenser and the *Magna Mater* Cybele," *Sixteenth Century Journal* 12, no. 3 (1981): 51–64. Hawkins reminds us that Isabel Rathborne long ago conjectured that Cybele was one of the literary ancestors of Gloriana: see her *Meaning of Spenser's Fairyland* (New York: Columbia University Press, 1937), 35. I am indebted to Hawkins' discussion of Cybele for the more general sense here of a link with *FQ* 2.12.

12. See Maureen Quilligan, *Milton's Spenser: The Politics of Reading* (Ithaca: Cornell University Press, 1983), 67ff.; and Louis Adrian Montrose, "'Shaping Fantasies': Figurations of Gender and Power in Elizabethan Culture," *Representations* 1, no. 2 (1983): 61–94.

13. The Muses' lament indicts the English nobility in phrases that directly recall the Bower of Bliss from the first installment of *The Faerie Queene* ("loathly idlenesse" [335]; "base slothfulnesse" [99]; "men depriv'd of sense and minde" [156]; together with an image of navigation that parallels that of the journey of Guyon and his Palmer guide: "But he that is of reasons skill bereft, / And wants the staffe of wisdome him to stay, / Is like a ship in midst of tempest left / Withouten helme or Pilot her to sway" [139ff]).

14. See the influential discussion of the Bower of Bliss in Stephen Greenblatt, *Renaissance Self-fashioning* (Chicago: University of Chicago Press, 1980), 165ff.

15. See Francis Bacon, "On the Fortunate Memory of Elizabeth Queen of England," trans. James Spedding, in *The Works of Francis Bacon*, ed. Spedding and Robert Ellis (London: Longman, 1857–74), 6:317; and Greenblatt, *Renaissance Self-fashioning*, 166–67.

16. See Sir John Harington's "Remembrauncer," *Nugae Antiquae* (1779; reprint, Hildesheim: Georg Olms, 1968), 2:211, cited in Louis Adrian Montrose, "The Elizabethan Subject and the Spenserian Text," in *Literary Theory/Renaissance Texts*, ed. Patricia Parker and David Quint (Baltimore: Johns Hopkins University Press, 1986), 326, and Montrose's larger discussion there of the dynamic of subjection and remastery, esp. 317–26.

17. Nancy Vickers, "Diana Described: Scattered Woman and Scattered Rhyme," in *Writing and Sexual Difference*, ed. Elizabeth Abel (Chicago: University of Chicago Press, 1982), 265–79. I am indebted to Vickers' suggestive discussion of the "scattering"

of Laura and of the Orpheus-like respite between seeing and dismemberment. See below.

18. Leonard Barkan, "Diana and Actaeon: The Myth as Synthesis," *English Literary Renaissance* 10, no. 3 (1980): 328, notes the Latin pun and George Sandys' explication of the myth as illustrating "how dangerous a curiosity it is to search into the secrets of Princes." See Sandys, *Ovid's "Metamorphosis" Englished, Mythologiz'd and Represented in Figures* (Oxford, 1632), 151–52.

19. See Mariann Sanders Regan, *Love Words: The Self and the Text in Medieval and Renaissance Poetry* (Ithaca: Cornell University Press, 1982), 50–82.

20. Montrose, "'Shaping Fantasies,'" 77.

21. See, for example, Greenblatt, *Renaissance Self-fashioning*, 177.

22. Laura Mulvey, "Visual Pleasure and Narrative Cinema," *Screen* 16, no. 3 (1978): 6–18.

23. See Mulvey, "Visual Pleasure," 12 ff.; and A. Bartlett Giamatti, "Spenser: From Magic to Miracle," in *Four Essays on Romance,* ed. Herschel Baker (Cambridge, Mass.: Harvard University Press, 1971).

24. Greenblatt, *Renaissance Self-fashioning,* 177, also notes this sense of implicit repetition or reenactment, remarking on "why Acrasia cannot be destroyed, why she and what she is made to represent must continue to exist, forever the object of the destructive quest. For were she not to exist as a constant threat, the power Guyon embodies would also cease to exist." My analysis would also invoke this sense of reencounter, but it would shift the emphasis more clearly to the specifically sexual politics of this episode.

Stephen Orgel

Shakespeare and the Cannibals

I

Almost as soon as Caliban appears in *The Tempest*, he is charged
by Prospero, and even more startlingly by Miranda, with savagery
and ingratitude. The denunciations are provoked by the recollection
of an attempt by Caliban to rape Miranda. But Caliban only com-
pounds the offense by acting both unrepentant and retrospectively
lecherous:

> O ho, O ho! would't had been done!
> Thou didst prevent me; I had peopled else
> This isle with Calibans.

[1.2.351–53]

I want to use this recollected moment of sexual imperialism as a locus
of assumptions about exploration and empire.

In act 2, scene 1 of *The Tempest,* Gonzalo has a utopian fantasy that
brings into the play a whole range of Renaissance thought about the
relation of Europeans to newly discovered lands and to their native
populations. These matters would have been especially timely in 1611
because of the recent formation of the Virginia Company, which in
1609 sent a fleet across the Atlantic bearing four hundred new colo-
nists. The results of this undertaking were little short of disastrous;
and at least one episode in the voyage provided Shakespeare with
material for *The Tempest:* during a hurricane near the Virginia coast,
the governor's ship was separated from the rest of the fleet and was
driven to Bermuda. The passengers got safely ashore, and wintered
comfortably there. William Strachey's account of the adventure, in a
widely circulated letter sent from Virginia in the summer of 1610, is
echoed in several places in the play.

The Strachey letter, however, does not account for all the New
World overtones in *The Tempest*. Caliban's god Setebos was a Patagon-
ian deity; the name appears in accounts of Magellan's voyages and is

clear evidence that the Americas were in Shakespeare's mind when he was inventing his islander. Travel narratives provided Shakespeare with a broad variety of models, both for the behavior of New World natives and for European responses to them.

Certain elements of the play relate to a New World topos persisting from the earliest accounts until well into the seventeenth century. Hugh Honour, in *The New Golden Land,* gives an excellent summary of the topos and reproduces a German broadsheet of 1505 that gives a particularly clear statement of its key elements (figure 1).[1] A wood-cut shows a group of natives wearing feathers and standing beneath a trellis from which hang human limbs. The text, in translation, reads:

The people are naked, handsome, brown, well-built, their heads, necks, arms, genitals, feet of both women and men are lightly covered with feathers. The men also have many precious stones on their faces and breasts. No one owns anything, but all things are held in common. And the men have as wives whoever pleases them, whether they are mothers, sisters or friends; they make no distinction between them. They also war with each other. They also eat each other, even those who have been killed, and hang their flesh in smoke. They live one hundred and fifty years, and have no government.

Cannibalism, Utopia, and free love reappear throughout the century as defining elements of New World societies. Cannibalism especially became part of the standard iconography of America and was described and depicted with varying degrees of luridness. Amerigo Vespucci, in his famous letter to his Medici patron (1500), notes his discovery that the American natives are cannibals as a point of exotic interest eliciting no particular distaste; but as the century progressed, scenes of the evisceration of corpses, the dressing of human flesh, and human barbecues grew to be stock elements of the American land-scape as it was represented for European audiences. Philippe Galle's personification of America elegantly straddles the fence (figure 2). If the figure's grisly attribute seems discordant, the fearful implications may in fact have heightened her attractiveness: Othello found stories of the anthropophagi effective aids in the wooing of Desdemona.

If Shakespeare were looking for accounts of New World natives, an

FIG. 1. New World natives, woodcut, Augsburg (?), c. 1505.
Bayerische Staatsbibliothek, Munich.

obvious place for him to turn would be to an essay on cannibals. We
know he did in fact turn to Montaigne's, where he found the other
elements of the topos as well: that the natives have a utopian government and sanction adultery. The latter observation is especially relevant, because the practice of free love in the New World is regularly
treated as an instance not of the lust of savages but of their edenic in-
nocence; and it helps to explain why Caliban is not only unrepentant
for his attempt on Miranda, but incapable of seeing that there is anything to repent for.

But the age's view of the relation of the New to the Old World goes
deeper than this: it is historical and typological as well. When Thomas
Harriot published his account of his voyage to Virginia, he included
as an appendix a set of engravings of the ancient Britons by Theodore
de Bry, "for to show," he explains, "how that the inhabitants of the

FIG. 2. Philippe Galle, *America,* engraving, c. 1500.
Metroplitan Museum of Art, New York, Harris Brisbane Dick Fund, 1953
(53.601.14[121]). Reproduced by permission.

Great Britain have been in times past as savage as those of Virginia."[2]
The Truue Picture of One Picte (figure 3) bears a striking similarity to
Galle's *America*. There is no suggestion in Harriot's accompanying
text that the early Britons were cannibals, but the analogy between
the cultures is clear from the iconography. De Bry was copying a set
of watercolors by the artist and naturalist John White, who had ac-
companied Harriot on his expedition, and the ancient Picte in White's
original is even more savage (figure 4). In the New World, Europe
could see its own past, itself in embryo: Prospero at the conclusion
of *The Tempest* acknowledges Caliban as his own.

These assumptions work in odd and interesting ways on the imagination of Renaissance Europe. Giulio Parigi's design for a 1608 Floren-
tine masque about the New World shows Amerigo Vespucci's ship en-
tering the most exotic of harbors, met by fabulous sea-monsters and
welcomed by a cloud full of deities (figure 5). As soon as one scratched
the surface of such a conceit, the exotic began to look very familiar.
Consider, for example, the Indian town of Secota, again from Harriot
on Virginia (figure 6). Harriot's text says that "their houses are scattered here and there," but de Bry's engraving is modeled on a neat
English village, with its high street and market gardens. This is the
European imagination refining and interpreting: John White's original drawing shows the village as much less tidily civilized. Similarly,
the figures at the center of a native dance depicted in Harriot (figure
7) are reminiscent of traditional representations of the three Graces—
again, however, only in de Bry's engraving, not in White's original
watercolor (figure 8), where the scene looks more like a witches'
coven, and there is nothing classically elegant about the three central
figures. The double vision of savage America is beautifully summed
up in a 1551 Spanish map of South America reproduced by Honour,
full of exotic wildlife and breechclouted savages, but personifying the
New World, at the heart of its jungle, as a classical deity.[3]

And, of course the assumptions we have been considering also
worked in reverse: the Europeans also saw themselves as versions of
the Indians. Inigo Jones designed feathered torchbearers for George
Chapman's masque of Virginian Indians, presented by the Inns of

Fig. 3. Theodore de Bry, after John White, *The Truue Picture of One Picte,* from Thomas Harriot, *A Briefe and True Report of the New Found Land of Virginia* (Frankfurt, 1590).

Fig. 4. John White, an ancient picte, watercolor, c. 1590.
British Museum. Reproduced by permission.

FIG. 5. Remigio Cantagallina, after Giulio Parigi, the ship of Amerigo Vespucci on the shores of the New World, design for the Fourth Intermezzo of *Il Giudizio di Paride*, etching, Florence 1606.

Court at Whitehall in 1613 as part of the wedding festivites for Princess Elizabeth and the Elector Palatine—*The Tempest* had also been performed several months earlier to entertain the royal fiancés. The Indian in figure 9 is a London lawyer. Indian headdresses became fashionable for court ladies at this period, and Simon van de Passe engraved a thoroughly anglicized Pocahontas (figure 10), who was happily resident at the English court for two years. Indeed, the domestication of the Indian was rather too successful in her case, and she had to be forced—unsuccessfully, as it turned out—to go home to Virginia. She died of a fever on board ship near the mouth of the Thames and is buried in Gravesend.

FIG. 6. Theodore de Bry, after John White, *The Town of Secota*, from Thomas Harriot, *A Briefe and True Report of the New Found Land of Virginia* (Frankfurt, 1590).

Fig. 7. Theodore de Bry, after John White, *Their Dances Which They Use att Their Hyghe Feastes*, from Thomas Harriot, *A Briefe and True Report of the New Found Land of Virginia* (Frankfurt, 1590).

It is worth observing that the English almost never do this sort of impersonation and domestication with Africans. The one time Queen Anne tried it, in Jonson's *Masque of Blackness* (1605), there was a great deal of disapproval. The African nymph in Inigo Jones' costume design (figure 11) has been civilized, exoticized—perhaps the most appropriate term, if we think again of *Othello,* is *disarmed*—by giving her eastern trappings, a Persian headdress and silk robes. It must be to the point, too, that the Europeans do not think of New World Indians as black, only as sunburned: it was claimed that if Indian babies were kept out of the sun, they would grow up white.

Fig. 8. John White, Indians dancing (detail), watercolor, c. 1590.
British Museum. Reproduced by permission.

Fig. 9. Inigo Jones, an Indian torchbearer, watercolor, costume design for George Chapman's *Masque of the Middle Temple and Lincoln's Inn*, 1613. Chatsworth, Devonshire Collection. Reproduced by permission of the Trustees of the Chatsworth Settlement.

MATOAKA ALS REBECCA FILIA POTENTISS · PRINC · POWHATANI IMP · VIRGINIÆ.
Ætatis suæ 21. A° 1616
Matoaks als Rebecka daughter to the mighty Prince Powhatan Emperour of Attanoughkomouck als virginia converted and baptized in the Christian faith, and wife to the wor.ll Mr. Joh Rolff.
S. Passe sculp:
Compton Holland exc.

FIG. 10. Simon van de Passe, Matoaka, or Pocahontas, engraving, 1616.

Fig. 11. Inigo Jones, an African nymph, one of the daughters of Niger, watercolor, costume design for Ben Jonson's *Masque of Blackness,* 1605. Chatsworth, Devonshire Collection. Reproduced by permission of the Trustees of the Chatsworth Settlement.

One of the *loci classici* for Renaissance concepts of New World natives is Montaigne's essay "On Cannibals." We know that Shakespeare
was familiar with this essay, because Gonzalo's imagined utopia includes, almost verbatim, a passage from John Florio's translation of
it. But Caliban has almost nothing in common with the prelapsarian
savages described by Montaigne. He owes more to concepts of the
natural depravity of New World populations, such as are found in
explorers' accounts from Purchas to Captain John Smith. In Montaigne, on the contrary, it is the Europeans who are predatory and
savage; Shakespeare, as he so often does, dramatizes both sides of the
debate and in the process renders a resolution to it impossible. Montaigne's point in introducing Plato's ideal republic is that if philoso-
phers could see savage societies, they would have to abandon their
utopian fantasies: New World natives have created an ideal community that outdoes Plato's imagined one. But Caliban provides no
counterargument to Gonzalo's fantasy. Shakespeare has taken everything from Montaigne except the point.

II

And yet, in the context of Gonzalo's commonwealth, with its assumption that any new land is there for the taking and refashioning,
Caliban does constitute a significant counterclaim to Prospero's
authority. The island, he asserts, is rightly his, and Prospero is an in-
vader and usurper. Caliban has, in fact, a double claim to the island,
both through inheritance from his mother, Sycorax, the first settler,
and through prior possession. Prospero implicitly disallows the claim
from inheritance by calling Caliban a bastard, but he never disputes
the second claim (which Caliban also never articulates), nor does he
ever argue the legitimacy of his own rule. In Renaissance terms, Caliban's claim to the island is, on either ground, a good one, even if the
charge of bastardy is held to be valid: there were by Shakespeare's
time numerous royal precedents, including the two previous queens

of England, Elizabeth and her half-sister, Mary Tudor, both of whom were technically illegitimate.

From this perspective—the one from which Caliban is king of the island—the assault on Miranda with which I began may be seen not as destructive and uncivilized but as an act of political economy, dictated by the same impulse that prompted Romulus to promote the rape of the Sabine women. Miranda, in Caliban's eyes, will not merely serve to satisfy his lust; she will also be the breeding stock for his empire and people the isle with Calibans. Moreover, however abhorrent the attempt on Miranda's chastity may be to Prospero, the essential, enabling idea behind it can only have come from him. We are sexual creatures by instinct; we have to be *taught* that sex is related to reproduction. If Prospero taught Caliban everything he knows, that is how Caliban learned of the demographic advantages of sex with the only woman on the island. Here is another context for Caliban's unrepentant lechery. Imperial rapes, once they get into history, are a source not of shame but of national pride: the rape of the Sabines, wedding as it did the lands beyond the Tiber to the empire, remained an outrage only to the Sabines.

Miranda has two royal suitors, and Caliban is one of them. If Prospero is unable explicitly to acknowledge the legitimacy of the suit, he implicitly does so by equating Ferdinand with Caliban, making him perform his servant's tasks, accusing him of usurpation and treason, and especially, inveighing against Ferdinand's lust for Miranda, which has not been at all apparent in the play. Any suitor—that is, even the suitor of Prospero's choice—is Caliban.

The point, and with it the clear relation between imperial and libidinous ambitions, is emphasized in that other marriage in the play's background, between Alonso's daughter Claribel and the King of Tunis. This is the wedding from which the Neapolitans were returning when the shipwreck occurred. It was not a happy occasion, but one to which the bride went unwillingly and of which the court as a whole disapproved; among the Neapolitans, only Alonso, the bride's father, favored the match. No reasons are given for the general dismay, but the King of Tunis would have been both a Moslem and black. The King of Naples presumably saw him as a desirable son-in-law for geopolitical rather than romantic reasons: an alliance between the kingdoms of Naples and Tunis in the sixteenth century would have controlled the eastern end of the Mediterranean. Caliban too, surely not coincidentally, is originally Tunisian: Sycorax was pregnant with him when she was exiled from Algiers, the western end of the kingdom of Tunis. Clearly Naples and Tunis have powerful interests in common; and, judging from the match arranged for Claribel, if Alonso had been marooned on the island instead of Prospero, he might well have taken a different view of Caliban as a suitor for his daughter.

III

Caliban's name seems to be related to the word *Carib*, the name of a fierce West Indian tribe, who were said to have been cannibals, and from which the word *cannibal* derives; and Caliban may be intended simply as an anagram of cannibal. The implicit assumptions in the choice of the name are clear enough; and they are Prospero's assumptions. But criticism has generally seen much more in Caliban than Prospero does—in the eighteenth century Joseph Warton observed kindness in his character,[4] and to Coleridge he was "in some respects a noble being: the poet has raised him far above contempt"[5]—far, that is, above Prospero's contempt. Frank Kermode, in the introduction to the Arden edition, does something similar, relating him to the European *wodewose*, the wild or savage man, bred in the woods but, despite his uncivilized manners, human and educable. Kermode uses some very dubious linguistic evidence to support his claim; but, evidence aside, the view of Caliban as a familiar European figure is symptomatic of a widespread critical attempt, which is prompted by the play itself, to humanize and domesticate Caliban, to rescue him from Prospero's view of him—to succeed with him where Prospero has failed. Auden was responding to the same impulse when, in his interesting and very sentimental gloss on the play *The Sea and the Mirror*, he made Caliban the embodiment of suffering humanity.

Caliban constitutes the most important instance in the play where what Prospero says and what we perceive fail to coincide. "You taught me language and my profit on't/Is I know how to curse" (1.2.365–66): that famous riposte summarizes and justifies Prospero's view of Caliban. But we hear much more than curses in Caliban's language; he is the other great poet of the play.

> Be not afeard, the isle is full of noises,
> Sounds and sweet airs that give delight and hurt not.
> Sometimes a thousand twangling instruments
> Will hum about mine ears, and sometimes voices,
> That, if I then had waked after long sleep,
> Will make me sleep again; and then, in dreaming,
> The clouds methought would open, and show riches
> Ready to drop upon me; that, when I waked,
> I cried to dream again.
>
> [3.2.133–41]

We see little enough of this side of Caliban, but Prospero's fear and loathing render him utterly blind to it.

The stage tradition has presented Caliban more often as clownish than frightening, thereby implicitly undercutting the seriousness of Prospero's fears and invective. With Stephano and Trinculo, the role became a popular comic turn in the late eighteenth century. A century later, Beerbohm Tree's famous 1904 production, in which Tree played Caliban, portrayed him as a sensitive and potentially noble creature, aboriginal humanity, and made much of his love of music (figure 12). The role, which in the play is very short, was greatly expanded by adding dances and pantomime to it. Frank Benson, at Stratford in 1891, had similarly presented Caliban as a Darwinian missing link and based his performance on the movements of great apes—both these interpretations are Victorian versions of Harriot finding in Virginia his own England in embryo. And by the last quarter of the nineteenth century, the rehabilitation of Caliban was so successful that it had become the great role in the play, the part that virtuoso actors chose, rather than that of Prospero.

IV

Dynastic issues, questions of legitimacy, and royal authority have an epic as well as a political dimension in the play. In particular, allusions to and echoes of the *Aeneid* are insistent in *The Tempest*, though few commentators have felt sure of what to make of them. There are certainly obvious points of contact between the two, the most obvious being Ferdinand's reaction to his first sight of Miranda with Aeneas' words on seeing Venus, "o dea certe"[6]—"Most sure the goddess." (1.2.424). Gonzalo, Antonio, and Sebastian, in an exchange that has proved baffling to editors, invoke "widow Dido" and "widower Aeneas" and argue over whether Tunis and Carthage are the same place; Ariel and his spirits appearing as harpies at Alonso's banquet are reenacting a Virgilian episode;[7] and so forth. The geographical world in which the play is located is largely that of the *Aeneid:* Alonso's shipwreck interrupts a voyage retracing Aeneas', from Carthage/ Tunis to Naples. Shakespeare's imagination in this was the imagination of Renaissance imperialism as well: if Alonso coveted a Tunisian alliance enough to marry his daughter to a Moslem king, Spain took more militant measures, sending invading warships to Tunis several times during the sixteenth century; and the mid-sixteenth-century chronicler of exploration Richard Eden records that the Spanish named a harbor in the West Indies Carthago—the newest empire validating itself by replicating the oldest.[8]

As for the notorious exchange about "widow Dido," it has proved baffling only because editors and critics have limited their attention to Virgil. From antiquity until well into the seventeenth century there were two traditions concerning Dido. In the older, which was considered the historical one, she was a princess of Tyre married to her uncle Sychaeus, a priest of Hercules. Her brother Pygmalion, the

Fig. 12.   Charles A. Buchel, Sir Herbert Beerbohm Tree as Caliban, 1904.
From *The Sketch*. Photo Lois Thornhill.

tyrant of Tyre, murdered her husband for his enormous wealth, and she fled by ship, taking with her both his gold and a group of discontented noblemen. On Cyprus she collected fifty women, who were raped and abducted by her followers, to provide, like the Sabine women for the Romans, the breeding stock for the new realm. The imperial mythology, in which rape is essential to the foundation of empire, is part of the Dido story too.

Dido then sailed to North Africa, where through a combination of shrewd bargaining and deceptiveness she obtained the land to found Carthage. She was an exemplary ruler, famous for her chastity and her devotion to the memory of her murdered husband. She committed suicide to prevent her forced marriage to a local king. Mantegna depicted her standing before her funeral pyre holding the urn containing her husband's ashes (figure 13). The painting is one of a pair, the other being the parallel Biblical heroine of impeccable and militant virtue, Judith.

It is Virgil who introduces Aeneas into the legend and thereby transforms Dido from a model of heroic chastity to an example of the dangers of erotic passion. Later commentators generally account for the transformation as Virgil's way of explaining the traditional enmity between Carthage and Rome—Hannibal, in this reading, is Dido's revenge. In antiquity both Macrobius and Servius rejected the historicity of the Virgilian story, and the Church Fathers regularly treated Dido as a proto-Christian for her absolute fidelity to her marriage vows. Petrarch in *The Triumph of Chastity* explicitly denies that Aeneas had anything to do with Dido's death, and Boccaccio in his book of heroines, *De Claris Mulieribus,* rebukes Virgil for lying about her.

George Sandys, in his commentary on book 14 of the *Metamorphoses,* summarizes the tradition in which Shakespeare was working. Regarding Virgil's Dido, he writes that "others upon better grounds have determined that this was merely a fiction of Virgil's, and that Aeneas never came thither." Other English writers, observing that Dido's given name was Elissa, found in her an easy analogue for Elizabeth; and by 1595 the name in Charles Stephanus' *Dictionarium His-*

Fig. 13. Andrea Mantegna, *Dido,* tempera and gold on linen, c. 1500.
Montreal Museum of Fine Arts, Purchase, Tempest Fund (920.104). Reproduced by permission.

toricum, a standard source book for the age, had become *Eliza. Dido* is an epithet applied to her after her death, usually explained as meaning "valiant." In the Sieve Portrait now in Siena (figure 14), Elizabeth appears flanked by miniature scenes from the story of Dido and Aeneas. Since the British crown traced its descent from Aeneas, the epic iconography here ingeniously provided the queen with both her heroic ancestor and the prototype of her chastity. The sieve, emblem of the Roman vestals and thus symbolic of Elizabeth's virginity, declares that this Dido will resist the temptations of any modern Aeneas.

This is the heroic and moral tradition that Gonzalo is invoking in his comparison of Claribel to "widow Dido." The cynical Antonio and Sebastian undercut the allusion by invoking the alternative tradition, in which Dido abandons her chastity to an equally unchaste "widower Aeneas"; there are many sympathetic readings of the Virgilian episode in the period, but there was no getting around the fact that Virgil's Dido ends as a fallen woman, conscious of her sin,[9] betrayed and abandoned. Brief as it is, the exchange, with its tiny dialectic of ethical and cynical, encapsulates the play's thematic ambivalence toward human nature and toward the past. It is relevant, too, to Prospero's compulsive fears for his daughter's chastity; and insofar as the play's Virgilian overtones encourage us to see Ferdinand as another Aeneas, Prospero's anxiety will strike us as justified.

Antonio's cynical reading of the Dido story, however, points in another direction too, away from the classical and heroic and toward Elizabethan assumptions about Renaissance Italy: the Machiavellian and diabolical figure as largely in the world of the play as the noble and philosophical. Shakespeare expresses a similar double vision of Italy in *Cymbeline.* Attempts to find a source for the play's modern history comparable to the *Aeneid* for its classicism have been on the whole unrewarding. In 1868 Halliwell called attention to William Thomas' *Historie of Italie* (1549), where there is an account of Prospero Adorno, a Milanese lieutenant who became Duke of Genoa, allied himself with Ferdinand, King of Naples, and was overthrown and expelled.[10] Recently William Slights has found a version of the

FIG. 14.   Cornelius Ketel (?), *Elizabeth I* (The Sieve Portrait), oil on canvas,
c. 1580.
Pinacoteca di Siena. Photo Soprintendenza B.A.S. Siena.

story told about another Prospero, surnamed Colonna, in Remigio Nannini's *Civill Considerations upon Many and Sundrie Histories* (London, 1601), which adds the name of Ferdinand's father—Alphonso (of which Alonso is a variant)—and in a nearby chapter discusses communication with spirits, though not by Prospero.[11] If either of these is really a source for the play, it is chiefly valuable as an indication of how little Shakespeare was controlled by the history he was reading; but in any case, such accounts, like the travel narratives, are less significant as the basis for a few names and details than as models for contemporary Italian political behavior.

The search for historical figures behind the play in fact offers some unexplored possibilities that resonate tantalizingly, but they seem to have more relevance to Caliban than to Prospero: the King of Naples in the Prospero Colonna story is Alphonso V of Aragon (1416–58), who claimed the throne of Naples not by descent from his father but under the will of his mother, Joanna II, and asserted his right by conquest. His son Ferdinand, who succeeded him as King of Naples, was illegitimate. If we are going to take history seriously as a source for the play, this is surely relevant to the way Prospero turns Ferdinand into a version of Caliban.

V

Prospero the illusionist, moving his drama toward reconciliation and a new life, presents in the betrothal masque his own version of Gonzalo's utopia, a vision of orderly nature and bountiful fruition. The performance opens with benign deities: Iris, bringing together Ceres and Juno to celebrate the royal betrothal, reconstitutes the fragmented world of the play. As Prospero had incorporated mother and wife in coming to the island with Miranda, so his art now figures them forth in forms of power and benignity, the primal mother and the wife of Jupiter. Goddess of earth and goddess of air,[12] patronesses of agriculture and of marriage, opposites and complements, together they resolve the dramatic tension implicit in Caliban and Ariel. When earth is seen as Ceres, it is no longer intractable, but productive and nurturing; when air is seen as Juno, it is no longer volatile, but universal and majestic. Even Prospero's libidinous fears are put to rest here: Iris assures Ceres that Venus and Cupid, plotters of the rape of her daughter Proserine, have fled from the scene, confounded by the chaste vows of Ferdinand and Miranda.

Ceres presides here because Prospero's masque is a civilizing vision, and, in constrast to the bounty of the island, the fertility it invokes is controlled and orderly. Caliban, the provider of Prospero's food, is a forager, hunter, and fisherman; the islanders are sustained by wild things and live as predators on nature. But the masque celebrates agriculture and refers us to a sophisticated society. Ceres even remarks on "this short-grassed green" (5.1.83): this action takes place on a well-tended lawn—or on the Blackfriars' stage, which was covered with green rushes, or the court dancing floor, with its green felt carpeting. The season adduced is, to begin with, "spongy April," the start of the agricultural year. Crops are not yet sprouting; the nymphs are "cold" and "chaste," the bachelor with spring fever is "lass-lorn" (65–68). Within fifty lines, however, Ceres is invoking the full barns and garners of high summer, "Vines with clust'ring bunches growing;/ Plants with goodly burden bowing" (112–13); and shortly before Prospero stops the performance, Iris summons "sunburned sicklemen, of August weary" (134). A whole season of growth, fruition, and harvest has been encompassed in the masque's brief span.

This entertainment, for all its lightness, is reenacting central concerns of the play as a whole. It invokes a myth in which the crucial act of destruction is the rape of a daughter; it finds in the preservation of virginity the promise of civilization and fecundity; and it presents as its patroness of marriage not Hymen, but Juno, the goddess who symbolizes royal power as well. This is Prospero's vision, symbolically expressing how deeply the fears for Miranda's chastity are implicated with his sense of his own power, how critical an element she is in his plans for the future. But she is valuable to him, and an extension of his authority, only so long as she remains a virgin, a potential bride for the husband of his choice.

The underlying assumptions here are not unique to Prospero, or to this play, or to Shakespeare. They inform Elizabethan and Jacobean political behavior generally and its enterprise in the New World. They are clearly implicit in Ralegh's selection of the name *Virginia* for his new colony (rather than, say, *Eliza* or *Tudoria*). The epithet acknowledges the extent to which virginity had become, in Elizabeth's reign, a crucial attribute of royal power and had become for James, striving like Prospero and Alonso for political alliances through the marriage of his children, an essential royal bargaining chip. In the potential of virginity lay not only civilization but the promise of infinite bounty within a hegemonic order. But the epithet expresses as well the darker truth of imperial ambitions. Ralegh's designs on the virgin land, appropriately carried out on the authority of the new Dido, were as much Caliban's as Prospero's.

NOTES

Some of the material in this essay also appears in my introduction to the Oxford *Tempest* (forthcoming).

1. Hugh Honour, *The New Golden Land* (New York: Pantheon Books, 1975), fig. 7, p. 12.

2. Thomas Harriot, *A Briefe and True Report of the New Found Land of Virginia* (Frankfurt, 1590), sig. E^r.

3. Honour, *New Golden Land*, pl. 8, p. 38.

4. Joseph Warton, *The Adventurer*, no. 97 (9 October 1753).

5. *Coleridge's Shakespearean Criticism*, ed. T. M. Raysor (London: Constable, 1930), 2:178.

6. Virgil, *Aeneid*, 1.328.

7. Ibid., 3.225ff.

8. Richard Eden, *The Decades of the New World* (London, 1555), 51–52. The name Setebos also appears in this book.

9. Virgil, *Aeneid*, 4.172.

10. William Thomas, *Historie of Italie* (London, 1549), fol. 181^V.

11. William Slights, "A Source for *The Tempest* and the Context of the *Discorsi*," *Shakespeare Quarterly* 36 (1985): 68–70.

12. Juno is regularly explained as air in Renaissance mythographies: see, for example, Vincenzo Cartari, *Imagini* (Venice, 1571), 172.

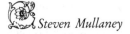 *Steven Mullaney*

Brothers and Others,
or the Art of Alienation

I

On his first voyage to Meta Incognita in 1576, Martin Frobisher captured a Baffin Island Eskimo who would serve, or so it was hoped, as a cultural go-between on two fronts: first as a much-needed native interpreter, and then as an exportable token of the voyage, capable of testifying at home to the wonders and riches of Frobisher's new-found-land. The native in question, however, proved less than cooperative. "Upon finding himself in captivitie," as George Best observed, "for very choller and disdain, he bit his tong in twayne within his mouth."[1] On the voyage back to England, as if to demonstrate the many senses in which alien "resistance" could thwart the desires of Elizabethan enterprise, he caught what would be his death of cold. Mute and ailing, the man survived in London for little more than a day—in the space of which he was displayed before an admiring populace, presented to the Queen, and even made to sit for a visiting painter, Lucas de Heere, who represented his waning subject not once but twice, in both native dress and courtly Elizabethan costume.[2]

The following spring, when Frobisher embarked upon a return voyage, he went forewarned about the potential power of native "choller and disdain"; thanks to de Heere's palette, however, he also went forearmed, taking with him the more faithful portrait of his adamantly un-Elizabethan alien. In due course a second member of the same tribe was captured, but at the first signs of despondency, the new captive was duly introduced to his predecessor. Here is Best's account of the ensuing engagement between the imaginary and the real:

For afterwardes, when we showed him the picture of his countreyman . . . he was upon the suddayne much amazed thereat, and beholding advisedly the same with silence a good while, as though he would streyne courtesie whether [he] shoulde begin the speech (for he thought him no doubte a lively creature), at length began to question with him, as with his companion, and finding him dumme and mute, seemed to suspect him, as with one disdaynful, and would with little helpe have growen into choller at the matter, until at last by feeling and handling, he founde him but a deceiving picture. And then with great noyse and cryes, ceased not wondering, thinking that we coulde make men live or die at our pleasure.[3]

In his unceasing wonder, Frobisher's second captive would prove a willing and even eager interpreter—impressed into service, as it were, by the simple yet dramatic expedient of holding the mirror up to nature.

When we speak today of art reflecting society or culture, we usually have in mind a less literal example; we rarely envision an effect as antithetical as the one produced here. But then, reflection theory was never particularly adept at grasping cultural practices, or at considering the effects of reproducing cultural images, norms, and ideologies—what might be called the surplus use-value of representation. Frobisher and his men obviously adhere to a more dynamic model of cultural representation. In their hands and from their perspective, what is for us a common but problematic critical metaphor becomes a far from predictable yet potent form of cultural production. Reflection here hardly reaffirms what is reproduced but instead produces a moment of cultural feedback such as might be described in information, as opposed to reflection, theory. The captive is confronted by an image of his own kind, and with a touching naïveté he responds in kind. However touching or naïve from our perspective, however, his initial hesitation and subsequent efforts to communicate with his presumed fellow must also be recognized as expressions of kinship and community, intended tokens of cultural recognition; his actions, that is to say, manifest a code of socially inscribed behavior of the kind that serves to define any given cultural community and to set it apart from all others—a decorum Best recognizes as "courtesie." Such overtures are unreciprocated, of course, but this lack of reciprocity is also, and more crucially, observed by others. From the native's perspective he has been drawn out of himself and left exposed, not only spurned but also humiliated, and his manifested desire for fellow-ship gives way to an equally powerful sense of outrage and betrayal. His comrade in captivity changes before his eyes, transformed into an image of the Other as this betrayal is first projected onto his "disdayn-ful" companion and then reproduced and acted out by the native him-self, in a choler directed not at his captors but at an emblem of his own cultural identity. Although the betrayal proves illusory, the ali-enation he has been induced to act out is all too real, and his wonder at the close is not altogether naïve. What has indeed lived and died at the pleasure of these Elizabethans—what has been elicited, then sub-verted by the "dumbe oratory" of art, if I may borrow Thomas Hey-wood's quite felicitous phrase[4]—is nothing less than the native's sense of himself, of those tribal loyalties that had, up until this moment, de-fined and produced in him any sense of self he possessed. Far from naïve, his unceasing wonder is in fact the enduring sign of his aliena-tion: produced at the moment when he realizes his error, it marks the distance between his former naïveté and a new perspective that comes from seeing himself, in error, through the eyes of his captors.

The scene of conversion is a remarkable one, and for my purposes it is not less but rather all the more significant if we recognize that Best's account is of dubious credibility. Whatever took place on the shores of Meta Incognita, the record we have is in large part a projec-tion of expectations and anxieties fostered the year before, a resolu-tion—perhaps imaginary, perhaps not—of the dilemma posed by Fro-bisher's first captive. In all likelihood, the first captive's violent loss of tongue was an accident, as far beyond his control as his lack of im-munity to European microbes. To his captors, however, it was a will-ful if ultimately Pyrrhic act of subversion, a hostile and telling expres-sion of native intransigence motivated by "choller and disdain," and it is no accident that such a perspective informs Best's account of the second voyage. Native intransigence is reproduced—willfully mute in life, Frobisher's first captive is no less unresponsive in pictorial effigy—but is also turned back upon its source; "choller and disdain," the signs of alien resistance and Pyhrric subversion, are artfully in-duced, displaced, and turned to Elizabethan advantage in a scene that,

whether it took place in the manner described or not, nonetheless unfolds with a certain social and psychological plausibility—especially,
one must assume, when viewed from the perspective of the Elizabethan audience for whom Best wrote, and with whom he shared certain assumptions about the manner in which social selves are created
and recreated, constructed and reconstructed.

From such a perspective, at any rate, what Best records is an act of
cultural speculation rather than mere reflection: a Renaissance version
of a mirror-stage, which is to say a mirror-stage precipitated at a cultural level rather than at the infantile threshold of the cultural, and
one, moreover, that is fractured at a critical moment to produce a
colonial form of transference, resulting in the displacement and re-
alignment of an already constituted cultural identity. However we describe it, the process of internal colonization that Best depicts was
hardly limited to the realm of colonial wish-fulfillment; nor was it
only on the margins of the known world or when dealing with such
naïve subjects that the period relied upon the power of fiction, of cultural representation and performance in various forms and forums, to
manage and redefine problematic boundaries of kinship and authority.[5] "Power can neither see, work, nor devise," as Fulke Greville
notes in *Mustapha*, "Without the people's hands, hearts, wit, and eyes"
(*Chorus Secundus*, 207–8).[6] It is an astute anatomy, born as it is of the
recognition that power is never merely a coercive force, that it must,
in order to be effective, act not only upon its subjects but through
them as well—through their hands, hearts, wit, eyes, and even
tongues, inducing them to participate and even to become the primary actors in the ongoing drama of their own subjection. Implicit
in Greville's anatomy, but close to the surface, is the further recognition that power thus conceived is always and already a collective fiction, or rather, that it operates at and upon the boundary that
separates the fictive from the actual, the imaginary from the real.
Viewing himself through his captors' eyes, Frobisher's Eskimo feels
that boundary expand to include himself: he sees himself, that is to
say, as if onstage, perceived not as a fiction but as a cultural construct,

a theatrically conceived subject in the psychoanalytic as well as the political sense of the term.

Thus conceived, our sixteenth-century Eskimo is not as isolated a figure as he might at first appear. Some years ago, Norbert Elias provided some illuminating studies of the cultural forces that were reshaping the social and psychological configuration of the subject in late sixteenth- and early seventeenth-century Europe.[7] Although Elias restricted his *History of Manners* to behavior manuals and etiquette books, he argued that the pressures and constraints upon the social self-evident in such sources were not only new in structure and effect but were also symptomatic of a larger "civilizing process"—a phrase he employs with a fine irony—necessitated by the expansion and solidification of dominant European cultures and by their increasing need to control and contain the residual and marginal cultures around them, both at home and abroad. What Frobisher's Eskimo is subjected to, whether in actuality or in an Elizabethan projection of the familiar upon the strange, is a twofold internal dynamic set in motion by the induced incorporation of an alien and superior perspective upon oneself and concluded by the resultant projection of mastery onto those who, whether imaginary or real, command that perspective; as Elias suggests, such a dynamic can be found at work throughout European culture in various forms and forums during the period, and at work to produce new forms of internal constraint and self-apprehension—to produce, that is to say, something like the modern subject.

What Elias does not address in his own work, however, is the inherent theatricality of such a transaction between the self and the Other and the place of such theatricality in what might be called the genealogy of the modern subject. The internal distantiation experienced by Frobisher's Eskimo creates a theater of and within the self, in which he views himself through the eyes of a judgmental and superior Other. Human subjects are always cultural constructs, but their articulation and the constitutive restraints upon them—what Michel Foucault has called "the techniques of the subject"[8]—vary from one culture to another, one period to the next; in the early modern period, the boundary that power speculates upon and with most prominently and significantly is the space of the theatrical. It is a space that is at once public and private, externally manifested and powerfully, affectively internalized; it is also an ambivalent and protean domain, as the two figures who occupied it most prominently in Elizabethan England knew most acutely. Those figures are of course Elizabeth and Shakespeare, each of whom was significantly invested in both the powers of fiction and the art of alienation, and each of whom played a role, however different, in the act of cultural speculation commonly known as *The Merchant of Venice*.

II

At the turn of this century, literary historians tended to date *The Merchant of Venice* late in 1594. It was in that year that one Roderigo Lopez, born a Portuguese Jew but living in England as a convert and court physician to Elizabeth, was convicted of conspiring against the life of the Queen and put to death before a large and festive crowd, which took a special delight in Lopez' dying assertion that "hee loved the Queene as well as Christ Jesus." According to Camden's account, the declaration "being spoken by a Jew, as it was, was but onely laughed at by the people"; according to Sir Sidney Lee and others, Shakespeare heard them, and wrote a "play of the hour" to capitalize upon the antisemitic spirit of the times.[9]

Today we gravitate toward a later date and, more significantly, a less settled sense of the play, to the extent that *The Merchant of Venice* has recently provided Norman Rabkin with an appropriately problematic introduction to *Shakespeare and the Problem of Meaning*. The Lopez trial is still routinely invoked as a historical context for the play, but still invoked by rote, as a context assumed to need no interpretation itself. Trials for high treason and public executions, however, were among the most prominent stages on which the early modern state attempted to work out, upon and around the figure of the condemned, its own problems of meaning—attempted, that is to say, to articulate and define the boundaries within which its own interpretation could take place, and to make manifest a secure and unclouded image of the authority of the prince, an image no longer in question but restored to its full and dramaturgically enacted potency. I say attempted, not only because in the Lopez case the image of power and authority thus projected was one that neither coincided with nor supplemented the Queen's own, but also because I want to emphasize the instability and especially the vulnerability inherent in a form of power that was, by necessity, theatrically conceived, negotiated, and maintained—a vulnerability to its own theatrically conceived conditions of possibility. The poetics of Elizabethan power, as Stephen Greenblatt has noted, is inseparable from a poetics of the theater; that poetics is also

> inseparably bound up with the figure of Queen Elizabeth, a ruler without a standing army, without a highly developed bureaucracy, without an extensive police force, a ruler whose power is constituted in theatrical celebrations of royal glory and theatrical violence visited upon the enemies of that glory. . . . Elizabethan power . . . depends upon its privileged visibility. As in a theatre, the audience must be powerfully engaged by this visible presence while at the same time held a respectful distance from it. "We princes," Elizabeth told a deputation of Lords and Commons in 1586, "are set upon stages in the sight and view of all the world."[10]

Elizabeth's pronouncement has come to be one of the most commonly cited sentences in recent Renaissance criticism, oftentimes given an air of bold assertion, of a power overcoming its inadequacies to achieve a full and even exultant mastery over the dramaturgical demands upon it. In context, however, Elizabeth's assertion was a rather vexed and apprehensive complaint. The deputation of Lords and Commons was demanding that she sign a death warrant for Mary, Queen of Scots; Elizabeth wanted the execution to go forward, but without her explicit order for the death of a sister-monarch and kinswoman.[11] What sets Elizabeth on stage is one of the more momentous genealogical crises of authority in the sixteenth century;

her visibility is not a sign of privilege or potency but of her own discomfiting subjection to the sight and view of all the world, and her
apprehension over what that world will make of her hand in Mary's
death. At the beginning of the controversy, Elizabeth had declared,
"I know what it is to be a subject, what to be a Soveraigne";[12] by its
end, when announcing her stage presence, she had discovered what it
was like to be both at once. Power in this instance, as on the shores
of Meta Incognita, resides not in the figure onstage but in the eye of
the beholder.

Or more precisely, the power wielded by such a monarch, the
power she was invested with, was to a large degree invested in her by
the gaze of her subjects; the royal image and identity were not wholly
at the Queen's command, but in part the projection and hence the
product of those subjects. Properly staged, early modern sovereignty
produced not a sense of mastery but of awe or wonder, a reaffirmation of the distance between audience and monarchical spectacle, subject and sovereign, but Elizabeth was keenly aware that her
subjects' desire for mastery was one of the necessary conditions for
their proper and respectful subjection.[13] She maintained her tenuous
position as the female ruler of a patriarchal state, in fact, by eliding
the vulnerability of power with the vulnerability of gender and turning both to her own advantage, styling herself as the unattainable,
hence endlessly pursued, Virgin Queen, adapting the conventions of
pastoral romance to restructure and manage the shape of her subjects'
sexual as well as political desires. She ruled not so much by "the
arduous and constant wooing of the body politic," as Wallace Mac-
Caffrey once suggested, as by inducing it to woo her.[14]

Not all her suitors were easily ruled, however, or content to linger
on the threshold indefinitely. In 1594, presented with the warrant for
Lopez' death, Elizabeth again resisted attaching her name and thus her
countenance to such a document; here her concern was not with the
bonds of official kinship that would be violated by ordering the death
of a sister-monarch, but with the bonds of a somewhat unofficial
kinship—that is to say, with the increasingly troublesome power,
place, and privileged relationship accorded to the Earl of Essex,

her current favorite and the instigator of the charges against her physician. A few years earlier Essex had been attempting to expand his power with and over the Queen by developing his own network of Spanish spies, hoping thereby to supplant the influence of Elizabeth's council; when he approached Lopez, however, the doctor not only refused to cooperate but also communicated the solicitation to the Queen, who was not amused. Lopez continued to resist and embarrass Essex and developed such an animosity toward one of the Earl's spies, a refugee from the Spanish court by the name of Antonio Perez, that he swore Don Antonio would not survive the next illness that befell him. Thinking it had found a kindred spirit, Spain inquired as to the possibility of the Queen's death as well; Lopez rebuffed the offer and even attempted to inform Elizabeth, but without success. Essex was more attentive, but when he revealed the plot to poison the Queen, he accused Lopez of being at the center of it. Elizabeth seems to have understood the motives behind the charge quite well, for she lashed out at Essex as "a rash and temerarious youth to enter into a matter against the poor man";[15] on the basis of testimony from suspects on the rack, however, Essex succeeded in forcing a trial and a judgment against the troublesome physician, and although it took months, he also eventually succeeded in bringing enough pressure to bear on the Queen that she had no choice but to sign the warrant for execution. Lopez went to the scaffold and Essex returned to the Queen's graces, but Elizabeth did exercise her sovereign rights to register, in a less spectacular forum than the scaffold, a dissenting perspective. For the rest of her life she wore at her girdle for all to see a gem that had belonged to Lopez, thereby granting him a position denied to Essex in the "virgin-knot" of jewels that, in the royal iconography of Elizabeth's body, at once set off and emblematized the inviolability of the Virgin Queen; the doctor's remaining possessions and property, which in a case of treason should have gone to the state, she allowed his widow to retain, and she went even further by granting Lopez' son Anthony "a parsonage of 30l. a year . . . for his maintainance at school."[16]

Lopez' hanging and dismemberment were not merely the occasion of popular and antisemitic entertainment; they were more pointedly and significantly the culmination of a power struggle whose initial acts took place in the royal council and courts, and as far as Elizabeth was concerned what was displayed on the scaffold was not the restoration of her own authority, but rather its manipulation and even usurpation. When Essex not only won the backing of all her council but also broadly publicized his version of the incident, she was compelled to save face and go along with the circulating fiction of her triumph and redemption, to choose not only between her favorite and her physician but also between her own autonomy and the demands placed upon her by the skillful manipulation of her sovereign image—what had become a compelling public drama of a Christian monarch saved from alien designs. Once placed in circulation, opened to interpretation and response, whether licensed or not, the monarchical spectacle wielded a certain power of its own.

A Christian state brought into crisis by an alien and Jew (whose conversion was never questioned, merely beside the point); the antagonism and plot against the life of an agent of Essex named Antonio—it is such elements that have produced limited topical readings of *The Merchant of Venice* in the past. The problem is not that such an appetite for reductive topicality is illegitimately imported into the past; as any reader of Jonson knows, it was difficult to prevent an Elizabethan audience from searching out or inventing topical allusions, and Elizabeth herself would feel the reductive power of the topical when, on the eve of the Essex uprising in 1601, the conspirators treated her to a revival of Shakespeare's *Richard II*. "I am Richard II, know ye not that?" In 1596 or 1597, when *The Merchant of Venice* was composed, the Lopez trial and execution were still current enough in print and in the popular imagination that Shakespeare's audience would have been drawn into a search for such pointed and contained correspondences, only to find themselves drawn into a less familiar world than the one they had anticipated: one structured around a crisis of state that, as in the Lopez case, is at least a partial fiction and, for Portia as for Essex, a crisis that is as much an opportunity as it is a dilemma—an opportunity to restructure bonds of official and unofficial kinship and to make persons as alienable as purses, by speculating upon and with what Antonio calls the commodity of strangers.

III

When Antonio declares himself at the mercy of Venetian law, he clarifies one of the city's reigning contradictions. Although a Christian state founded upon rigorous discriminations between brother and other, citizen and noncitizen, Venice is also dependent upon what it excludes from the benefits of Christian community — upon what it excludes, ostensibly, *for* the benefit of that community. The Duke cannot save Antonio,

> For the commodity that strangers have
> With us in Venice, if it be denied,
> Will much impeach the justice of the state,
> Since that the trade and profit of the city
> Consisteth of all nations.

[3.3.27–31]

The use-value of any commodity is determined by its alienability; the benefits that accrue to Venice from its various strangers stem from their definition as strangers, aliens who, like Shylock and Tubal, can circulate outside the city's moral economy to provide the capital necessary for its commercial ventures, meaning both its maritime and its marital speculations. In his generosity, Antonio declares himself to be useless; the tainted wether of the flock, he is willing to sacrifice himself for Venice and for Bassanio. It soon becomes clear, however, that Antonio is eager to turn his lack into an accomplishment, his impoverishment into a form of power, his generosity into a bond that can be neither canceled nor repaid. He acknowledges that all the world is a stage, the part he has to play already written and a sad one, but his role will be more than gratifying if it serves to reveal to Portia "Whether Bassanio had not once a love" (4.1.273). He is about to learn, however, that a theatrically conceived self is not a fixed and static identity but a mobile one; that once put into circulation and thus ventured upon, his image of himself as an emblem of Christian generosity can be turned back upon itself, revalued so that it functions not to bind Bassanio to him with an infinitely indebted love that rivals and overwhelms the bond with Portia, but rather to bind Antonio himself to their marital union and Bassanio's fidelity, "My soul upon the forfeit" (5.1.252). He is about to learn, that is to say, something that another celibate figure, a royal monarch rather than a royal merchant, learned in the Lopez controversy: that he is as much the subject of his own carefully maintained image as he is its master or sovereign, that the commodity of strangers defines a symbolic as well as a commercial economy, which under the aegis of one well versed in the art of alienation will expand to include his own person.

Going to Venice to see the Merchant and the Jew—both the man to whom Bassanio has confessed a prior engagement and that man's apparent nemesis ("I have engag'd myself to a dear friend,/Engag'd my friend to his mere enemy" [3.2.260-61])—Portia assures Nerissa that they can pass well enough in male disguise that their husbands "shall think we are accomplished/With that we lack" (3.4.62-63). Her joke reverberates far beyond the confines of a transvestite stage, even beyond its general political context in the longstanding rule of a Queen who maintained and negotiated power by persuading her subjects that she, too, was accomplished with what she lacked, not only in terms of coercive and regulatory force but also in terms of gender. Elizabeth did not sport a codpiece, but she did lay claim to a sort of ideological cross-dressing, asserting that she had that within which passeth the exterior show of what her subjects would regard as a mere woman. "I know I have the body of a weak and feeble woman, but I have the heart and stomach of a king, and of a king of England too."[17] Like Elizabeth, Portia is also, as she puts it, "Queen o'er [her]self" only so long as she remains on the threshold of marriage, the object of amorous admiration and the shaper of suitors' fantasies. There the similarities cease, for Portia, like the heroines of many romantic comedies of the 1590s, applies her androgynous power to the alienation of herself in marriage, the conversion, as she puts it, of herself and what is hers to Bassanio.

Noting the degree to which cultural productions of the 1580s and 1590s elaborate certain aspects of Queen Elizabeth's personal mythology, Louis Montrose has suggested that the effect was not a celebration of the royal image, an adulatory or even neutral reflection of Elizabethan ideology, but rather a critical and sometimes subversive displacement and multiplication of that image. "The texts of Spenser and other Elizabethan courtly writers," as Montrose puts it, "often fragment the royal image, reflecting aspects of the Queen 'in mirrours more than one.'"[18] What Elizabeth would have seen in *The Merchant of Venice* was not a simple political allegory of the sort she encountered when *Richard II* was revived in 1601, but rather a more refractory and overdetermined speculation on the situation of an aging Virgin Queen, who found herself increasingly limited in her capacity to induce and control the desires of her subjects and suitors, to limit and prohibit their own marriages (as she attempted to do not only with her courtiers but even with her chambermaids)[19] and to make herself the focus of all alliances, political and erotic. Antonio is not a figure for the Queen, but, at the end of a play structured around the threat of an alien and Jew, he does occupy a position that recalls Elizabeth's own in the Lopez case, and it is a position Shakespeare emphasizes in diverging from his sources—eliminating Antonio's role as Bassanio's adoptive father, developing the rivalry between Antonio and Portia, excluding Antonio from the series of marriages at the close. In Portia, Elizabeth would have found a more complex figure: one who incorporates certain aspects of her royal image and reigning mythology, but who commands the stage at the end only by fully embracing what Harry Berger has called her "role of commodity in the alliance market,"[20] and who achieves her final conquest of Bassanio not only by displacing and rearticulating his bond with Antonio, but also by making full use of that commodity of the bond market known as Shylock.

IV

As in the New World narrative with which I began, we encounter in Shylock a figure caught up in another's quest for gain, in an Elizabethan venture for the "goulden fleece"—as Ralegh described the riches of the New World sought by men like Martin Frobisher, and as Bassanio, reappropriating the colonial appropriation of the phrase, describes his own quest to win the riches and the lady of Shakespeare's Belmont. And like Frobisher's first captive, Shylock also represents a pronounced cultural intransigence, an insistence on retaining his own cultural identity and genealogical heritage, a refusal to cross the boundaries that separate and distinguish brother from other, alien from citizen, Jew from gentile. Whatever else he is—viewed from varying perspectives, a very devil incarnation, a sentimental widower, an oppressive and unmusical father, a vengeful and usurious breeder of metal—from his own perspective he is an alien to "gentle" Venice, and he defines himself proudly in terms of the ethnic and religious differences upon which he grounds his cultural identity.

However proud or contentious, Shylock's assertions of cultural particularity and difference make him a unique figure in Elizabethan portrayals of Jews; in Christian Venice, however, such assertions are both difficult to convey and to maintain. The "gentles" of the city use language to discriminate, we might say, only when it is to their financial, racial, or religious advantage; otherwise language is a medium with which to obscure and mystify differences and contradictions, as in the constant and ideologically powerful pun between gentle and gentile, or Bassanio's confusion of the ethical and financial meanings of Shylock's query as to whether Antonio is "a good man." Bassanio's invitation to dinner, his assumption that business and social transactions are fully compatible and complementary, forces Shylock to remind him of what he seems to have forgotten—that he is speaking to a Jew.

Yes, to smell pork, to eat of the habitation which your prophet the Nazarite conjured the devil into: I will buy with you, sell with you, talk with

you, walk with you, and so following: but I will not eat with you, drink
with you, nor pray with you. (1.3.29–33)

Similarly, in his dispute with Antonio over the taking of interest,
over who is a brother and who an other, Shylock attempts to identify
himself as the latter, but to no avail.

   Shy. When Jacob grazed his uncle Laban's sheep,—
        This Jacob from our holy Abram was
        (As his wise mother wrought in his behalf)
        The third possessor: ay, he was the third—
   Ant. And what of him? did he take interest?

                                                    [1.3.66–71]

Antonio hears only what the editor of the Arden Shakespeare hears,
a meaningless digression. What Antonio interrupts, however, is Shylock's racial and religious genealogy, the narrative of his own kind, by
which he identifies and distinguishes himself from his gentle but
impatient antagonist.

The exclusion of Christian practices and the insistence on his own
identity as an alien in Venice are prominent enough that it comes as
some surprise that we next see Shylock on his way to dinner with
Antonio, bothered by the notion that he is going to feed with Christians but finding his appetite whetted, his dietary scruples dulled, by
the desire to feed upon the royal merchant. The boundary between
Christian and Jew first becomes blurred, however, in the bond scene
itself, when Shylock offers "kindness" to Antonio, a loan made not
as to an other, but as to a brother. W. H. Auden first pointed out
what many critics still overlook, namely that Shylock's bond is not
a usurious one.[21] Auden remarks that Shylock is acting unprofes-
sionally, refusing to take interest and establishing instead a relation
with Antonio that is one of debtor and creditor; Marc Shell has
pointed out that the equation between money and flesh, purse and
person, that characterizes Shylock's "merry sport" is an equation
more in keeping with Christian than with Jewish jurisprudence, a
fundamental aspect of Roman law and the rationale behind such
Western phenomena as debtors' prisons.[22] As an alien and a Jew,

Shylock wants both revenge and reaffirmation; to achieve either, however, he must recognize that his capacities as an alien and a Jew are limited, that in Christian Venice, if he wishes to win a public as well as a private sense of superiority to Antonio, he must align himself with his other, adopt a practice more Christian than Jewish, and play out what he intends to be a mock and limited sort of conversion. "The Hebrew will turn Christian," as Antonio himself recognizes, "he grows kind" (1.3.174).

Later, in his "Hath not a Jew eyes?" speech, Shylock will equate vengeance itself with "kindness," with the practice as opposed to the doctrine of Christian humility and sufferance. As a Jew, Shylock claims generic membership in the human race, an assertion that does not violate the difference upon which he founds his identity; as a Jew in Venice, however, he blurs that difference by claiming the right to follow Christian example—the right, as Kenneth Burke once suggested, to use the rhetoric of Christian sufferance and humility as Christians in Venice typically use it, to serve the rhetoric of property. Shylock's perspective on himself is doubled, but not merely contradictory; Burke as usual is keen in his recognition of the dialectical nature of the conflict between the two roles Shylock is attempting to combine. The "humility" of Shylock's situation, Burke suggests, lies in relinquishing his self-definition for the time, accepting the definition and the rules of the game as viewed from his opponent's perspective, in the hopes of turning the tables on Antonio and thereby "lifting himself above his disadvantages as a Jew while in the very same act he reaffirms his status."[23] Like Portia's cross-dressing, Shylock's self-induced alienation attempts to translate a culturally inscribed weakness and disadvantage into a source of power; Shylock, however, is trapped in the role he has attempted to improvise, not only by having his demands met all too well in court but also by finding his own self-image as an alien held up to him, reaffirmed but in the very same act appropriated from him, by the one figure in the play who is better versed in the art and the law of alienation, in the commodity of strangers, than Shylock himself.

Portia proves a very Daniel in court: that is to say, she speaks to

Shylock in his own terms, adopting his insistence on a strictly literal interpretation of the bond but "submitting to its rigor more rigorously than even the Jew."[24] A stranger in Venice herself, she reveals a remarkable capacity for assimilation into another culture and manipulation of cultural others, a capacity that Richard Carew identified, in terms that are at once linguistic and colonial, as the "Excellencie" or "towardness" of sixteenth-century Englishmen:

> A Stranger, though ever so long conversant among us, carrieth evermore a Watchword upon his tongue, to descry him by; but turn an *Englishman* at any time of his Age into what Country soever, allowing him due respite, and you shall see him profit so well, that the imitation of his Utterance will in nothing differ from the Pattern of that native language, the want of which towardness cost the *Ephraimites* their skins.[25]

Portia's "towardness" has its limits—her plea for mercy seems a genuine effort to dissuade Shylock from his vengeance, but framed as it is in terms of specifically Christian salvation, it is unwittingly addressed to everyone onstage except Shylock—but when better managed, her "towardness" also extends beyond hoisting the Jew with his own legalistic petard, or resolving the crisis precipitated by Shylock's bond. That crisis has drawn Shylock on, and ourselves as well; Portia no sooner resolves it, however, than she reveals our compelling crisis to have been an engaging fiction—by pulling from the sleeve of her law clerk's robe an Alien Law of Venice, whose existence is not only absent from Shakespeare's sources but is also apparently news to the Duke of Venice himself.

Shylock's possessions and life are forfeit, not if he spills a drop of blood unspecified in his bond or takes more or less than a pound of flesh, but because he is what he always claimed to be—an alien in Venice.

> It is enacted in the laws of Venice,
> If it be proved against an alien,
> That by direct, or indirect attempts
> He seek the life of any citizen,
> The party 'gainst the which he doth contrive,
> Shall seize one half his goods, the other half

Comes to the privy coffer of the state,
And the offender's life lies at the mercy
Of the Duke only, 'gainst all other voice.

[4.1.344–52]

The case was never in question; the verdict against Shylock was always there, from the time he first proposed his bond to Antonio. More discomfiting for Shylock than the decision against him is his alienation, at this moment, from precisely what he has embraced as a cultural identity distinct from Christian Venice. Portia's Alien Law is unnecessary to resolve the crisis in Venice but is necessary to subject Shylock fully; it is the legal equivalent of Frobisher's pictorial act of cultural speculation. Shylock's early insistence on a radical ethnic, religious, and cultural difference is here reflected back upon him and at the same time taken from him. He is all that he claimed he was, but only because Venice declares him to be so: an alien, but one defined and constituted by Venetian authority.

The controversy surrounding Elizabeth's physician, Roderigo Lopez, centered on a fiction of a different order; unlike his historical predecessor, who had no hand in the plot against the royal monarch, Shylock does conspire against the life of his royal merchant. If we tend to view Shylock with greater sympathy than the spectators around the scaffold viewed Lopez in 1594, we have nonetheless been drawn into the play by the threat Shylock presents to Antonio and to the state, and we are engaged by the dramatic impetus of that threat. The Alien Law shatters this dramatic impetus, if only for a moment, by reminding us that we have all been engaged, onstage and off, by a compelling and powerful fiction—one that recalls and silently comments upon the fiction that was played out on a different scaffold a few years earlier in Elizabethan London.

V

I do not mean to suggest that such a fine speculation on recent affairs of state had a significant impact on Shakespeare's audience, if

indeed it had any; I do want to emphasize the fact that the Elizabethan stage was one of many forums for cultural speculation in the
period, and that it conceived of itself as an alternative one. It was a
forum that the Court both helped to maintain and regarded with a
certain suspicion—a suspicion channeled into explicit forms of censor-
ship that outlawed the representation of the current monarch or
religious controversies of the moment, but which proved wholly inadequate to address or contain the affective powers of such a stage,
in such a period.

Where the royal image was concerned, the prohibition against
bringing the current monarch onstage could not contain the demys-
tifying effect of staging and restaging the mysteries of state, the rise
and fall of monarchs both historical and imaginary, images of greatness made so familiar, as Sir Henry Wotton observed of *Henry VIII*,
as to be ridiculous.[26] In more general terms, the Elizabethan theater
represented a significant and unprecedented expansion of what had
been a relatively limited symbolic economy, a cultural phenomenon
of recent enough vintage that its novelty and impact were difficult to
gauge, much less delimit or control. It was in 1576, the year of Martin
Frobisher's first New World voyage, that James Burbage made a more
limited excursion beyond the confines of London to construct the
first of that city's popular playhouses; at the moment when Frobisher
was employing the affective powers of representation to transform a
recalcitrant captive into a willing and malleable subject, Burbage's
Theatre had already begun to present its own audience with new and
unfamiliar versions of itself. The coincidence of dates is a matter of
historical accident. It can serve to draw our attention, however, to
something that the period only partially apprehended and that is especially easy to overlook from our own perspective, after four centuries
of the Shakespeare industry at work. The drama that would evolve
on the boards of Burbage's stage was in itself a radical new development, as novel in its way and for its audience as a relatively faithful
painting was for a sixteenth-century Eskimo. The period was ac-
customed to a more abstract mode of dramatic representation, to the
personification of absolute states of being—Vice and Virtue, Sedition

and Youth, ad infinitum—characteristic of the morality play, a tradition of drama whose genealogy extends most prominently not to the Elizabethan stage but to the increasingly elaborate pageantry, ceremonies, and masques of the Elizabethan and Jacobean court.

By contrast, the stage that we associate with Shakespeare's name developed and refined a new mode of dramatic representation, whose individualized and concrete characterization of the dramatic subject made new demands upon its audience—demands familiar to us, but a compelling novelty and, I would argue, a significant if unpredictable cultural force in the larger civilizing process of the period. Here is Thomas Heywood, registering his sense of the new:

> What English blood seeing the person of any bold English presented and doth not hug his fame and hunny at his valor, pursuing him in his enterprise with his best wishes and as being wrapt in contemplation, offers him in his heart all prosperous performance, as if the performer were the man personated? so bewitching a thing is lively and well-spirited action, that it hath power to new mould the hearts of the spectators.[27]

Observing artificial others in such a fashion requires and induces enhanced powers of observation and identification; such a theatrical transaction necessarily blurs the boundary between the observing subject and the dramatic subject, the actual and the artificial person, the real and the imaginary. According to Heywood, the effect of such a mode of apprehension is to make the audience apprehensive themselves: by making men "see and shame at their faults," he suggests, drama induces them to reform themselves, "lest they should happen to become the like subject of general scorne to an auditory." They see and shame at *their* faults, meaning both their own and those of their fictional counterparts; they incorporate and turn upon themselves this combined perspective of self and other, "lest they should happen to become the like subject of general scorne to an auditory." Writing a defense of the stage, Heywood couches his discussion in terms of vice and virtue, but the theatrical transaction he describes, like the stage he defends, achieves its effect only by dismantling such absolute and abstract dichotomies. It may at times produce in the audience a vicarious sense of dread or shame, but it does so only by producing a different sort of apprehension, a sense in its viewers of being observed themselves—as was indeed the case, insofar as the drama that developed in the late sixteenth century fostered a vicarious participation and identification that made the spectators, in an imaginary but potent sense, the object of their own gaze.

Of *The Merchant of Venice*, Norman Rabkin has remarked that it comes at a stage in Shakespeare's career marked by an enhanced ability to create characters with authentic voices and an increasing exploration of his power to effect mercurial and kaleidoscopic shifts in the emotions of his audience.[28] Such a development was not merely an aesthetic phenomenon, however. Given the period, it represented an expanded threshold not only of dramatic representation but also of self-representation, not only of the fictional construction of character but also of the social construction of the self. The power of the stage was precisely the power of fiction: the power to induce an audience to view themselves and those around them, from commoner to monarch, as actors in their own lives, as artificial and artfully manipulated constructions, as indeed they were, whether they existed onstage or off, whether they were constituted by a playwright or by larger forces of cultural determination. If such a power produces what Norbert Elias would call an expanded domain of the superego, and hence an expanded avenue of access for forces of social and cultural control, it also produces an expanded self-awareness that the period in question was not fully equipped to manage or turn to its own advantage. But that is an issue beyond the range of closing comments, which these are. In closing, I would suggest that the Renaissance stage did not merely reflect the larger civilizing process of its times. The destabilizing dialectic between self and other, audience and play, social and psychological constitutions of the subject, which defined the complex theatrical transaction we know as Elizabethan and Jacobean drama, was in itself an influential forum and laboratory for the production of what would become the modern subject. If from our perspective and place in history we still feel a special kinship with Shakespearean modes of characterization, it is at least in part because Shakespeare's characters had a considerable role in producing us.

NOTES

1. George Best, *The Three Voyages of Martin Frobisher,* ed. R. Collinson (London: Hakluyt Society, 1863), 74.

2. For a discussion of one of de Heere's portraits, see William C. Sturtevant, "First Images of Native America," in *First Images of America,* ed. Fredi Chiappelli (Berkeley & Los Angeles: University of California Press, 1976), 1:441.

3. Best, *Three Voyages,* 138.

4. Thomas Heywood, *An Apology for Actors* (London, 1612); reprinted in *Shakespeare Society's Papers* (London, 1843), 20.

5. New World accounts often provide illuminating glimpses of significant but otherwise obscure cultural practices and assumptions, and several recent studies have illuminated the role that the New World played as a staging ground for domestic techniques of social containment and control. Among other works, see my "Strange Things, Gross Terms, Curious Customs: The Rehearsal of Cultures in the Late Renaissance," *Representations* 3 (1983): 40–67; Tzvetan Todorov, *The Conquest of America: The Question of the Other,* trans. Richard Howard (New York: Harper & Row, 1984); and the recent work of Stephen Greenblatt, in both *Renaissance Self-Fashioning: From More to Shakespeare* (Chicago: University of Chicago Press, 1980), 193–254, and a recent essay, "Invisible Bullets: Renaissance Authority and Its Subversion, *Henry IV* and *Henry V,*" in *Political Shakespeare: New Essays in Cultural Materialism,* ed. Jonathan Dollimore and Alan Sinfield (Ithaca: Cornell University Press, 1985), 18–47.

6. The edition of *Mustapha* can be found in *Selected Writings of Fulke Greville,* ed. Joan Rees (London: Athlone Press, 1973).

7. See Norbert Elias, *The History of Manners,* trans. Edmund Jephcott (New York: Pantheon, 1978).

8. See Michel Foucault, *The Use of Pleasure,* trans. Robert Hurley (New York: Pantheon, 1985).

9. For Camden's account, see his *Tomus Alter, & Idem: Or the Historie of the Life and Reigne of that Famous Princesse, Elizabeth* (London, 1629), 105. The case and its relation to the play are discussed by Sidney Lee, although Lee does not perceive the maneuvering by Essex as such, which I detail later in this essay; see Lee's entry under "Lopez" in *The Dictionary of National Biography* (London, 1893), 5:132–33, and his essay "The Original of Shylock," *Gentleman's Magazine* 246 (1880): 185–200.

10. Greenblatt,"Invisible Bullets," 44.

11. For documents relevant to the execution, see Arthur Kinney, ed., *Elizabethan Backgrounds: Historical Documents of the Age of Elizabeth I* (Hamden, Conn.: Archon Books, 1975), 213–36.

12. Ibid., 226.

13. On the issue of monarchical visibility and the exorbitancy of the theatrical, see Christopher Pye, "The Sovereign, the Theater, and the Kingdome of Darknesse: Hobbes and the Spectacle of Power," *Representations* 8 (1984): 85–106.

14. Wallace T. MacCaffrey, "Place and Patronage in Elizabethan Politics," in *Elizabethan Government and Society*, ed. S. T. Bindoff et al. (London: Athlone Press, 1961), 97; on the cultural dynamics of Elizabeth's reign, see Louis Adrian Montrose, "'Eliza, Queene of Shepheardes,' and the Pastoral of Power," *English Literary Renaissance* 10 (1980): 153–82; and "Gifts and Reasons: The Contexts of Peele's *Arraygnement of Paris*," *ELH* 47 (1980): 433–61.

15. Quoted in Sidney Lee, *Dictionary of National Biography* (London, 1893), 5:134.

16. Ibid.

17. The quotation is from Elizabeth's Armada speech; cited in an unpublished essay by Louis Adrian Montrose, "The Elizabethan Subject and the Spenserian Text," 23.

18. Louis Adrian Montrose, "'Shaping Fantasies': Figurations of Gender and Power in Elizabethan Culture," *Representations* 2 (1983): 85.

19. On Elizabeth's manipulation of marriages, see Leonard Tennenhouse, "Representing Power: *Measure for Measure* in Its Time," *Genre* 15 (1982): 150–51.

20. Harry Berger, Jr., "Marriage and Mercifixion in *The Merchant of Venice:* The Casket Scene Revisited," *Shakespeare Quarterly* 32 (1981): 156.

21. W. H. Auden, *The Dyer's Hand and Other Essays* (New York: Vintage, 1968), 227–28.

22. Marc Shell, *Money, Language, and Thought: Literary and Philosophic Economies from the Medieval to the Modern Era* (Berkeley & Los Angeles: University of California Press, 1982), 64–67.

23. Kenneth Burke, *A Rhetoric of Motives* (Berkeley & Los Angeles: University of California Press, 1969), 193–94.

24. Sigurd Burckhardt, *Shakespearean Meanings* (Princeton: Princeton University Press, 1968), 210.

25. "The Excellencie of the English Tongue" (1596?), in *The Survey of Cornwall*, ed. F. E. Halliday (London: A. Melrose, 1953), 305.

26. On the ambivalent relation between the Crown and the stage, see Stephen Orgel, "Making Greatness Familiar," *Genre* 15 (1982): 41–48; also relevant, but at times overstated in its exclusive focus on tragedy, is Franco Moretti, "'A Huge Eclipse': Tragic Form and the Deconsecration of Sovereignty," *Genre* 15 (1982): 7–40.

27. Heywood, *Apology*, 21.

28. Norman Rabkin, *Shakespeare and the Problem of Meaning* (Chicago: University of Chicago Press, 1981), 6–7.

Janet Adelman

"Born of Woman"

FANTASIES OF MATERNAL POWER IN *MACBETH*

In the last moments of any production of *Macbeth*, as Macbeth feels himself increasingly hemmed in by enemies, the stage will resonate hauntingly with variants of his repeated question, "What's he/ That was not born of woman?" (5.7.2–3; for variants, see 5.3.4, 6; 5.7.11, 13; 5.8.13, 31).[1] Repeated seven times, Macbeth's allusion to the witches' prophecy—"none of woman born/Shall harm Macbeth" (4.1.80–81)—becomes virtually a talisman to ward off danger; even after he has begun to doubt the equivocation of the fiend (5.5.43), mere repetition of the phrase seems to Macbeth to guarantee his invulnerability. I want in this essay to explore the power of these resonances, particularly to explore how Macbeth's assurance seems to turn itself inside out, becoming dependent not on the fact that all men are, after all, born of woman but on the fantasy of escape from this universal condition. The duplicity of Macbeth's repeated question—its capacity to mean both itself and its opposite—carries such weight at the end of the play, I think, because the whole of the play represents in very powerful form both the fantasy of a virtually absolute and destructive maternal power and the fantasy of absolute escape from this power; I shall argue in fact that the peculiar texture of the end of the play is generated partly by the tension between these two fantasies.

Maternal power in *Macbeth* is not embodied in the figure of a particular mother (as it is, for example, in *Coriolanus*); it is instead diffused throughout the play, evoked primarily by the figures of the witches and Lady Macbeth. Largely through Macbeth's relationship to them, the play becomes (like *Coriolanus*) a representation of primitive fears about male identity and autonomy itself,[2] about those looming female presences who threaten to control one's actions and one's mind, to constitute one's very self, even at a distance. When Macbeth's first words echo those we have already heard the witches speak—"So fair and foul a day I have not seen" (1.3.38); "Fair is foul, and foul is fair"

(1.1.11)—we are in a realm that questions the very possibility of autonomous identity. The play will finally reimagine autonomous male identity, but only through the ruthless excision of all female presence, its own peculiar satisfaction of the witches' prophecy.

In 1600, after the Earl of Gowrie's failed attempt to kill James VI, one James Weimis of Bogy, testifying about the earl's recourse to necromancy, reported that the earl thought it "possible that the seed of man and woman might be brought to perfection otherwise then by the *matrix* of the woman."[3] Whether or not Shakespeare deliberately recalled Gowrie in his portrayal of the murderer of James's ancestor,[4] the connection is haunting: the account of the conspiracy hints that, for Gowrie at least, recourse to necromancy seemed to promise at once invulnerability and escape from the maternal matrix.[5] The fantasy of such escape in fact haunts Shakespeare's plays. A few years after Macbeth, Posthumus will make the fantasy explicit: attributing all ills in man to the "woman's part," he will ask, "Is there no way for men to be, but women/Must be half-workers?" (*Cymbeline*, 2.5.1–2).[6] The strikingly motherless world of *The Tempest* and its potent image of absolute male control answers Posthumus' questions affirmatively: there at least, on that bare island, mothers and witches are banished and creation belongs to the male alone.

Even in one of Shakespeare's earliest plays, male autonomy is ambivalently portrayed as the capacity to escape the maternal matrix that has misshaped the infant man.[7] The man who will become Richard III emerges strikingly as a character for the first time as he watches his brother Edward's sexual success with the Lady Grey. After wishing syphilis on him so that he will have no issue (a concern that anticipates Macbeth's), Richard constructs his own desire for the crown specifically as compensation for his failure at the sexual game. Unable to "make [his] heaven in a lady's lap," he will "make [his] heaven to dream upon the crown" (*3 Henry VI*, 3.2.148,169). But his failure to make his heaven in a lady's lap is itself understood as the consequence of his subjection to another lady's lap, to the misshaping power of his mother's womb:

> Why, love forswore me in my Mother's womb;
> And, for I should not deal in her soft laws,
> She did corrupt frail nature with some bribe
> To shrink mine arm up like a withered shrub;
> To make an envious mountain on my back.
>
> [3.2.153–57]

Richard blames his deformity on a triad of female powers: Mother, Love, and Nature all fuse, conspiring to deform him as he is being formed in his mother's womb. Given this image of female power, it is no wonder that he turns to the compensatory heaven of the crown. But the crown turns out to be an unstable compensation. Even as he shifts from the image of the misshaping womb to the image of the crown, the terrifying enclosure of the womb recurs, shaping his attempt to imagine the very political project that should free him from dependence on ladies' laps:

> I'll make my heaven to dream upon the crown
> And, whiles I live, t'account this world but hell
> Until my misshaped trunk that bears this head
> Be round impalèd with a glorious crown.
> And yet I know not how to get the crown,
> For many lives stand between me and home;
> And I—like one lost in a thorny wood,
> That rents the thorns and is rent with the thorns,
> Seeking a way and straying from the way,
> Not knowing how to find the open air
> But toiling desperately to find it out—
> Torment myself to catch the English crown;
> And from that torment I will free myself
> Or hew my way out with a bloody axe.
>
> [3.2.168–81]

The crown for him is "home," the safe haven. But through the shifting meaning of "impalèd," the crown as safe haven is itself transformed into the dangerous enclosure: the stakes that enclose him protectively turn into the thorns that threaten to impale him.[8] Strikingly, it is not his head but the trunk that bears his head that is so impaled by crown and thorns: the crown compensatory for ladies' laps fuses with the image of the dangerous womb in an imagistic nightmare in which the lap/womb/home/crown become the thorny wood from which he desperately seeks escape into the open air. Through this imagistic transformation, these lines take on the config-uration of a birth fantasy, or more precisely a fantasy of impeded birth, a birth that the man-child himself must manage by hewing his way out with a bloody axe.[9] Escape from the dangerous female is here achieved by recourse to the exaggeratedly masculine bloody axe. This, I will argue, is precisely the psychological configuration of *Macbeth*, where dangerous female presences like Love, Nature, Mother are given embodiment in Lady Macbeth and the witches, and where Macbeth wields the bloody axe in an attempt to escape their domin-ion over him.

At first glance, Macbeth seems to wield the bloody axe to comply with, not to escape, the dominion of women. The play constructs Macbeth as terrifyingly pawn to female figures. Whether or not he is rapt by the witches' prophecies because the horrid image of Duncan's murder has already occurred to him, their role as gleeful prophets constructs Macbeth's actions in part as the enactments of their will. And he is impelled toward murder by Lady Macbeth's equation of masculinity and murder: in his case, the bloody axe seems not an escape route but the tool of a man driven to enact the ferociously masculine strivings of his wife.[10] Nonetheless, the weight given the image of the man not born of woman at the end suggests that the underlying fantasy is the same as in Richard's defensive con-struction of his masculinity: even while enacting the wills of women, Macbeth's bloody masculinity enables an escape from them in fan-tasy—an escape that the play itself embodies in dramatic form at the end. I will discuss first the unleashing of female power and Macbeth's compliance with that power, and then the fantasy of escape.

In the figures of Macbeth, Lady Macbeth, and the witches, the play gives us images of a masculinity and a femininity that are terribly dis-turbed; this disturbance seems to me both the cause and the conse-quence of the murder of Duncan. In *Hamlet*, Shakespeare had recon-structed the Fall as the death of the ideal father; here, he constructs a revised version in which the Fall is the death of the ideally androgynous parent. For Duncan combines in himself the attributes of both father and mother: he is the center of authority, the source of lineage and honor, the giver of name and gift; but he is also the source of all nurturance, planting the children to his throne and making them grow. He is the father as androgynous parent from whom, singly, all good can be imagined to flow, the source of a benign and empowering nurturance the opposite of that imaged in the witches' poisonous cauldron and Lady Macbeth's gall-filled breasts. Such a father does away with any need for a mother: he is the image of both parents in one, threatening aspects of each controlled by the presence of the other.[11] When he is gone, "The wine of life is drawn, and the mere lees/Is left this vault to brag of" (2.3.93–94): nurturance itself is spoiled, as all the play's imagery of poisoned chalices and interrupted feasts implies. In his absence male and female break apart, the female becoming merely helpless or merely poisonous and the male merely bloodthirsty; the harmonious relation of the genders imaged in Duncan fails.

In *Hamlet*, the absence of the ideal protecting father brings the son face to face with maternal power. The absence of Duncan similarly unleashes the power of the play's malevolent mothers. But this father-king seems strikingly absent even before his murder. Heavily idealized, he is nonetheless largely ineffectual: even while he is alive, he is unable to hold his kingdom together, reliant on a series of bloody men to suppress an increasingly successful series of rebellions.[12] The witches are already abroad in his realm; they in fact constitute our introduction to that realm. Duncan, not Macbeth, is the first person to echo them ("When the battle's lost and won" [1.1.4]; "What he hath lost, noble Macbeth hath won" [1.2.69]). The witches' sexual ambiguity terrifies: Banquo says of them, "You should be women,/And yet your beards forbid me to interpret/That you are so" (1.3.45–47). Is their androgyny the shadow-side of the King's, enabled perhaps by his failure to maintain a protective masculine authority? Is their strength a consequence of his weakness? (This is the configuration of *Cymbeline*, where the power of the witch-queen-stepmother is so depen-

dent on the failure of Cymbeline's masculine authority that she ob-
ligingly dies when that authority returns to him.) Banquo's question
to the witches may ask us to hear a counterquestion about Duncan,
who should be man. For Duncan's androgyny is the object of
enormous ambivalence: idealized for his nurturing paternity, he is
nonetheless killed for his womanish softness, his childish trust, his inability to read men's minds in their faces, his reliance on the fighting
of sons who can rebel against him. Macbeth's description of the dead
Duncan—"his silver skin lac'd with his golden blood" (2.3.110)—
makes him into a virtual icon of kingly worth; but other images surrounding his death make him into an emblem not of masculine
authority, but of female vulnerability. As he moves toward the
murder, Macbeth first imagines himself the allegorical figure of
murder, as though to absolve himself of the responsibility of choice.
But the figure of murder then fuses with that of Tarquin:

> wither'd Murther,
> . . . thus with his stealthy pace,
> With Tarquin's ravishing strides, towards his design
> Moves like a ghost.
>
> [2.1.52–56]

These lines figure the murder as a display of male sexual aggression
against a passive female victim: murder here becomes rape; Macbeth's
victim becomes not the powerful male figure of the king, but the
helpless Lucrece.[13] Hardened by Lady Macbeth to regard maleness
and violence as equivalent, that is, Macbeth responds to Duncan's
idealized milky gentleness as though it were evidence of his femaleness. The horror of this gender transformation, as well as the horror
of the murder, is implicit in Macduff's identification of the king's
body as a new Gorgon ("Approach the chamber, and destroy your
sight/With a new Gorgon" [2.3.70–71]). The power of this image lies
partly in its suggestion that Duncan's bloodied body, with its multiple
wounds, has been revealed as female and hence blinding to his sons:
as if the threat all along was that Duncan would be revealed as female
and that this revelation would rob his sons of his masculine protection and hence of their own masculinity.[14]

In *King Lear,* the abdication of protective paternal power seems to release the destructive power of a female chaos imaged not only in Goneril and Regan, but also in the storm on the heath. Macbeth virtually alludes to Lear's storm as he approaches the witches in act 4, conjuring them to answer though they "untie the winds, and let them fight/Against the Churches," though the "waves/Confound and swallow navigation up," though "the treasure/Of Nature's germens tumble all together/Even till destruction sicken" (4.1.52–60; see *King Lear,* 3.2.1–9). The witches merely implicit on Lear's heath have become in *Macbeth* embodied agents of storm and disorder,[15] and they are there from the start. Their presence suggests that the absence of the father that unleashes female chaos (as in *Lear*) has already happened at the beginning of *Macbeth*; that absence is merely made literal in Macbeth's murder of Duncan at the instigation of female forces. For this father-king cannot protect his sons from powerful mothers, and it is the son's—and the play's—revenge to kill him, or, more precisely, to kill him first and love him after, paying him back for his excessively "womanish" trust and then memorializing him as the ideal androgynous parent.[16] The reconstitution of manhood becomes a central problem of the play in part, I think, because the vision of manhood embodied in Duncan has already failed at the play's beginning.

The witches constitute our introduction to the realm of maternal malevolence unleashed by the loss of paternal protection; as soon as Macbeth meets them, he becomes (in Hecate's probably non-Shakespearean words) their "wayward son" (3.5.11). This maternal malevolence is given its most horrifying expression in Shakespeare in the image through which Lady Macbeth secures her control over Macbeth:

> I have given suck, and know
> How tender 'tis to love the babe that milks me:
> I would, while it was smiling in my face,
> Have pluck'd my nipple from his boneless gums,
> And dash'd the brains out, had I so sworn
> As you have done to this.

[1.7.54–59]

This image of murderously disrupted nurturance is the psychic equivalence of the witches' poisonous cauldron; both function to subject Macbeth's will to female forces.[17] For the play strikingly constructs the fantasy of subjection to maternal malevolence in two parts, in the witches and in Lady Macbeth, and then persistently identifies the two parts as one. Through this identification, Shakespeare in effect locates the source of his culture's fear of witchcraft in individual human history, in the infant's long dependence on female figures felt as all-powerful: what the witches suggest about the vulnerability of men to female power on the cosmic plane, Lady Macbeth doubles on the psychological plane.

Lady Macbeth's power as a female temptress allies her in a general way with the witches as soon as we see her. The specifics of that implied alliance begin to emerge as she attempts to harden herself in preparation for hardening her husband: the disturbance of gender that Banquo registers when he first meets the witches is played out in psychological terms in Lady Macbeth's attempt to unsex herself. Calling on spirits ambiguously allied with the witches themselves, she phrases this unsexing as the undoing of her own bodily maternal function:

> Come, you Spirits
> That tend on mortal thoughts, unsex me here,
> And fill me, from the crown to the toe, top-full
> Of direst cruelty! make thick my blood,
> Stop up th'access and passage to remorse;
> That no compunctious visitings of Nature
> Shake my fell purpose, nor keep peace between
> Th'effect and it! Come to my woman's breasts,
> And take my milk for gall, you murth'ring ministers.
>
> [1.5.40–48]

In the play's context of unnatural births, the thickening of the blood and the stopping up of access and passage to remorse begin to sound like attempts to undo reproductive functioning and perhaps to stop the menstrual blood that is the sign of its potential.[18] The metaphors in which Lady Macbeth frames the stopping up of remorse, that is, suggest that she imagines an attack on the reproductive passages of her own body, on what makes her specifically female. And as she invites the spirits to her breasts, she reiterates the centrality of the attack specifically on maternal function: needing to undo the "milk of human kindness" (1.5.18) in Macbeth, she imagines an attack on her own literal milk, its transformation into gall. This imagery locates the horror of the scene in Lady Macbeth's unnatural abrogation of her maternal function. But latent within this image of unsexing is the horror of the maternal function itself. Most modern editors follow Johnson in glossing "take my milk for gall" as "take my milk in exchange for gall," imagining in effect that the spirits empty out the natural maternal fluid and replace it with the unnatural and poisonous one.[19] But perhaps Lady Macbeth is asking the spirits to take her milk *as* gall, to nurse from her breast and find in her milk their sustaining poison. Here the milk itself is the gall; no transformation is necessary. In these lines Lady Macbeth focuses the culture's fear of maternal nursery—a fear reflected, for example, in the common worries about the various ills (including female blood itself) that could be transmitted through nursing and in the sometime identification of colostrum as witch's milk.[20] Insofar as her milk itself nurtures the evil spirits, Lady Macbeth localizes the image of maternal danger, inviting the identification of her maternal function itself with that of the witch. For she here invites precisely that nursing of devil-imps so central to the current understanding of witchcraft that the presence of supernumerary teats alone was often taken as sufficient evidence that one was a witch.[21] Lady Macbeth and the witches fuse at this moment, and they fuse through the image of perverse nursery.

It is characteristic of the play's division of labor between Lady Macbeth and the witches that she, rather than they, is given the imagery of perverse nursery traditionally attributed to the witches. The often noted alliance between Lady Macbeth and the witches constructs malignant female power both in the cosmos and in the family; it in effect adds the whole weight of the spiritual order to the condemnation of Lady Macbeth's insurrection.[22] But despite the superior cosmic status of the witches, Lady Macbeth seems to me finally the more frightening figure. For Shakespeare's witches are an odd mixture of the terrifying and the near comic. Even without consideration of the Hecate scene (3.5) with its distinct lightening of tone and its incipient comedy of discord among the witches, we may begin to feel a shift toward the comic in the presentation of the witches: the specificity and predictability of the ingredients in their dire recipe pass over toward grotesque comedy even while they create a (partly pleasurable) shiver of horror.[23] There is a distinct weakening of their power after their first appearances: only halfway through the play, in 4.1, do we hear that they themselves have masters (4.1.63). The more Macbeth claims for them, the less their actual power seems: by the time Macbeth evokes the cosmic damage they can wreak (4.1.50–60), we have already felt the presence of such damage, and felt it moreover not as issuing from the witches but as a divinely sanctioned nature's expressions of outrage at the disruption of patriarchal order. The witches' displays of thunder and lightning, like their apparitions, are mere theatrics compared to what we have already heard; and the serious disruptions of natural order—the storm that toppled the chimneys and made the earth shake (2.3.53–60), the unnatural darkness in day (2.4.5–10), the cannibalism of Duncan's horses (2.4.14–18)—seem the horrifying but reassuringly familiar signs of God's displeasure, firmly under His—not their—control. Partly because their power is thus circumscribed, nothing the witches say or do conveys the presence of awesome and unexplained malevolence in the way that Lear's storm does. Even the process of dramatic representation itself may diminish their power: embodied, perhaps, they lack full power to terrify: "Present fears"—even of witches—"are less than horrible imaginings" (1.3.137–38). They tend thus to become as much containers for as expressions of nightmare; to a certain extent, they help to exorcise the terror of female malevolence by localizing it.

The witches may of course have lost some of their power to terrify through the general decline in witchcraft belief. Nonetheless, even when that belief was in full force, these witches would have been less frightening than their Continental sisters, their crimes less sensational. For despite their numinous and infinitely suggestive indefinability,[24] insofar as they are witches, they are distinctly English witches; and most commentators on English witchcraft note how tame an affair it was in comparison with witchcraft belief on the Continent.[25] The most sensational staples of Continental belief from the *Malleus Maleficarum* (1486) on—the ritual murder and eating of infants, the attacks specifically on the male genitals, the perverse sexual relationship with demons—are missing or greatly muted in English witchcraft belief, replaced largely by a simpler concern with retaliatory wrongdoing of exactly the order Shakespeare points to when one of his witches announces her retaliation for the sailor's wife's refusal to share her chestnuts.[26] We may hear an echo of some of the Continental beliefs in the hint of their quasi-sexual attack on the sailor with the uncooperative wife (the witches promise to "do and do and do," leaving him drained "dry as hay") and in the infanticidal contents of the cauldron, especially the "finger of birth-strangled babe" and the blood of the sow "that hath eaten/Her nine farrow." The cannibalism that is a staple of Continental belief may be implicit in the contents of that grim cauldron; and the various eyes, toes, tongues, legs, teeth, livers, and noses (indiscriminately human and animal) may evoke primitive fears of dismemberment close to the center of witchcraft belief. But these terrors remain largely implicit. For Shakespeare's witches are both smaller and greater than their Continental sisters: on the one hand, more the representation of English homebodies with relatively small concerns; on the other, more the incarnation of literary or mythic fates or sybils, given the power not only to predict but to enforce the future. But the staples of Continental witchcraft belief are not altogether missing from the play: for the most part, they are transferred away from the witches and recur as the psychological issues evoked by Lady Macbeth in her relation to Macbeth. She becomes the inheritor of the realm of primitive relational and bodily disturbance: of infantile vulnerability to maternal power, of dismemberment and its developmentally later equivalent, castration. Lady Macbeth brings the witches' power home: they get the cosmic apparatus, she gets the psychic force. That Lady Macbeth is the more frightening figure—and was so, I suspect, even before belief in witchcraft had declined—suggests the firmly domestic and psychological basis of Shakespeare's imagination.[27]

The fears of female coercion, female definition of the male, that are initially located cosmically in the witches thus find their ultimate locus in the figure of Lady Macbeth, whose attack on Macbeth's virility is the source of her strength over him and who acquires that strength, I shall argue, partly because she can make him imagine himself as an infant vulnerable to her. In the figure of Lady Macbeth, that is, Shakespeare rephrases the power of the witches as the wife/mother's power to poison human relatedness at its source; in her, their power of cosmic coercion is rewritten as the power of the mother to misshape or destroy the child. The attack on infants and on the genitals characteristic of Continental witchcraft belief is thus in her returned to its psychological source: in the play these beliefs are localized not in the witches but in the great central scene in which Lady Macbeth persuades Macbeth to the murder of Duncan. In this scene, Lady Macbeth notoriously makes the murder of Duncan the test of Macbeth's virility; if he cannot perform the murder, he is in effect reduced to the helplessness of an infant subject to her rage. She begins by attacking his manhood, making her love for him contingent on the murder that she identifies as equivalent to his male potency: "From this time/Such I account thy love" (1.7.38–39); "When you durst do it, then you were a man" (1.7.49). Insofar as his drunk hope is now "green and pale" (1.7.37), he is identified as emasculated, exhibiting the symptoms not only of hangover, but also of the greensickness, the typical disease of timid young virgin women. Lady Macbeth's argument is, in effect, that any signs of the "milk of human kindness" (1.5.17) mark him as more womanly than she; she proceeds to enforce his masculinity by demonstrating her willingness to dry up that milk in herself, specifically by destroying her nursing infant in fantasy: "I would, while it was smiling in my face,/Have pluck'd my nipple from his boneless gums,/And dash'd the brains out" (1.7.56–58). That this image has no place in the plot, where the Macbeths are strikingly childless, gives some indication of the inner necessity through which it appears. For Lady Macbeth expresses here not only the hardness she imagines to be male, not only her willingness to unmake the most essential maternal relationship; she expresses also a deep fantasy of Macbeth's utter vulnerability to her. As she progresses from questioning Macbeth's masculinity to imagining herself dashing out the brains of her infant son,[28] she articulates a fantasy in which to be less than a man is to become interchangeably a woman or a baby,[29] terribly subject to the wife/mother's destructive rage.

By evoking this vulnerability, Lady Macbeth acquires a power over Macbeth more absolute than any the witches can achieve. The play's central fantasy of escape from woman seems to me to unfold from this moment; we can see its beginnings in Macbeth's response to Lady Macbeth's evocation of absolute maternal power. Macbeth first responds by questioning the possibility of failure ("If we should fail?" [1.7.59]). Lady Macbeth counters this fear by inviting Macbeth to share in her fantasy of omnipotent malevolence: "What cannot you and I perform upon/Th'unguarded Duncan?" (1.7.70–71). The satiated and sleeping Duncan takes on the vulnerability that Lady Macbeth has just invoked in the image of the feeding, trusting infant;[30] Macbeth releases himself from the image of this vulnerability by sharing in the murder of this innocent. In his elation at this transfer of vulnerability from himself to Duncan, Macbeth imagines Lady Macbeth the mother to infants sharing her hardness, born in effect without vulnerability; in effect, he imagines her as male and then reconstitutes himself as the invulnerable male child of such a mother:

> Bring forth men-children only!
> For thy undaunted mettle should compose
> Nothing but males.
>
> [1.7.73–75]

Through the double pun on *mettle/metal* and *male/mail,* Lady Macbeth herself becomes virtually male, composed of the hard metal of which the armored male is made.[31] Her children would necessarily be men, composed of her male mettle, armored by her mettle, lacking the female inheritance from the mother that would make them vulnerable. The man-child thus brought forth would be no trusting infant; the very phrase *men-children* suggests the presence of the adult man even at birth, hence the undoing of childish vulnerability.[32] The mobility of the imagery – from male infant with his brains dashed out to Macbeth and Lady Macbeth triumphing over the sleeping, trusting Duncan, to the all-male invulnerable man-child, suggests the logic of the fantasy: only the child of an all-male mother is safe. We see here the creation of a defensive fantasy of exemption from the woman's part: as infantile vulnerability is shifted to Duncan, Macbeth creates in himself the image of Lady Macbeth's hardened all-male man-child; in committing the murder, he thus becomes like Richard III, using the bloody axe to free himself in fantasy from the dominion of women, even while apparently carrying out their will.

Macbeth's temporary solution to the infantile vulnerability and maternal malevolence revealed by Lady Macbeth is to imagine Lady Macbeth the all-male mother of invulnerable infants. The final solution, both for Macbeth and for the play itself, though in differing ways, is an even more radical excision of the female: it is to imagine a birth entirely exempt from women, to imagine in effect an all-male family, composed of nothing but males, in which the father is fully restored to power. Overtly, of course, the play denies the possibility of this fantasy: Macduff carries the power of the man not born of woman only through the equivocation of the fiends, their obstetrical joke that quibbles with the meaning of *born* and thus confirms circuitously that all men come from women after all. Even Macbeth, in whom, I think, the fantasy is centrally invested, knows its impossibility: his false security depends exactly on his commonsense assumption that everyone is born of woman. Nonetheless, I shall argue, the play curiously enacts the fantasy that it seems to deny: punishing Macbeth for his participation in a fantasy of escape from the maternal matrix, it nonetheless allows the audience the partial satisfaction of a dramatic equivalent to it. The dual process of repudiation and enactment of the fantasy seems to me to shape the ending of *Macbeth* decisively; I will attempt to trace this process in the rest of this essay.

The witches' prophecy has the immediate force of psychic relevance for Macbeth partly because of the fantasy constructions central to 1.7:

Be bloody, bold, and resolute: laugh to scorn
The power of man, for none of woman born
Shall harm Macbeth.

[4.1.79–81]

The witches here invite Macbeth to make himself into the bloody and invulnerable man-child he has created as a defense against maternal malevolence in 1.7: the man-child ambivalently recalled by the accompanying apparition of the Bloody Child. For the apparition alludes at once to the bloody vulnerability of the infant destroyed by Lady Macbeth and to the bloodthirsty masculinity that seems to promise escape from this vulnerability, the bloodiness the witches urge Macbeth to take on. The doubleness of the image epitomizes exactly the doubleness of the prophecy itself: the prophecy constructs Macbeth's invulnerability in effect from the vulnerability of all other men, a vulnerability dependent on their having been born of woman. Macbeth does not question this prophecy, even after the experience of Birnam Wood should have taught him better, partly because it so perfectly meets his needs: in encouraging him to "laugh to scorn/The power of men," the prophecy seems to grant him exemption from the condition of all men, who bring with them the liabilities inherent in their birth. As Macbeth carries the prophecy as a shield onto the battlefield, his confidence in his own invulnerability increasingly reveals his sense of his own exemption from the universal human condition. Repeated seven times, the phrase *born to woman* with its variants begins to carry for Macbeth the meaning "vulnerable," as though vulnerability itself is the taint deriving from woman; his own invulnerability comes therefore to stand as evidence for his exemption from that taint. This is the subterranean logic of Macbeth's words to Young Siward immediately after Macbeth has killed him:

Thou wast born of woman:—
But swords I smile at, weapons laugh to scorn,
Brandish'd by man that's of a woman born.

[5.7.11–13]

Young Siward's death becomes in effect proof that he was born of woman; in the logic of Macbeth's psyche, Macbeth's invulnerability is the proof that he was not. The *but* records this fantasied distinction: it constructs the sentence "You, born of woman, are vulnerable; but I, not born of woman, am not."[33]

Insofar as this is the fantasy embodied in Macbeth at the play's end, it is punished by the equivocation of the fiends: the revelation that Macduff derives from woman, though by unusual means, musters against Macbeth all the values of ordinary family and community that Macduff carries with him. Macbeth, "cow'd" by the revelation (5.8.18),[34] is forced to take on the taint of vulnerability; the fantasy of escape from the maternal matrix seems to die with him. But although this fantasy is punished in Macbeth, it does not quite die with him; it continues to have a curious life of its own in the play, apart from its embodiment in him. Even from the beginning of the play, the fantasy has not been Macbeth's alone: as the play's most striking bloody man, he is in the beginning the bearer of this fantasy for the all-male community that depends on his bloody prowess. The opening scenes strikingly construct male and female as realms apart; and the initial descriptions of Macbeth's battles construe his prowess as a consequence of his exemption from the taint of woman.

In the description of his battle with Macdonwald, what looks initially like a battle between loyal and disloyal sons to establish primacy in the father's eyes is oddly transposed into a battle of male against female:

> Doubtful it stood;
> As two spent swimmers, that do cling together
> And choke their art. The merciless Macdonwald
> (Worthy to be a rebel, for to that
> The multiplying villainies of nature
> Do swarm upon him) from the western isles
> Of Kernes and Gallowglasses is supplied;
> And Fortune, on his damned quarrel smiling,
> Show'd like a rebel's whore: but all's too weak;
> For brave Macbeth (well he deserves that name),
> Disdaining Fortune, with his brandish'd steel,
> Which smok'd with bloody execution,
> Like Valour's minion, carv'd out his passage,

Till he fac'd the slave;
Which ne'er shook hands, nor bade farewell to him,
Till he unseam'd him from the nave to th' chops,
And fix'd his head upon our battlements.

[1.2.7–23]

The two initially indistinguishable figures metaphorized as the swimmers eventually sort themselves out into victor and victim, but only by first sorting themselves out into male and female, as though Macbeth can be distinguished from Macdonwald only by making Macdonwald functionally female. The "merciless Macdonwald" is initially firmly identified; but by the time Macbeth appears, Macdonwald has temporarily disappeared, replaced by the female figure of Fortune, against whom Macbeth seems to fight ("brave Macbeth, . . . Disdaining Fortune, with his brandish'd steel"). The metaphorical substitution of Fortune for Macdonwald transforms the battle into a contest between male and female; it makes Macbeth's deserving of his name contingent on his victory over the female. We are prepared for this transformation by Macdonwald's sexual alliance with the tainting female, the whore Fortune;[35] Macbeth's identification as valor's minion redefines the battle as a contest between the half-female couple Fortune/Macdonwald and the all-male couple Valor/Macbeth. Metaphorically, Macdonwald and Macbeth take on the qualities of the unreliable female and the heroic male; Macbeth's battle against Fortune turns out to be his battle against Macdonwald because the two are functionally the same. Macdonwald, tainted by the female, becomes an easy mark for Macbeth, who demonstrates his own untainted manhood by unseaming Macdonwald from the nave to the chops. Through its allusions both to castration and to Caesarian section, this unseaming furthermore remakes Macdonwald's body as female, revealing what his alliance with Fortune has suggested all along.

In effect, then, the battle that supports the father's kingdom plays out the creation of a conquering all-male erotics that marks its conquest by its triumph over a feminized body, simultaneously that of Fortune and Macdonwald. Hence, in the double action of the passage, the victorious unseaming happens twice: first on the body of Fortune and then on the body of Macdonwald. The lines descriptive of Macbeth's approach to Macdonwald—"brave Macbeth . . . Disdaining Fortune, with his brandish'd steel . . . carved out his passage"—make that approach contingent on Macbeth's first carving his passage through a female body, hewing his way out. The language here perfectly anticipates Macduff's birth by Caesarian section, revealed at the end of the play: if Macduff is ripped untimely from his mother's womb, Macbeth here manages in fantasy his own Caesarian section,[36] carving his passage out from the unreliable female to achieve heroic male action, in effect carving up the female to arrive at the male. Only after this rite of passage can Macbeth meet Macdonwald: the act of aggression toward the female body, the fantasy of self-birth, marks his passage to the contest that will be definitive of his maleness partly insofar as it is definitive of Macdonwald's tainted femaleness. For the all-male community surrounding Duncan, then, Macbeth's victory is allied with his triumph over femaleness; for them, he becomes invulnerable, "lapp'd in proof" (1.2.55) like one of Lady Macbeth's armored men-children.[37] Even before his entry into the play, that is, Macbeth is the bearer of the shared fantasy that secure male community depends on the prowess of the man in effect not born of woman, the man who can carve his own passage out, the man whose very maleness is the mark of his exemption from female power.[38]

Ostensibly, the play rejects the version of manhood implicit in the shared fantasy of the beginning. Macbeth himself is well aware that his capitulation to Lady Macbeth's definition of manhood entails his abandonment of his own more inclusive definition of what becomes a man (1.7.46); and Macduff's response to the news of his family's destruction insists that humane feeling is central to the definition of manhood (4.3.221). Moreover, the revelation that even Macduff had a mother sets a limiting condition on the fantasy of a bloody masculine escape from the female and hence on the kind of manhood defined by that escape. Nonetheless, even at the end, the play enables one version of the fantasy that heroic manhood is exemption from the female even while it punishes that fantasy in Macbeth. The key figure in whom this double movement is vested in the end of the play is Macduff; the unresolved contradictions that surround him are, I think, marks of ambivalence toward the fantasy itself. In insisting that mourning for his family is his right as a man, he presents family feeling as central to the definition of manhood; and yet he conspicuously leaves his family vulnerable to destruction when he goes off to offer his services to Malcolm. The play moreover insists on reminding us that he has inexplicably abandoned his family: both Lady Macduff and Malcolm question the necessity of this abandonment (4.2.6–14; 4.3.26–28); and the play never allows Macduff to explain himself. This unexplained abandonment severely qualifies Macduff's force as the play's central exemplar of a healthy manhood that can include the possibility of relationship to women: the play seems to vest diseased familial relations in Macbeth and the possibility of healthy ones in Macduff; and yet we discover dramatically that Macduff has a family only when we hear that he has abandoned it. Dramatically and psychologically, he takes on full masculine power only as he loses his family and becomes energized by the loss, converting his grief into the more "manly" tune of vengeance (4.3.235); the loss of his family here enables his accession to full masculine action even while his response to that loss insists on a more humane definition of manhood.[39] The play here pulls in two directions. It reiterates this doubleness by vesting in Macduff its final fantasy of exemption from woman. The ambivalence that shapes the portrayal of Macduff is evident even as he reveals to Macbeth that he "was from his mother's womb / Untimely ripp'd" (5.8.15–16): the emphasis on untimeliness and the violence of the image suggest that he has been prematurely deprived of a nurturing maternal presence; but the prophecy construes just this deprivation as the source of Macduff's strength.[40] The prophecy itself both denies and affirms the fantasy of exemption from women: in affirming that Macduff has indeed had a mother, it denies the fantasy of male self-generation; but in attributing his power to his having been untimely ripped from that mother, it sustains the sense that violent separation from the mother is the mark of the successful male. The final battle between Macbeth and Macduff thus replays the initial battle between Macbeth and Macdonwald. But Macduff has now taken the place of Macbeth: he carries with him the male power given him by the Caesarian solution, and Macbeth is retrospectively revealed as Macdonwald, the woman's man.

The doubleness of the prophecy is less the equivocation of the fiends than Shakespeare's own equivocation about the figure of Macduff and about the fantasy vested in him in the end. For Macduff carries with him simultaneously all the values of family and the claim that masculine power derives from the unnatural abrogation of family, including escape from the conditions of one's birth. Moreover, the ambivalence that shapes the figure of Macduff similarly shapes the dramatic structure of the play itself. Ostensibly concerned to restore natural order at the end,[41] the play bases that order upon the radical exclusion of the female. Initially construed as all-powerful, the women virtually disappear at the end, Lady Macbeth becoming so diminished a character that we scarcely trouble to ask ourselves whether the report of her suicide is accurate or not, the witches literally gone from the stage and so diminished in psychic power that Macbeth never mentions them and blames his defeat only on the equivocation of their male masters, the fiends; even Lady Macduff exists only to disappear. The bogus fulfillment of the Birnam Wood prophecy suggests the extent to which the natural order of the end depends on the exclusion of the female. Critics sometimes see in the march of Malcolm's soldiers bearing their green branches an allusion to the Maying festivals in which participants returned from the woods bearing branches, or to the ritual scourging of a hibernal figure by the forces of the oncoming spring.[42] The allusion seems to me clearly present; but it serves, I think, to mark precisely what the moving of Birnam Wood is not. Malcolm's use of Birnam Wood is a military maneuver. His drily worded command (5.4.4–7) leaves little room for suggestions of natural fertility or for the deep sense of the generative world rising up to expel its winter king; nor does the play later enable these associations except in a scattered and partly ironic way.[43] These trees have little resemblance to those in the Forest of Arden; their branches, like those carried by the apparition of the "child crowned, with a tree in his hand" (4.1.86), are little more than the emblems of a strictly patriarchal family tree.[44] This family tree, like the march of Birnam Wood itself, is relentlessly male: Duncan and sons, Banquo and son, Siward and son. There are no daughters and scarcely any mention of mothers in these family trees. We are brought as close as possible here to the fantasy of family without women.[45] In that sense, Birnam Wood is the perfect emblem of the nature that triumphs at the end of the play: nature without generative possibility, nature without women. Malcolm tells his men to carry the branches to obscure themselves, and that is exactly their function: insofar as they seem to allude to the rising of the natural order against Macbeth, they obscure the operations of male power, disguising them as a natural force; and they simultaneously obscure the extent to which natural order itself is here reconceived as purely male.[46]

If we can see the fantasy of escape from the female in the play's fulfillment of the witches' prophecies—in Macduff's birth by Caesarian section and in Malcolm's appropriation of Birnam Wood—we can see it also in the play's psychological geography. The shift from Scotland to England is srikingly the shift from the mother's to the father's terrain.[47] Scotland "cannot/Be call'd our mother, but our grave" (4.3.165–66), in Rosse's words to Macduff: it is the realm of Lady Macbeth and the witches, the realm in which the mother *is* the grave, the realm appropriately ruled by their bad son Macbeth. The escape to England is an escape from their power into the realm of the good father-king and his surrogate son Malcolm, "unknown to woman" (4.3.126). The magical power of this father to cure clearly balances the magical power of the witches to harm, as Malcolm (the father's son) balances Macbeth (the mother's son). That Macduff can cross from one realm into the other only by abandoning his family suggests the rigidity of the psychic geography separating England from Scotland. At the end of the play, Malcolm returns to Scotland mantled in the power England gives him, in effect bringing the power of the fathers with him: bearer of his father's line, unknown to woman, supported by his agent Macduff (empowered by his own special immunity from birth), Malcolm embodies utter separation from women and as such triumphs easily over Macbeth, the mother's son.

The play that begins by unleashing the terrible threat of destructive maternal power and demonstrates the helplessness of its central male figure before that power thus ends by consolidating male power, in effect solving the problem of masculinity by eliminating the female. In the psychological fantasies that I am tracing, the play portrays the failure of the androgynous parent to protect his son, that son's consequent fall into the dominion of the bad mothers, and the final victory of a masculine order in which mothers no longer threaten because they no longer exist. In that sense, *Macbeth* is a recuperative consolidation of male power, a consolidation in the face of the threat unleashed in *Hamlet* and especially in *King Lear* and never fully contained in those plays. In *Macbeth,* maternal power is given its most virulent sway and then abolished; at the end of the play we are in a purely male realm. We will not be in so absolute a male realm again until we are in Prospero's island-kingdom, similarly based firmly on the exiling of the witch Sycorax.

NOTES

1. All references to *Macbeth* are to the new Arden edition, edited by Kenneth Muir, (London: Methuen, 1972).

2. I have written elsewhere about Coriolanus' doomed attempts to create a self that is independent of his mother's will; see my "'Anger's My Meat': Feeding, Dependency, and Aggression in *Coriolanus*," in *Representing Shakespeare: New Psychoanalytic Essays,* ed. Murray M. Schwartz and Coppélia Kahn (Baltimore: Johns Hopkins University Press, 1980), 129–49. Others have noted the extent to which both *Macbeth* and *Coriolanus* deal with the construction of a rigid male identity felt as a defense against overwhelming maternal power; see particularly Coppélia Kahn, *Man's Estate: Masculine Identity in Shakespeare* (Berkeley & Los Angeles: University of California Press, 1981), 151–92, whose chapter title–"The Milking Babe and the Bloody Man in *Coriolanus* and *Macbeth*"–indicates the similarity of our concerns. Linda Bamber argues, however, that the absence of a feminine Other in *Macbeth* and *Coriolanus* prevents the development of manliness in the heroes, since true manliness "involves a detachment from the feminine" (*Comic Women, Tragic Men: A Study of Gender and Genre in Shakespeare* [Stanford: Stanford University Press, 1982], 20, 91–107).

3. "Gowries Conspiracie: A Discoverie of the unnaturall and vyle Conspiracie, attempted against the Kings Maiesties Person at Sanct-Iohnstoun, upon Twysday the

Fifth of August, 1600," in *A Selection from the Harleian Miscellany* (London: C. & G. Kearsley, 1793), 196.

4. Stanley J. Kozikowski argues strenuously that Shakespeare knew either the pamphlet cited above ("Gowries Conspiracie," printed in Scotland and London in 1600) or the abortive play on the conspiracy, apparently performed twice by the King's Men and then canceled in 1604 ("The Gowrie Conspiracy against James VI: A New Source for Shakespeare's *Macbeth,*" *Shakespeare Studies* 13 [1980]: 197–211). Although I do not find his arguments entirely persuasive, it seems likely that Shakespeare knew at least the central facts of the conspiracy, given both James's annual celebration of his escape from it and the apparent involvement of the King's Men in a play on the subject. See also Steven Mullaney's suggestive use of the Gowrie material as an analogue for *Macbeth* in its link between treason and magical riddle ("Lying Like Truth: Riddle, Representation and Treason in Renaissance England," *ELH* 47 [1980]: 32, 38).

5. After the failure of the conspiracy, James searched the dead earl's pockets, finding nothing in them "but a little close parchment bag, full of magicall characters, and words of inchantment, wherin, it seemed, that he had put his confidence, thinking him selfe never safe without them, and therfore ever carried them about with him; beeing also observed, that, while they were uppon him, his wound whereof he died, bled not, but, incontinent after the taking of them away, the blood gushed out in great aboundance, to the great admiration of al the beholders" ("Gowries Conspiracie," 196). The magical stopping up of the blood and the sudden return of its natural flow seem to me potent images for the progress of Macbeth as he is first seduced and then abandoned by the witches' prophecies; that Gowrie's necromancer, like the witches, seemed to dabble in alternate modes of generation increases the suggestiveness of this association for *Macbeth.*

6. All references to Shakespeare's plays other than *Macbeth* are to the revised Pelican edition, *William Shakespeare: The Complete Works,* ed. Alfred Harbage (Baltimore, Penguin Books, 1969).

7. Richard Wheeler, Michael Neill, and Coppélia Kahn similarly understand Richard III's self-divided and theatrical masculinity as a defensive response to real or imagined maternal deprivation. See Wheeler, "History, Character and Conscience in *Richard III,*" *Comparative Drama* 5 (1971–72): 301–21, esp. 314–15; Neill, "Shakespeare's Halle of Mirrors: Play, Politics, and Psychology in *Richard III,*" *Shakespeare Studies* 8 (1975): 99–129, esp. 104–6; and Kahn, *Man's Estate,* 63–66.

8. *Impale* in the sense of "to enclose with pales, stakes or posts; to surround with a pallisade" (*OED*'s first meaning) is of course the dominant usage contemporary with *Macbeth.* But the word was in the process of change. *OED*'s meaning 4, "to thrust a pointed stake through the body of, as a form of torture or capital punishment," although cited first in 1613, clearly seems to stand behind the imagistic transformation here. The shift in meaning perfectly catches Richard's psychological process, in which any protective enclosure is ambivalently desired and threatens to turn into a torturing impalement.

9. Robert N. Watson notes the imagery of Caesarian birth here and in *Macbeth* (*Shakespeare and the Hazards of Ambition* [Cambridge, Mass.: Harvard University Press, 1984], esp. 19-20, 99-105); the metaphors of Caesarian section and Oedipal rape are central to his understanding of ambitious self-creation insofar as both imagine a usurpation of the defining parental acts of generation (see, for example, pp. 3-5). Though it is frequently very suggestive, Watson's account tends too easily to blur the distinction between matricide and patricide: in fantasies of rebirth, the hero may symbolically replace the father to re-create himself, but he does so by means of an attack specifically on the maternal body. In Shakespeare's images of Caesarian birth, the father tends to be conspicuously absent; indeed, I shall argue, precisely his absence—not his defining presence—creates the fear of the engulfing maternal body to which the fantasy of Caesarian section is a response. This body tends to be missing in Watson's account, as it is missing in his discussion of Richard's Caesarian fantasy here.

10. In an early essay that has become a classic, Eugene Waith established the centrality of definitions of manhood and Lady Macbeth's role in enforcing Macbeth's particularly bloodthirsty version, a theme that has since become a major topos of *Macbeth* criticism ("Manhood and Valor in Two Shakespearean Tragedies," *ELH* 17 [1950]: 262-73). Among the ensuing legions, see, for example, Matthew N. Proser, *The Heroic Image in Five Shakespearean Tragedies* (Princeton: Princeton University Press, 1965), 51-91; Michael Taylor, "Ideals of Manhood in *Macbeth*," *Etudes Anglaises* 21 (1968): 337-48 (unusual in its early emphasis on the extent to which the culture is complicit in defining masculinity as aggression); D. W. Harding, "Women's Fantasy of Manhood: A Shakespearean Theme," *Shakespeare Quarterly* 20 (1969): 245-53 (significant especially in its stress on women's responsibility for committing men to their false fantasy of manhood); Paul A. Jorgensen, *Our Naked Frailties: Sensational Art and Meaning in "Macbeth"* (Berkeley & Los Angeles: University of California Press, 1971), esp. 147ff.; Jarold Ramsey, "The Perversion of Manliness in *Macbeth*," *SEL* 13 (1973): 285-300; Carolyn Asp, "'Be bloody, bold, and resolute': Tragic Action and Sexual Stereotyping in *Macbeth*," *Studies in Philology* 25 (1981): 153-69 (significant especially for associating Macbeth's pursuit of masculinity with his pursuit of omnipotence); Harry Berger, Jr., "Text Against Performance in Shakespeare: The Example of *Macbeth*," in *The Forms of Power and the Power of Forms in the Renaissance*, ed. Stephen Greenblatt, special issue of *Genre* (15[1982]), esp. 67-75; and Robert Kimbrough, "Macbeth: The Prisoner of Gender," *Shakespeare Studies* 16 (1983): 175-90. Virtually all these essays recount the centrality of 1.7 to this theme; most see Macbeth's willingness to murder as his response to Lady Macbeth's nearly explicit attack on his male potency. Dennis Biggins and James J. Greene note particularly the extent to which the murder itself is imagined as a sexual act through which the union of Macbeth and Lady Macbeth is consummated; see Biggins, "Sexuality, Witchcraft, and Violence in *Macbeth*," *Shakespeare Studies* 8 (1975): 255-77; Greene, "Macbeth: Masculinity as Murder," *American Imago* 41 (1984): 155-80; see also Watson, *Shakespeare and the Hazards of Ambition*, 90. My account differs from most of these largely in stressing the infantile components of Macbeth's susceptibility

to Lady Macbeth. The classic account of these pre-Oedipal components in the play is David B. Barron's brilliant early essay "The Babe That Milks: An Organic Study of *Macbeth*," originally published in 1960 and reprinted in *The Design Within*, ed. M. D. Faber (New York: Science House, 1970), 253–79. For similar readings, see Marvin Rosenberg, *The Masks of Macbeth* (Berkeley & Los Angeles: University of California Press, 1978), 81–82, 270–72, and especially Kahn, *Man's Estate*, 151–55, 172–92, and Richard P. Wheeler, *Shakespeare's Development and the Problem Comedies* (Berkeley & Los Angeles: University of California Press, 1981), 144–49; as always, I am deeply and minutely indebted to the two last named.

11. Harry Berger, Jr., associates both Duncan's vulnerability and his role in legiti-mizing the bloody masculinity of his thanes with his status as the androgynous supplier of blood and milk ("The Early Scenes of *Macbeth*: Preface to a New Interpretation," *ELH* 47 [1980]: 26–28). Murray M. Schwartz and Richard Wheeler note specifically the extent to which the male claim to androgynous possession of nurturant power reflects a fear of maternal power outside male control (Schwartz, "Shakespeare through Con-temporary Psychoanalysis," in *Representing Shakespeare*, 29. Wheeler, *Shakespeare's De-velopment*, 146. My discussion of Duncan's androgyny is partly a consequence of my having heard Peter Erickson's rich account of the Duke's taking on of nurturant func-tion in *As You Like It* at MLA in 1979; this account is now part of his *Patriarchal Struc-tures in Shakespeare's Drama* (Berkeley & Los Angeles: University of California Press, 1985); see esp. pp. 27–37.

12. Many commentators note that Shakespeare's Duncan is less ineffectual than Holingshed's; others note the continuing signs of his weakness. See especially Harry Berger's brilliant account of the structural effect of Duncan's weakness in defining his (and Macbeth's) society ("The Early Scenes," 1–31).

13. Many note the appropriateness of Macbeth's conflation of himself with Tarquin, given the play's alliance of sexuality and murder. See, for example, Ian Robinson, "The Witches and Macbeth," *Critical Review* 11 (1968): 104; Biggins, "Sexuality, Witchcraft, and Violence," 269; and Watson, *Shakespeare and the Hazards of Ambition*, 100. Arthur Kirsch works extensively with the analogy, seeing the Tarquin of *The Rape of Lucrece* as a model for Macbeth's ambitious desire ("Macbeth's Suicide," *ELH* 51 [1984]: 269–96). Commentators on the analogy do not in general note that it transforms Macbeth's kingly victim into a woman; Norman Rabkin is the exception (*Shakespeare and the Problem of Meaning* [Chicago: Chicago University Press, 1981], 107).

14. Wheeler sees the simultaneously castrated and castrating Gorgon-like body of Duncan as the emblem of the world Macbeth brings into being (*Shakespeare's Develop-ment*, 145); I see it as the emblem of a potentially castrating femaleness that Macbeth's act of violence reveals but does not create.

15. The witches' power to raise storms was conventional; see, for example, Reginald Scot, *The Discoverie of Witchcraft* (London 1584; reprint, with an introduction by Hugh Ross Williamson, Carbondale: Southern Illinois University Press, 1964), 31; King James's *Daemonologie* (London, 1603), 46; and the failure of the witches to raise a storm

in Jonson's *Masque of Queens*. Jonson's learned note on their attempt to disturb nature gives his classical sources for their association with chaos: see *Masque,* 11.134–37, 209–20, and Jonson's note to l.134, in *Ben Jonson: The Complete Masques,* ed. Stephen Orgel (New Haven: Yale University Press, 1969), 531–32.

16. Many commentators, following Freud, find the murder of Duncan "little else than parricide" ("Those Wrecked by Success," in *The Standard Edition of the Complete Psychological Works of Sigmund Freud,* trans. and ed. James Strachey [London, Hogarth Press, 1957], 14: 321); see, for example, Rabkin, *Shakespeare and the Problem of Meaning,* 106–9, Kirsch, "Macbeth's Suicide," 276–80, 286, and Watson, *Shakespeare and the Hazards of Ambition,* esp. 85–88, 98–99 (the last two are particularly interesting in understanding parricide as an ambitious attempt to redefine the self as omnipotently free from limits). In standard Oedipal readings of the play, the mother is less the object of desire than "the 'demon-woman,' who creates the abyss between father and son" by inciting the son to parricide (Ludwig Jekels, "The Riddle of Shakespeare's *Macbeth,*" in *The Design Within,* 240). See also, for example, L. Veszy-Wagner, "*Macbeth:* 'Fair Is Foul and Foul Is Fair,'" *American Imago* 25 (1968): 242–57; Norman N. Holland, *Psychoanalysis and Shakespeare* (New York: Octagon Books, 1979), 229; and Patrick Colm Hogan's very suggestive account of the Oedipal narrative structure, "*Macbeth:* Authority and Progenitorship," *American Imago* 40 (1983): 385–95. My reading differs from these Oedipal readings mainly in suggesting that the play's mothers acquire their power because the father's protective masculine authority is already significantly absent; in my reading, female power over Macbeth becomes the sign (rather than the cause) of that absence.

17. For those recent commentators who follow Barron in seeing pre-Oedipal rather than Oedipal issues as central to the play, the images of disrupted nurturance define the primary area of disturbance; see, for example, Barron, "The Babe That Milks," 255; Schwartz, "Shakespeare through Psychoanalysis," 29; Berger, "The Early Scenes," 27–28; Joan M. Byles, "Macbeth: Imagery of Destruction," *American Imago* 39 (1982): 149–64; Wheeler, *Shakespeare's Development,* 147–48; and Kirsch, "Macbeth's Suicide," 291–92. Although Madelon Gohlke (now Sprengnether) does not specifically discuss the rupture of maternal nurturance in *Macbeth,* my understanding of the play is very much indebted to her classic essay, "'I wooed thee with my sword': Shakespeare's Tragic Paradigms," in which she establishes the extent to which masculinity in Shakespeare's heroes entails a defensive denial of the female (in *Representing Shakespeare:* 170–87); in an unfortunately unpublished essay, she discusses the traumatic failure of maternal protection imaged by Lady Macbeth here. In his brilliant essay "Phantasmagoric *Macbeth*" (forthcoming in *ELR*), David Willbern locates in Lady Macbeth's image the psychological point of origin for the failure of potential space that Macbeth enacts. Erickson, noting that patriarchal bounty in *Macbeth* has gone awry, suggestively locates the dependence of that bounty on the maternal nurturance that is here disturbed (*Patriarchal Structures,* 116–21). Several critics see in Macbeth's susceptibility to female influence evidence of his failure to differentiate from a maternal figure, a failure psychologically the consequence of the abrupt and bloody weaning imaged by Lady Macbeth; see,

for example, Susan Bachmann, "'Daggers in Men's Smiles'—The 'Truest Issue' in *Macbeth*," *International Review of Psycho-Analysis* 5 (1978): 97–104; and particularly the full and very suggestive accounts of Barron, "The Babe That Milks," 263–68, and Kahn, *Man's Estate*, 172–78. In the readings of all these critics, as in mine, Lady Macbeth and the witches variously embody the destructive maternal force that overwhelms Macbeth and in relation to whom he is imagined as an infant. Rosenberg notes intriguingly that *Macbeth* has twice been performed with a mother and son in the chief roles (*Masks of Macbeth*, 196).

18. Despite some overliteral interpretation, Alice Fox and particularly Jenijoy La Belle usefully demonstrate the specifically gynecological references of "passage" and "visitings of nature," using contemporary gynecological treatises. (See Fox, "Obstetrics and Gynecology in *Macbeth*," *Shakespeare Studies* 12 [1979]: 129; and La Belle, "'A Strange Infirmity': Lady Macbeth's Amenorrhea," *Shakespeare Quarterly* 31 [1980]: 382, for the identification of *visitings of nature* as a term for menstruation; see La Belle, 383, for the identification of *passage* as a term for the neck of the womb. See also Barron, who associates Lady Macbeth's language here with contraception ["The Babe That Milks," 267].)

19. *For* is glossed as "in exchange for" in the following editions, for example: *The Complete Signet Classic Shakespeare*, ed. Sylvan Barnet (New York: Harcourt, Brace, Jovanovich, 1972); *The Complete Works of Shakespeare*, ed. Hardin Craig (Chicago: Scott, Foresman, 1951), rev. ed. edited by David Bevinton (Chicago: Scott, Foresman, 1973); *The Riverside Shakespeare*, ed. G. Blakemore Evans (Boston: Houghton Mifflin, 1974); *William Shakespeare: The Complete Works*, ed. Alfred Harbage (Baltimore: Penguin, 1969); *The Complete Works of Shakespeare*, ed. George Lyman Kittredge (Boston: Ginn, 1936), rev. ed. edited by Irving Ribner (Boston: Ginn, 1971). Muir demurs, preferring Keightley's understanding of *take* as "infect" (see the Arden edition, p. 30).

20. Insofar as syphilis was known to be transmitted through the nursing process, there was some reason to worry; see, for example, William Clowes's frightening account, "A brief and necessary Treatise touching the cure of the disease called Morbus Gallicus" (London, 1585, 1596), 151. But Leontes' words to Hermione as he removes Mamillius from her ("I am glad you did not nurse him./Though he does bear some signs of me, yet you/Have too much blood in him" [*The Winter's Tale*, 2.1.56–58]) suggest that the worry was not fundamentally about epidemiology. Worry that the nurse's milk determined morals was, of course, common; see, for example, Thomas Phaire, *The Boke of Chyldren* (1545; reprint, Edinburgh: E. & S. Livingstone, 1955), 18. The topic was of interest to King James, who claimed to have sucked his Protestantism from his nurse's milk; his drunkenness was also attributed to her. See Henry N. Paul, *The Royal Play of "Macbeth"* (New York: Macmillan Co., 1950), 387–88. For the identification of colostrum with witch's milk, see Samuel X. Radbill, "Pediatrics," in *Medicine in Seventeenth-Century England*, ed. Allen G. Debus (Berkeley & Los Angeles, University of California Press, 1974), 249. The fear of maternal functioning itself, not simply of its

perversions, is central to most readings of the play in pre-Oedipal terms; see the critics cited in note 17 above.

21. Many commentators on English witchcraft note the unusual prominence given to the presence of the witch's mark and the nursing of familiars; see, for example, Barbara Rosen's introduction to the collection of witchcraft documents she edited (*Witchcraft* [London: Edward Arnold, 1969], 29–30). She cites contemporary documents on the nursing of familiars, for example, pp. 187–88, 315; the testimony of Joan Prentice, one of the convicted witches of Chelmsford in 1589, is particularly suggestive: "at what time soever she would have her ferret do anything for her, she used the words 'Bid, Bid, Bid, come Bid, come Bid, come Bid, come suck, come suck, come suck'" (p. 188). Katharine Mary Briggs quotes a contemporary (1613) story about the finding of a witch's teat (*Pale Hecate's Team* [New York: Arno Press, 1977], 250); see also Wallace Notestein, *A History of Witchcraft in England from 1558 to 1718* (Washington: American Historical Association, 1911), 36; and George Lyman Kittredge, *Witchcraft in Old and New England* (New York: Russell & Russell, 1956), 179. Though he does not refer to the suckling of familiars, King James believed in the significance of the witch's mark, at least when he wrote the *Daemonologie* (see p. 33). M. C. Bradbrook notes that Lady Macbeth's invitation to the spirits is "as much as any witch could do by way of self-dedication" ("The Sources of *Macbeth*," *Shakespeare Survey* 4 [1951]: 43).

22. In a brilliant essay, Peter Stallybrass associates the move from the cosmic to the secular realm with the ideological shoring up of a patriarchal state founded on the model of the family ("*Macbeth* and Witchcraft," in *Focus on "Macbeth,"* ed. John Russell Brown [London: Routledge & Kegan Paul, 1982], esp. 196–98).

23. Wilbur Sanders notes the extent to which "terror is mediated through absurdity" in the witches (*The Dramatist and the Received Idea* [Cambridge: Cambridge University Press, 1968], 277); see also Berger's fine account of the scapegoating reduction of the witches to a comic and grotesque triviality ("Text Against Performance," 67–68). Harold C. Goddard (*The Meaning of Shakespeare* [Chicago: University of Chicago Press, 1951], 512–13), Robinson ("The Witches and Macbeth," 100–103), and Stallybrass, ("*Macbeth* and Witchcraft," 199) note the witches' change from potent and mysterious to more diminished figures in act 4.

24. After years of trying fruitlessly to pin down a precise identity for the witches, critics are increasingly finding their dramatic power precisely in their indefinability. The most powerful statements of this relatively new critical topos are those by Sanders (*The Dramatist and the Received Idea*, 277–79), Robert H. West (*Shakespeare and the Outer Mystery* [Lexington: University of Kentucky Press, 1968], 78–79), and Stephen Booth (*"King Lear," "Macbeth," Indefinition, and Tragedy* [New Haven: Yale University Press, 1983], 101–3).

25. For their "Englishness", see Stallybrass, "*Macbeth* and Witchcraft," 195. Alan Macfarlane's important study of English witchcraft, *Witchcraft in Tudor and Stuart England* (New York: Harper & Row, 1970), frequently notes the absence of the Continental

staples: if the witches of Essex are typical, English witches do not fly, do not hold Sabbaths, do not commit sexual perversions or attack male potency, do not kill babies (see pp. 6, 160, 180, for example).

26. Macfarlane finds the failure of neighborliness reflected in the retaliatory acts of the witch the key to the social function of witchcraft in England; see ibid., 168–76 for accounts of the failures of neighborliness—very similar to the refusal to share chestnuts—that provoked the witch to act. James Sprenger and Heinrich Kramer, *Malleus Maleficarum*, trans. Montague Summers (New York: Benjamin Blom, 1970), is the *locus classicus* for Continental witchcraft beliefs: for the murder and eating of infants, see pp. 21, 66, 99, 100–101; for attacks on the genitals, see pp. 47, 55–60, 117–19; for sexual relations with demons, see pp. 21, 112–14. Or see Scot's convenient summary of these beliefs (*Discoverie*, 31).

27. The relationship between cosmology and domestic psychology is similar in *King Lear;* even as Shakespeare casts doubt on the authenticity of demonic possession by his use of Harsnett's *Declaration of Egregious Popish Impostures,* Edgar/Poor Tom's identification of his father as "the foul Flibbertigibbet" (3.4.108) manifests the psychic reality and source of his demons. Characteristically in Shakespeare, the site of blessing and of cursedness is the family, their processes psychological.

28. Although *his* was a common form for the as yet unfamiliar possessive *its,* Lady Macbeth's move from "while it was smiling" to "his boneless gums" nonetheless seems to register the metamorphosis of an ungendered to a gendered infant exactly at the moment of vulnerability, making her attack specifically on a male child. That she uses the ungendered *the* a moment later ("the brains out") suggests one alternative open to Shakespeare had he wished to avoid the implication that the fantasied infant was male; Antony's crocodile, who "moves with it own organs" (*Antony and Cleopatra,* 2.7.42), suggests another. (*OED* notes that, although *its* occurs in the Folio, it does not occur in any work of Shakespeare published while he was alive; it also notes the various strategies by which authors attempted to avoid the inappropriate use of *his.*)

29. Lady Macbeth maintains her control over Macbeth through 3.4 by manipulating these categories: see 2.2.53–54 ("'tis the eye of childhood/That fears a painted devil") and 3.4.57–65 ("Are you a man? . . . these flaws and starts . . . would well become/A woman's story"). In his response to Banquo's ghost, Macbeth invokes the same categories and suggests their interchangeability: he dares what man dares (3.4.98); if he feared Banquo alive, he could rightly be called "the baby of a girl" (l. 105).

30. In "Phantasmagoric *Macbeth,*" David Willbern notes the extent to which the regicide is reimagined as a "symbolic infanticide" so that the image of Duncan fuses with the image of Lady Macbeth's child murdered in fantasy. Macbeth's earlier association of Duncan's power with the power of the "naked new-born babe,/Striding the blast" (1.7.21–22) prepares for this fusion. Despite their symbolic power, the literal babies of this play and those adults who sleep and trust like infants are hideously vulnerable.

31. See Kahn, *Man's Estate,* 173, for a very similar account of this passage.

32. Shakespeare's only other use of *man-child* is in a strikingly similar context:

Volumnia, reporting her pleasure in Coriolanus' martial success, tells Virgilia, "I sprang not more in joy at first hearing he was a man-child than now in first seeing he had proved himself a man" (*Coriolanus,* 1.3.15–17).

33. De Quincy seems to have understood this process: "The murderers are taken out of the region of human things, human purposes, human desires. They are transfigured: Lady Macbeth is 'unsexed'; Macbeth has forgot that he was born of woman" ("On the Knocking at the Gate in 'Macbeth,'" in *Shakespeare Criticism: A Selection, 1623–1840,* ed. D. Nichol Smith [London: Oxford University Press, 1946], 335). Critics who consider gender relations central to this play generally note the importance of the witches' prophecy for the figure of Macduff; they do not usually note its application to Macbeth. But see Kahn's suggestion that the prophecy sets Macbeth "apart from women as well as from men" (*Man's Estate,* 187) and Gohlke's central perception that, "to be born of woman, as [Macbeth] reads the witches' prophecy, is to be mortal" ("I wooed thee," 176).

34. See Kahn's rich understanding of the function of the term *cow'd* (*Man's Estate,* 191).

35. Many comment on this contamination; see, for example, Berger, "The Early Scenes of *Macbeth,*" 7–8; Hogan, "Macbeth," 387; Rosenberg, *The Masks of Macbeth,* 45; Biggins, "Sexuality, Witches, and Violence," 265.

36. Watson notes the suggestion of Caesarian section here, through not its aggression toward the female. Barron does not comment specifically on this passage but notes breaking and cutting imagery throughout and relates it to Macbeth's attempt to "cut his way out of the female environment which chokes and smothers him" ("The Babe That Milks," 269). I am indebted to Willbern's "Phantasmagoric *Macbeth*" specifically for the Caesarian implications of the unseaming from nave to chops.

37. The reference to Macbeth as "Bellona's bridegroom" anticipates his interaction with Lady Macbeth in 1.7: only the murderous man-child is fit mate for either of these unsexed, quasi-male figures.

38. To the extent that ferocious maleness is the creation of the male community, not of Lady Macbeth or the witches, the women are scapegoats who exist partly to obscure the failures of male community. For fuller accounts of this process, see Veszy-Wagner, "Macbeth," 244, Bamber, *Comic Women,* 19–20, and especially Berger, "Text Against Performance," 68–75. But whether or not the women are scapegoats insofar as they are (falsely) held responsible for Macbeth's murderous maleness, fear of the female power they represent remains primary (not secondary and obscurantist) insofar as the male community and, to some extent, the play itself define maleness as violent differentiation from the female.

39. A great many critics, following Waith ("Manhood and Valor," 266–67), find the play's embodiment of healthy masculinity in Macduff. They often register some uneasiness about his leaving his family, but they rarely allow this uneasiness to complicate their view of him as exemplary. But critics interested in the play's construction of masculinity as a defense against the fear of femaleness tend to see in Macduff's removal from

family a replication of the central fear of women that is more fully played out in Macbeth. See, for example, Wheeler, *Shakespeare's Development,* 146; and Berger, "Text Against Performance," 70. For these critics, Macduff's flight is of a piece with his status as the man not born of woman.

40. Critics interested in gender issues almost invariably comment on the centrality of Macduff's fulfillment of this prophecy, finding his strength here in his freedom from contamination by or regressive dependency on women: see, for example, Harding, "Women's Fantasy," 250; Barron, "The Babe That Milks," 272; Berger, "The Early Scenes," 28; Bachmann, "Daggers," 101; Kirsch, "Macbeth's Suicide," 293; Kahn, *Man's Estate,* 172-73; Wheeler, *Shakespeare's Development,* 146; and Victor Calef, "Lady Macbeth and Infanticide or 'How Many Children Had Lady Macbeth Murdered?'" *Journal of the American Psychoanalytic Association* 17 (1969): 537. For Barron and Harding, Macduff's status as the bearer of this fantasy positively enhances his manhood; but for many of these critics, it qualifies his status as the exemplar of healthy manhood. Perhaps because ambivalence toward Macduff is built so deeply into the play, several very astute critics see the fantasy embedded in Macduff here and nonetheless continue to find in him an ideal manhood that includes the possibility of relatedness to the feminine. See, for example, Kahn, *Man's Estate,* 191; and Kirsch, "Macbeth's Suicide," 294.

41. The triumph of the natural order has of course been a commonplace of criticism since the classic essay by G. Wilson Knight, "The Milk of Concord: An Essay on Life-Themes in *Macbeth,*" in his *Imperial Theme* (London: Methuen, 1965), esp. 140-53. The topos is so powerful that it can cause even critics interested in gender issues to praise the triumph of nature and natural sexuality at the end without noting the exclusion of the female; see, for example, Greene, "Macbeth," 172. But Rosenberg, for example, notes the qualifying effect of this exclusion (*Masks of Macbeth,* 654).

42. See, for example, Goddard, *Meaning of Shakespeare,* 520-21; Jekels, "Riddle," 238; John Holloway, *The Story of the Night* (London: Routledge & Kegan Paul, 1961), 66; Rosenberg, *Masks of Macbeth,* 626; and Watson, *Shakespeare and the Hazards of Ambition,* 89, 106-16. Even without sensing the covert presence of a vegetation myth, critics often associate the coming of Birnam Wood with the restoration of spring and fertility; see, for example, Knight, "Milk of Concord," 144-45; and Greene, "Macbeth," 169. Only Bamber demurs: in her account Birnam Wood rises up in aid of a male alliance, not the Saturnalian disorder of the Maying rituals (*Comic Women,* 106). My view coincides with hers.

43. When Malcolm refers to planting (5.9.31) at the play's end, for example, his comment serves partly to reinforce our sense of his distance from his father's generative power.

44. Paul attributes Shakespeare's use of the imagery of the family tree here to his familiarity with the cut of the Banquo tree in Leslie's *De Origine, Moribus, et Rebus Gestis Scotorum* (*Royal Play,* 175). But the image is too familiar to call for such explanation; see, for example, the tree described in *Richard II* (1.2.12-21).

45. As Wheeler notes, the description of Malcolm's saintly mother makes him "sym-

bolically the child of something approximating virgin birth" (*Shakespeare's Development*, 146)—in effect another version of the man not quite born of woman. Berger comments on the aspiration to be "a nation of bachelor Adams, of no woman born and unknown to women" ("Text Against Performance," 72) without noting the extent to which this fantasy is enacted in the play; Stallybrass calls attention to this configuration and describes the structure of antithesis through which "(virtuous) families of men" are distinguished from "antifamilies of women" ("*Macbeth* and Witchcraft," 198). The fantasy of escape from maternal birth and the creation of all-male lineage would probably have been of interest to King James, whose problematic derivation from Mary, Queen of Scots must occasionally have made him wish himself not born of (that particular) woman, no matter how much he was concerned publicly to rehabilitate her image. See Jonathan Goldberg's account of James's complex attitude toward Mary and especially his attempt to claim the Virgin Queen, Elizabeth, rather than Mary as his mother as he moved toward the English throne (*James I and the Politics of Literature* [Baltimore: Johns Hopkins University Press, 1983], 11–17, 25–26, 119); see also Goldberg's very suggestive discussions of James's poetic attacks on women (ibid., 24–25) and his imaging himself as a man taking control of a woman in becoming king of England (ibid., 30–31, 46). Stephen Orgel speculates brilliantly about the ways in which James's concerns about his own lineage and hence about the derivation of his royal authority are refle⁻ted in *The Tempest:* James "conceived himself as the head of a single-parent family," as a paternal figure who has "incorporated the maternal," in effect as a Prospero; the alternative model is Caliban, who derives his authority from his mother ("Prospero's Wife," *Representations* 8 [1984]: 8–9). Perhaps *Macbeth* indirectly serves a cultural need to free James from entanglement with the problematic memory of his witch-mother (portrayed thus, for example, by Spenser in book 5 of *The Faerie Queene*), tracing his lineage instead from a safely distanced and safely male forefather, Banquo.

46. Although neither Berger nor Stallybrass discusses the function of Birnam Wood specifically, I am indebted here to their discussions of the ideological function of the play's appeal to cosmology in the service of patriarchy, Berger seeing it as "a collective project of mystification" ("Text Against Performance," 64), Stallybrass as "a returning of the disputed ground of politics to the undisputed ground of Nature" ("*Macbeth* and Witchcraft," 205–6). If, as Bradbrook suggests, witches were thought able to move trees ("Sources," 42), then we have in Malcolm's gesture a literal appropriation of female power, an act of making the unnatural natural by making it serve patriarchal needs.

47. See Erickson's fine discussion of this geographic distinction (*Patriarchal Structures*, 121–22).

 *Marjorie Garber*

Shakespeare's Ghost Writers

As if a man were author of himself,
And knew no other kin.
— *Coriolanus* 5.3.36–37

Who is the author of Shakespeare's plays? To many members
of the profession, this question has the rhetorical status of the question "Who is buried in Grant's tomb?" It is greeted by orthodox Stratfordians with umbrage, derision, and contemptuous dismissal of so
intense an order as inevitably to raise another question: What is at
stake here? Why, in other words, has the doubt about Shakespeare's
authorship persisted so tenaciously, and why has it been so equally
tenaciously dismissed?

The issue, as participants in the controversy see it, is whether the
author of the plays is in fact the man who lived in Stratford, received
with his father a grant of arms making him a propertied gentlemen,
prospered and bought New Place, one of the finest houses in Stratford, married Anne Hathaway, and bequeathed her his second-best
bed. No one denies that a man named William Shakespeare lived in
Stratford; what is vigorously objected to in some quarters is that it
was this same man who wrote the plays. Is is argued that the very
paucity of literary biographical material suggests that the authorship
is in doubt, or, indeed, is itself a fiction, designed to obscure the "real"
author, who by virtue of rank or other disabling characteristics could
not with safety have claimed the plays for his (or her) own. Here,
very briefly, is the case against Shakespeare as Shakespeare, which, as
you will see, is both textual and biographical:

We know relatively little about the life, despite a significant collection of legal or business documents. Surely the greatest poet of his
time would have left a more vivid record, including the comments of
his contemporaries. No one in his hometown seems to have thought
of him as a celebrated author. Most of the encomia for "Shakespeare"

were written after the death of the Stratford man, and some, like Jonson's famous poem affixed to the Folio, praise "Shakespeare" but may not identify him with the prosperous citizen of rural Warwickshire.

The plays show a significant knowledge of the law, more than could have been acquired in a casual way. Francis Bacon was a lawyer; Bacon wrote the plays.

The plays were clearly written by someone at home with the court and the aristocracy, and could not have been written by a plebian. Edward de Vere, seventeenth Earl of Oxford, was a nobleman; Oxford wrote the plays. (If this belief held general sway, Stanley Wells would now be presiding over the publication of *The Oxford Oxford*.)

The plays show a significant degree of classical learning, and also a certain witty detachment about university education. The Shakespeare of Stratford may have picked up his small Latin and less Greek at the Stratford grammar school, but we have no records proving that Shakespeare attended the school, and several rival claimants (Marlowe, Bacon, Oxford, the Countess of Pembroke, Queen Elizabeth) had demonstrably more rigorous training in both language and the classics.

Finally, it is pointed out that there are extant only six signatures of Shakespeare, all of which are so crabbed and illegible as to suggest illiteracy or illness. Three of the signatures appear on his will and three others on business documents, none of them in a literary connection. One scene from *Sir Thomas More*, a play in six distinct manuscript hands, is said to be by Shakespeare: these 147 lines, ascribed to "Hand D," have been subjected to much scrutiny and have given rise to elaborate conjecture about Shakespeare's process of composition. Yet even G. Blakemore Evans, who goes so far as to include the lines in *The Riverside Shakespeare*, and who describes them as "affording us a unique view of what Shakespeare's 'foul papers' may have looked like,"[1] admits that the evidence for the attribution, which was in fact not suggested until 1871, is inconclusive.

Against these last two arguments, orthodox Stratfordians respond in a number of ways: first, by touting the excellence of the Stratford grammar school (according to James G. McManaway in the official Folger Library pamphlet on the controversy, its headmaster made as much money as his counterpart at Eton, and a person with equivalent training today would, in his words, be "a Ph.D. at Harvard"[2]); second, by insisting that Shakespeare's father would "never deny his first-born son the privileges of schooling to which his . . . position entitled him" (McManaway again);[3] and third, by asserting that the nonsurvival of Shakespeare's literary hand "has no bearing on the subject of authorship" (yet again McManaway).[4] Manuscripts that went to the print shop prior to 1700 were universally discarded once the plays were set in type, and other English Renaissance authors (e.g., Spenser, Ralegh, and Webster) left similarly scanty paper trails. Yet no one quarrels about Spenser's authorship, or Ralegh's, or Webster's, or Milton's.

This, of course, is precisely the point. Why is it different for Shakespeare? Why is so much apparently invested in finding the "real" ghost writer, or in resisting and marginalizing all attempts to prove any authorship other than that of "the poacher from Stratford" (to cite the title of a recent book on Shakespeare authorship)? "Without possibility of question," maintains the Folger ghost-buster, "the actor at the Globe and the gentleman from Stratford were the same man."[5] Then why does the question persist? *That* is the question, or at least it is the question that I would like to address. I would like, in other words, to take the authorship controversy seriously, not, as is usually done, in order to round up and choose among the usual suspects, but rather in order to explore the significance of the debate (or the "dissension") itself, to consider the ongoing existence of the polemic between pro-Stratford-lifers and prochoice advocates as an exemplary literary event in its own right.

One of the difficulties involved in taking the authorship question seriously has been that proponents of rival claims seem to have an uncanny propensity to appear a bit loony—literally. One of the most articulate defenders of the Earl of Oxford authorship is one John Thomas Looney (an "unfortunate name," commented *Life* magazine in an article on the authorship question—but, his defenders say, "an honorable one on the Isle of Man, where it is pronounced 'Loney.'"[6]

It was Looney, appropriately enough, who won Freud to the Oxford camp). Nor is Mr. Looney the only contender for unfortunateness of name: a zealous Shakespearean cryptographer, who proves by numerological analysis that the real author could be either Bacon or Daniel Defoe, is George M. Battey ("no more fortunately named than Mr. Looney," comments an orthodox chronicler of the controversy, "and, quite properly, no more deterred by it'"). Batty or loony, the ghost seekers' names are legion, and they have left an impressive legacy of monuments to human interpretive ingenuity.

It was not until the mid nineteenth century that the full energies of the authorship controversy declared themselves — on both sides of the Atlantic — with the 1857 publication of Delia Bacon's 675-page *Philosophy of the Plays of Shakespeare Unfolded* (arguing the case for Francis Bacon [no relation] and bearing a noncommittal preface by Hawthorne), William Henry Smith's *Bacon and Shakespeare,* and the first impassioned defense, *William Shakespeare Not an Impostor,* by George Henry Townsend.[8]

Out of these diverse beginnings has grown a thriving industry, which to this day shows no signs of abating. Some sense of its magnitude can be gleaned from the fact that when, in 1947, Professor Joseph Galland compiled his bibliography of the controversy, entitled *Digesta Anti-Shakespeareana,* no one could afford to publish the 1,500-page manuscript.[9] And that was forty years ago. The flood of publications has continued unabated to this day, culminating in the recent and highly acclaimed version of the Oxford case, *The Mysterious William Shakespeare: The Myth and the Reality,* by Charlton Ogburn, Jr.

What, then, can be said about this strange and massive fact of literary history? It is significant that the Shakespeare authorship controversy presents itself at exactly the moment Foucault describes as appropriate for appropriation: the moment when the "author-function" becomes, in the late eighteenth and early nineteenth centuries, an item of property, part of a "system of ownership" in which strict copyright rules define the relation between text and author in a new way. It is not until there is such a thing as property that violations of property can occur; it is not surprising that the claims for rival authorship arise at the moment at which, in Foucault's words, "the transgressive properties always intrinsic to the act of writing became the forceful imperative of literature."[10] It may well be, therefore, that an analysis of the Shakespeare case will shed light on the general question raised by Foucault: "What is an author?"

Instances of the appropriative, even mercantile nature of the controversy abound. Described by one observer as a kind of "middle-class affair,"[11] the debate has largely been waged by lawyers and medical men, followed by members of the clergy and retired army officers. Not surprisingly, it became a popular forensic topic and inevitably the subject of litigation. In 1892–93, the Boston monthly magazine the *Arena* sponsored a symposium that took testimony for fifteen months. (Among the pro-Baconian plaintiffs was Ignatius Donnelly, a Minnesota congressman who had written a book called *The Great Cryptogram*, in which he attempted at great length to apply a cipher invented by Bacon. Donnelly had come across the cipher in his son's copy of a children's magazine entitled *Every Boy's Book*. By means of Bacon's "bi-literal cipher," a secret "infolded" message could be placed within an innocent "infolding" text.) The twenty-five-member jury in the case, which included prominent Shakespearean scholars and actors, found for the man from Stratford. A different verdict, however, was forthcoming in the 1916 courtroom battle on the tercentenary of Shakespeare's death. Two convinced Baconians, the cryptographer Elizabeth Wells Gallup and her financial backer, Colonel Fabyan, were sued by a motion picture manufacturer, William N. Selig, who hoped to profit from the tercentenary by filming some of the plays and felt that the slur on the Stratfordian authorship would lessen the value of his product. In this case the judge, finding that "Francis Bacon is the author," awarded Colonel Fabyan $5,000 in damages. Although the verdict was later vacated, the case made legal history.

Since both of these cases involved claims for a secret cipher, this may be the moment to say something about the role of codes and ciphers in the anti-Stratfordian cause. The purported discovery of a latent message encrypted in the manifest text provides the grounds for

a startling number of cases of alternative authorship. The proliferation of ciphers can be seen as another transgressive correlative to the
conception of literature as property. Here, the property violation
happens not *to* the text but *within* the text. While copyright laws
attempt to demarcate the bounds of literary property, cryptographers
set out to uncover ghostlier demarcations, to show that the text itself
is haunted by signs of rival ownership. Such codes, ciphers, anagrams,
and acrostics can be as fanciful as Mrs. Windle's assertion that proof
of the existence of a cipher was to be found in *Othello*: the island of
Cyprus clearly was meant to be read by those in the know as "cipher
us."[12] Or they can be as complex as Dr. Owen's wheel, a remarkable
contraption the size of two large movie reels, across which some one
thousand pages of Renaissance literary texts could be wound and
stretched for the better application of the cipher. Strictly speaking,
Owen was not the inventor of the wheel—he credits that achievement
to Bacon himself, in Bacon's "Letter to the Decipherer," which Owen
found "infolded" in the text of the so-called Shakespeare plays. The
letter to the decipherer, which is in code, contains instructions for
cracking the code—useful, of course, only to one who had already
done so. Owen's commitment to the truth of his method ultimately
compelled him to believe that Bacon was the author not only of the
works of Shakespeare, Greene, Marlowe, and so on, but also of a post-
humous translation of one of his own Latin works, heretofore
credited to his literary secretary and executor, Dr. Rawley. During
the writing of his book on *Sir Francis Bacon's Cipher Story,* Dr. Owen
received periodic visitations from Bacon's ghost, thus becoming perhaps the first to pursue his research under the aegis of the ghost of
a ghost writer. Convinced that tangible proof of Baconian authorship
was to be found in a set of iron boxes, he obtained financial backing
from the ever optimistic Colonel Fabyan and began excavations for
them in the bed of the River Wye.

The search for buried treasure indeed often accompanies the un-
earthing of encrypted messages here, just as it does in Poe's *Gold Bug.*
Delia Bacon is notorious for having waited, shovel in hand, in Shakespeare's tomb, suddenly assailed by doubts about what she was

digging for. On that occasion, the ghost of Shakespeare (whoever he was) declined to unfold himself.

But if, on the one hand, the isolated Looneys and Batteys always seem to be out there with their shovels, on the other hand examination reveals a significant degree of institutional as well as financial investment in the question. As recently as 1974, the most articulate contemporary spokesman for the Oxford case, Charlton Ogburn, Jr., created a scandal by publishing an article urging his views in the *Harvard Magazine,* the alumni bulletin of his alma mater. The outcry was intense and prolonged. Harvard professors Gwynne Evans and Harry Levin published a scathing reply in a subsequent number of the magazine, and letters deploring the threat to *veritas* continued to pour in for months. ("I'm amazed, shocked, and disgusted that THE magazine of the world's greatest university should actually publish more of the stale old spinach on the Oxford lunacy"; "I am certain that Professor Kittredge is turning over in his grave"; "Charlton Ogburn is a fool and a snob"; and much more in the same vein.[13]) Reviving the notion of legal recourse to proof, Ogburn called for a trial to settle the issue. Philip S. Weld, a prominent newspaperman and former president and publisher of *Harvard Magazine,* offered to defray the costs of litigation, including "box lunches and sherry for the opposing players," and proposed that "if no one at Harvard wishes to argue the case for the Stratfordian, perhaps you could engage someone from the Yale English Department."[14]

In fact, a survey of the available literature on the "Shakespeare question" produces an uncanny number of references, often seemingly superfluous, to Harvard as an institution. The rhetorical role assigned to Harvard in the authorship controversy is not adventitious. The University becomes itself in effect a Ghost Underwriter, guaranteeing the legitimacy of whatever side invokes its name as a sign of power and authority. This is one reason why the outcry over Ogburn's article in *Harvard Magazine* became so heated, moving one letter writer to characterize the published defense by the Harvard professors of the Stratford man as "paranoid, shrill, and even hysterical."[15]

Something else is being defended—or attacked—here. What is the ghost that walks?

At this point it might be useful to hazard a few conjectures about the kinds of investment that motivate the controversy on both sides:

Institutional investments. Anti-Stratfordians accuse the "orthodox" of economic and egocentric commitment to such establishments as the Shakespeare Birthplace and the thriving tourist industry in Stratford, England; the Folger Shakespeare Library in Washington, with its handsome building, theater, and gift shop; and publishing projects like *The Riverside Shakespeare,* from which considerable financial benefit, as well as professional advancement, can be reaped. But there is institutionalization on the other side as well. Both Baconians and Oxfordians have established organizations to further their causes (the Bacon Society was founded in England in 1885; the Bacon Society of America in 1922; the Shakespeare Fellowship, later the Shakespeare Authorship Society, promoting the claims for Oxford, was formed in London in 1922, and its American counterpart, the Shakespeare Fellowship, in 1939). The *Shakespeare-Oxford Society Newsletter* and the *Shakespeare Authorship Review* are going concerns.

Professional investments. Related to such institutions is what might be called the guild mentality of the academic community. Professors who regularly lecture and publish on the plays of Shakespeare do not as a rule write books extolling rival claimants for authorship. A Shakespearean's identity seems to hinge on the identity of Shakespeare. This produces a schism that can be read in a number of ways: either as representatives of sanity protecting scholarly seriousness against the Looneys and Batteys, or as guardians of the ivy tower protecting their jobs and reputations against true intellectual openness and the subversive ideas of outsiders.

"Psychological" investments. For some combatants, "Shakespeare" represents a juggernaut, a monument to be toppled. Thus he is fragmented, marginalized into a committee (the group authorship theory), or even a conspiracy. As the author of *An Impartial Study of the Shakespeare Title* puts it, "no one man in the Sixteenth Century,

or in any century before or since, leaving out the God-man, our Savior, could use as many words as are found in the plays."[16] A related phenomenon follows the pattern of Freud's Family Romance, which involves the desire to subvert the father, or to replace a known parent figure with an unknown, greater one, in this case a member of the nobility instead of a country fellow from Stratford. S. Schoenbaum persuasively suggests this as one reason for Freud's own belief in the Oxford candidacy.[17]

"Territorial" investments. By far the greatest number of contributions, on both sides of the question, have come from Americans; in an 1884 bibliography containing 255 titles, almost two-thirds were written by Americans. In 1895 the Danish critic Georg Brandes fulminated against the "troop of half-educated people" who believed that Shakespeare did not write the plays, and bemoaned the fate of the profession. "Literary criticism," which "must be handled carefully and only by those who have a vocation for it," had clearly fallen into the hands of "raw Americans and fanatical women."[18] Delia Bacon, often credited with beginning the whole controversy, was of course both. But while she was ultimately confined to a mental hospital, she had succeeded in attracting to her defense—though not necessarily to her point of view—such distinguished allies as Hawthorne and Emerson. Nor can we ignore the redoubtable Maria Bauer, who in the late 1930s received permission to excavate in Williamsburg, Virginia for the proof of Bacon's authorship, and who, in her book *Foundations Unearthed,* exhorted her fellow Americans: "Cast your vote [for Bacon as] the great Founder, the empire-builder of your Nation and your Culture" by digging up the treasure trove in the "Bruton Vault."[19] This was the democratization of authorship with a vengeance.

Writers as different as John Greenleaf Whittier and Mark Twain, too, professed doubts about the Stratford man. Twain, who himself wrote under a pseudonym, and who had felt impelled to correct exaggerated reports of his own death, wrote an essay entitled "Is Shakespeare Dead?" in which he faults the Stratfordians for conjecturing a life story out of little or no evidence. Twain then goes on to declare himself a "Brontosaurian," theorizing an immense body from a few ambiguous bones. "The Brontosaurian doesn't really know which of them did it, but is quite composedly and contentedly sure that Shakespeare *didn't,* and strongly suspects that Bacon *did.*"[20] As Emerson wrote to his brother about the forthcoming publication of *Representative Men:* "Who dare print, being unlearned, an account of Plato . . . or, being uninspired, of Shakspeare? Yet there is no telling what we rowdy Americans, whose name is Dare, may do!"[21]

"We rowdy Americans" have had a variety of motivations for interest in the authorship question. First, there is what might be called an impulse to reverse colonization, a desire to recapture "Shakespeare" and make him new (and in some odd way "American") by discovering his true identity, something at which the British had failed. Second, and in some sense moving in the opposite direction, there is an ambivalent fascination with aristocracy, as something both admired and despised. Thus the great democrat, Walt Whitman, declares himself "firm against Shakespeare—I mean the Avon man, the actor."[22] Those "amazing works," the English history plays, could, he asserted, have had for their "true author" only "one of the 'wolfish earls' so plentiful in the plays themselves, or some born descendant and knower."[23] Charlie Chaplin, born in England but achieving success in America as the common man's hero, declared in his autobiography: "I'm not concerned with who wrote the works of Shakespeare . . . but I hardly think it was the Stratford boy. Whoever wrote them had an aristocratic attitude." Authorship of the autobiography is ascribed, on the title page, to Sir Charles Spencer Chaplin.[24]

A third American motivation might loosely be described as mythic or "Unitarian"—the desire to believe in Shakespeare as a kind of God, transcending ordinary biography and fact. Thus, taking a gently ironic view of the efforts of "the Shakespeare Society" to find salient facts about the poet, Emerson asserts, "Shakespeare is the only biographer of Shakespeare; and even he can tell nothing, except to the Shakespeare in us."[25] "He was," writes Emerson, "the farthest reach of subtlety compatible with an individual self—the subtlest of authors, and only just within the possibility of authorship."[26]

But attachments to Shakespeare have not always remained "on this

side idolatry," as the pious reference to the vocabulary of the God-
man (a Holy Ghost writer?) attests. Another American, Henry James,
confessing himself to be "sort of 'haunted' by the conviction that the
divine William is the biggest and most successful fraud ever practiced
on a patient world,"[27] fictionalized the skepticism as well as the fascination provoked by such bardolatry in a late short story entitled
"The Birthplace." The story is often described as being about the
tourist industry at Shakespeare's birthplace in Stratford. But the
proper names never, in fact, appear. The poet is referred to throughout as "He" and "Him" with a capital *H*, and his writing, similarly
capitalized, as "a Set of the Works." Far from casting doubt on the
story's referent, however, James's typical indirection is here the perfect vehicle for his subject: no direct naming could have represented
as well the paradoxes of the authorship controversy.

As the story opens, Mr. and Mrs. Morris Gedge have just been hired
as docents of the Birthplace. The Birthplace Trust appears in the story
as the "Body," the indwelling poet as the "Spirit," the process of ex-
hibition is known as the "Show," and the "Show" includes the telling
of certain "Facts" about which Gedge becomes increasingly dubious.
He suggests to his wife a modification of discourse that amounts to
an imposition of Jamesian style.

> Couldn't you adopt . . . a slightly more discreet method? what we can say
> is that things have been *said;* that's all *we* have to do with. "And is this
> really"—when they jam their umbrellas into the floor—"the very *spot* where
> He was born?" "So it has, from a long time back, been described as being."
> Couldn't we meet Them, to be decent a little, in some such way as that?[28]

In search of enlightenment, Gedge haunts the "Holy of Holies of the
Birthplace" the "Chamber of Birth," scene of the Primal Scene, which
should contain the Fact of Facts—the fact that He was born there—or
indeed, born at all. "He *had* to take it as the place where the spirit
would most walk and where He would therefore be most to be met,
with possibilities of recognition and reciprocity."[29] But the ghost
never appears. Like Gertrude in *Hamlet,* Gedge sees nothing at all. In
a proto–New Critical or proto-Foucauldian move, he finally confides

to a pair of visiting Americans that the author does not exist. "Practically, . . . there *is* no author; that is for us to deal with. There are all the immortal people—*in* the work; but there's nobody else."[30]

The rest of Gedge's career is instructive for academics, for he first makes the mistake of openly displaying his doubts—"giving the Show away," as the representative of the Body says when he arrives to reprove him. But once reminded of his jeopardy, Gedge turns completely around and, freed of the burden of an indwelling author, himself becomes one, gaining such fame as a raconteur that the Body doubles his stipend.

The crucial point here is the independence—in terms both of entrepreneurship and of artistic freedom—conferred upon the Morris Gedges of this world by the absence of the author—by the hole at the center of things. In a similar spirit, Mark Twain alleged rather gleefully about Shakespeare that *"he hadn't any history to record. There is no way of getting around that deadly fact."*[31] Emerson, we can recall, likewise rejoiced in the picture of a Shakespeare "only just within the possibility of authorship," and in his *Journals* he raises the question once more: "Is it not strange," he asks, "that the transcendent men, Homer, Plato, Shakespeare, confessedly unrivalled, should have questions of identity and of genuineness raised respecting their writings?"[32] This is in part what *makes* them transcendent.

In fact, poets and writers who address the "Shakespeare Question" in the nineteenth and twentieth centuries tend to embrace the question *as* a question, preferring its openness to the closure mandated by any answer. This is as true in England as it is in America. Dickens remarks—in a letter much cited by anti-Stratfordians—that "it is a great comfort, to my way of thinking, that so little is known concerning the poet. The life of Shakespeare is a fine mystery and I tremble every day lest something should turn up."[33] With this splendid reversal of Mr. Micawber, Dickens aligns himself with the Gedge camp.

Moreover, the most famous statements about Shakespeare as a creative artist—the ones we all grew up on—make very similar kinds of assertion. Coleridge characterizes him as "our myriad-minded Shakespeare."[34] Keats evolved his celebrated concept of "Negative Capabil-

ity" to describe the quality "which Shakespeare possessed so enor-
mously . . . that is, when a man is capable of being in uncertainties,
mysteries, doubts, without any irritable reaching after fact and
reason"[35] and wrote that "Shakespeare led a life of Allegory; his works
are the comments on it."[36] Dryden, in a phrase equally familiar, calls
Shakespeare "the man who of all modern, and perhaps ancient, poets
had the largest and most comprehensive soul."[37] The suggestion in all
of these cases is of a kind of transcendent ventriloquism. It is as
though Shakespeare *is* beyond authorship, beyond even the "plurality
of egos" that Foucault locates in all discourse that supports the
"author-function."[38] Matthew Arnold's sonnet on Shakespeare marks
out the issue clearly.

> Others abide our question. Thou art free.
> We ask and ask—Thou smilest and art still,
> Out-topping knowledge.[39]

The "foiled searching of mortality" fails to disclose the answer:
"Thou, who didst the stars and sunbeams know,/Self-schooled, self-
scanned, self-honored, self-secure/Didst tread on earth unguessed
at.—Better so!"[40] Better so indeed. We have described the investment
in various answers, but a great deal seems invested in *not* finding the
answer. It begins to become obvious that Shakespeare is the towering
figure he is for us not despite, but rather *because of,* the authorship
controversy. He is *defined* by that controversy, as, equally, he defines
it, making Foucault's use of him as an example almost tautologous.
Shakespeare is a present absence—which is to say, a ghost. Shakespeare as an author is the person who, were he more completely
known, would not be the Shakespeare we know.

Formulations like *What is an author?* and *the death of the author,*
which have engaged the imagination of contemporary theorists, draw
much of their power and fascination from "the kinship between writing and death"[41]—a little less than kin and more than kind. Freed from
the trammels of a knowable "authorial intention," the author paradoxically gains power rather than losing it, assuming a different kind
of authority that renders him in effect his own ghost. It begins to

become clear that to speak about "ghost writing" is not merely to play upon words. As Foucault puts it, "we find the link between writing and death manifested in the total effacement of the individual characteristics of the writer. . . . If we wish to know the writer in our day, it will be through the singularity of his absence and in his link to death, which has transformed him into a victim of his own writing."[42] If you want to know the author—*in* the text, as well as *of* or *behind* the text—look to see who's dead.

Consider, for example, the tradition that has grown up about Shakespeare as an actor in his own plays. Nicholas Rowe, in the *Life* printed with his 1709 edition of the *Works,* writes that "tho' I have inquir'd I could never meet with any further account of him this way, than that the top of his performance was the Ghost in his own *Hamlet.*"[43] Rowe's edition was published ninety-three years after Shakespeare's death—his information is hearsay, rumor, or better, but it is not an eyewitness account. It therefore belongs properly with the affect of the Shakespeare story rather than with its irreducible facts. A less reliable account reports that Will Shakespeare's younger brother, having been asked about the parts played by his celebrated sibling, described seeing him "act a part in one of his own comedies, wherein being to personate a decrepit old man, he wore a long beard, and appeared so weak and drooping and unable to walk, that he was forced to be supported and carried by another person to a table, at which he was seated among some company, who were eating, and one of them sung a song."[44] This part has been identified as that of Old Adam in *As You Like It,* who enters the scene in question (2.7) borne on Orlando's shoulders, like Anchises borne on the shoulders of his son Aeneas.

Both of these traditional accounts are suggestive. Each casts Shakespeare as a father figure advising his son, and placed at a disadvantage by age (or death) so that he requires the son to enact his will. Old Adam, in whom appears "the constant service of the antique world" (2.3.57) personates the dead Sir Rowland and his lost ways of civility. It is he who warns Orlando about treachery in the Duke's court and encourages him to seek safety in Arden. We may see this as appropriate to a playwright's role, giving his protagonist motive for action, so that the casting acts as a kind of metadramatic shadow or reflection of the relationship between author, actor, and plot. But the role of ghost writer here is doubled. Each of these figures achieves his own erasure, first presenting or representing the imperative of the father, then disappearing from the play.

Let us return, then, to our original question. Who is the author of Shakespeare's plays? Is it possible that, in this already overdetermined controversy, there is at least one more determining factor? Is there something in the nature of the plays themselves that somehow provokes, as it responds to, the authorship controversy? Are there, in other words, explicit scenes of ghost writing in the plays themselves? It has long been noted that Shakespeare's plays are full of questions of authority, legitimacy, usurpation, authorship, and interpretation. Indeed, drama as a genre not only permits but also encodes the dissemination of authority—this is in part what authorizes such formulations as "negative capability" and "myriad-minded"-ness. But can the more *particular* details of the authorship controversy as I have just documented it somehow be seen to be anticipated and overdetermined by the plays? Can the "Shakespeare Question" be situated within the text itself? Is the authorship controversy in part a textual effect?

There are in fact an uncanny number of ways in which the plays can be seen to dramatize the controversy. In the remainder of this essay, I will discuss only a small number of such scenes of encoded authorship, which encompass everything from ghosts that write and writers who function as ghosts, to handwriting analyses, signature controversies, the deciphering of codes, the digging of graves, the silencing of madwomen, the staging of plays that get away from their authors, and the thematizing of myriad other forms of doubt and discontinuity within authorial identity and control.

The most paradoxically vivid of Shakespeare's ghost writers are the ghosts within the plays, whose appearance is almost always juxtaposed to a scene of writing. Hamlet takes dictation from the ghost of his father: "My tables, meet it is I set it down/That one may smile,

and smile, and be a villain!" (1.5.107–8) Old Hamlet's script is a revenge tragedy, perhaps the ur-*Hamlet*. Hamlet will alter the script,
will himself sign and seal what he will describe as a "play" on the
voyage to England. But in this first encounter with the Ghost we see
a further rewriting of authority as well.

> I'll wipe away all trivial fond records,
> All saws of books, all forms, all pressures past
> That youth and observation copied there,
> And thy commandment all alone shall live
> Within the book and volume of my brain.
>
> [1.5.98–103]

"Thy commandment" (to revenge) replaces all the saws and pressures,
or seals, of the past. In this post-Mosaic transmission of the law from
father to son one kind of erasure (or "wiping away") is already taking
place. The Ghost himself is under erasure—"'tis here, 'tis here, 'tis
gone"—visible and invisible, potent and impotent. But *all* ghosts are
under erasure: that is their status. What Hamlet writes down in *his*
tables is the doubled plot of the Mousetrap play, for to smile and
smile and be a villain is a description not only of Claudius, but also
of Hamlet, just as Hamlet glosses the figure of "one Lucianus, nephew
to the King" in the Mouse-trap as both a sign of his knowledge of
Claudius' guilt in the past and a threat of his own revenge in the
future. The integration of the Ghost into the composite figure of
"Hamlet the Dane" begins with this scene of writing, as Hamlet
writes himself into the story and writes the Ghost out, revising the
revenge imperative (and the imperative of the revenge play).

The ghost of Julius Caesar is likewise appropriated as a ghost writer,
in this case by Mark Antony in the funeral oration. It is clear from
the moment of the assassination that the conspirators have killed the
wrong Caesar, the man of flesh and blood, and not the feared and
admired monarch. They have, so to speak, killed the wrong author-
function—the one associated with the proper name and not with the
works. Brutus' despairing cry, "O Julius Caesar, thou art mighty yet!/
Thy spirit walks abroad and turns our swords/In our own proper en-
trails" (5.3.94–96) records his sense of Caesar as uncanny omni-

presence and conflates his two sightings of the ghost with the self-destructive actions of the conspirators. Antony will himself become a "seizer" of opportunity, in the public reading of Caesar's *will*, "under Caesar's seal" (3.2.240), which leaves his money and pleasure-grounds to the people. In effect he makes Caesar, the dead and living Caesar of the author-function, his own ghost writer, the more effaced, the more powerful.

Brutus, who actually sees great Caesar's ghost, likewise participates in a crucial scene of writing and authorial appropriation, one that occurs, significantly, before the assassination itself, as Brutus walks at night in his orchard. A letter is thrown in at his window, and, as he reads it, he writes it:

> "Brutus, thou sleep'st; awake, and see thyself!
> Shall Rome, etc. Speak, strike, redress!"
> "Brutus, thou sleep'st; awake!"
> Such instigations have been often dropp'd
> Where I have took them up.
> "Shall Rome, etc." Thus must I piece it out:
> Shall Rome stand under one man's awe? What, Rome?
> My ancestors did from the streets of Rome
> The Tarquin drive when he was call'd a king.
> "Speak, strike redress!" Am I entreated
> To speak and strike? O Rome, I make thee promise,
> If the redress will follow, thou receivest
> Thy full petition at the hand of Brutus!
>
> [2.1.46–58]

Brutus supplies this anonymous document with what is in fact a dead (that is, inanimate) author—"Rome." "Rome" enjoins him to join the conspiracy. "Shall Rome, etc."—like many of Shakespeare ciphers—gives the interpreter considerable latitude to inscribe his own message ("thy full petition at the *hand* of Brutus"). The hand that rewrites here is of course also the hand that kills. The anonymity of the communication itself encodes authority—the importunings of a mere individual, like Cassius, are suspect because they are tied to a flawed human persona, and to personal motives. Receiving the letter, Brutus elects to ignore the possibility of a merely human agent and to regard it instead as an uncanny answer to his own latent thought, about himself and his love-relationship to Rome. Here Brutus becomes his own ghost writer and gives to the author he creates the pseudonym of "Rome."

Another kind of ghostly self-erasure can be seen in the famous "deposition scene" in *Richard II* (4.1). There Richard, denying any possibility of a split between persona and role, the king's two bodies (or the proper name of the author and his works, to use Foucault's division), sees himself as erased, transformed into a shadow or ghost of himself, when he is deposed by Bullingbrook:

> I have no name, no title,
> No, not that name was given me at the font,
> But 'tis usurp'd. . . .
> . . . .
> O that I were a mockery king of snow,
> Standing before the sun of Bullingbrook,
> To melt myself away in water-drops!
>
> [4.1.255–62]

A "deposition" is both a forced removal from office and a piece of testimony taken down for use in the witness's absence (as well as the term describing the lowering of Christ's body from the cross—Richard's view of the event). Richard here deposes at his own deposition, figuring himself as a snowman whose whiteness and impermanence are tragically vulnerable to the kingly sun. He is already a voice from the past, and the disembodied voice, the ghost of Richard II, will haunt the rest of the tetralogy with increasing power.

Bullingbrook has faulted the "skipping king" Richard for his availability to the people—he himself, by being seldom seen, will be more wondered at, more the stuff of legend, reverence, and fantasy. Like Arnold's vision of a Shakespeare "unguessed at—Better so!" this strategy locates power in absence—absence of personality, absence of fact, absence of peculiarity. But the question is also one of suitability, of fitting the role. Richard is the lineal king, the king by Divine Write, by Holy Writ. But Bullingbrook, like Bacon, fits the part, with his winning manners and his "fair discourse" (2.3.6). It is striking that one of his complaints against Richard is that the king has erased his name and coat of arms from the windows of the family estate, "leaving me no sign,/Save men's opinion and my living blood,/To show the world I am a gentleman" (3.1.25–27).

As with a "deposition," so with a "will"—the dead hand is a living voice replacing the original author, and open to interpretation. Thus Portia complains that in the mandatory casket choice "the will of a living daughter [is] curb'd by the will of a dead father" (*MV* 1.2.24–25). Shakespeare—if it is he—puns on his own name as an absent presence enforcing desire and authority (or failing to enforce them) throughout the *Sonnets*, and, as we have seen, Mark Antony makes of the "will" of the murdered Caesar read aloud to the plebians a document that encodes his own "will," his own authority over the original conspirators.

But if ghosts are often writers, so too are writers often ghosts. The question of Shakespeare's signature, especially as it appears (three times) on his will, can also be situated within the text. A signature, as Derrida has shown, is simultaneously a present absence and an absent presence, something that must be iterated to be recognizable, but that stands for its signator in that person's absence. "By definition, a written signature implies the actual or empirical nonpresence of the signer."[45] A signature, then, is very like a ghost, as will become explicitly the case when Hamlet on shipboard takes his father's signet, providentially carried in his purse, and signs the name of "Hamlet" to the letter he has forged in the careful calligraphy of a professional scribe. ("I once did hold it, as our statists do, a baseness to write fair ... but, sir, now/It did me yeman's service" [5.2.33–36]). The "changeling" letter that sends Rosencrantz and Guildenstern to their deaths is signed by Hamlet—but which Hamlet? It is the underwritten script of the Ghost's imperative superscribed by the son's educated hand.

Again, the plays are thematizing the authorship controversy: the question of the identification of signatures and handwriting (Could Shakespeare write? Could his parents? Could his daughters? Why have we no literary remains in his hand, or—if any—just the *Thomas*

More fragment?) is a question configured in the plays not only in Hamlet and Old Hamlet, but in Maria's forged letter to Malvolio in *Twelfth Night*, made possible by an uncanny resemblance between her handwriting and Olivia's, and in Edmund's forged letter purporting to come from his brother Edgar. "You know the character to be your brother's?" asks Gloucester, using the Renaissance term for handwriting, for letter of the alphabet, and also for cipher or code. "It is his hand, my lord; but I hope his heart is not in the contents" (*KL* 1.2.62; 67–68). The character, of course, is Edmund's, the letter a forgery of *his* jealousy and not of Edgar's. In these forgeries the text itself becomes a ghost writer: the scriptwriting capacity takes on a power of its own, supplementing the plot and radically altering it. And once more, as in the plays, so in the authorized biography. Critics search in vain for the "speech of some dozen lines, or sixteen lines" (2.2.541–42) that Hamlet asks the players to insert in "The Murder of Gonzago" as an indicator of his secret knowledge. In just the same way, editors have scrutinzed the manuscript of *Sir Thomas More* for undoubted proof of Shakespeare's authorship and have fixed at last on the 147 lines written by "Hand D."

The spectral presence of the "hand" haunts the editorial tradition in another way as well, in connection with a particularly compelling example of authorial fragmentation. Lavinia in *Titus Andronicus*, who enters the stage "*her hands cut off, and her tongue cut out, and ravish'd*" (2.4.SD) is assigned the task of writing *without* hands, and it is unsettling how often phrases like "on the one hand . . . and on the other" appear in the critical introductions to the play. T. S. Eliot calls it "a play in which it is incredible that Shakespeare had any hand at all"; M. C. Bradbrook observes that in the play "Shakespeare was trying his hand at the high style," and E. M. W. Tillyard points out admiringly that "the author holds everything in his head"—all textual effects, themselves, of the play's embarrassing power.[46] Titus' brother Marcus urges that he not "teach Lavinia to lay such violent hands upon her life," and Titus (who has himself been tricked into cutting off one of his own hands) turns angrily upon him: "What violent hands can she lay upon her life?" (since she has none):

Ah, wherefore doest thou urge the name of hands. . . .
. . . .
O handle not the theme, to talk of hands,
Lest we remember still that we have none.
Fie, fie, how franticly I square my talk,
As if we should forget we have no hands,
If Marcus did not name the word of hands!

[3.2.25–33]

In the very next scene (4.1) Lavinia begins to rifle through her
nephew Lucius' books with her stumps, in quest of a means of communication. Her father, uncle, and nephew are puzzled, but it soon
transpires that she is turning the leaves of—what else?—Ovid's *Metamorphoses,* indicating the "tragic tale of Philomel . . . of Tereus' treason and his rape" (4.1.47–48) as the narratives of her own experience.
"Give signs, sweet girl," implores Titus (4.1.61), and Marcus devises
a better plan. As so often in this play, the stage direction says it all:
"*He writes his name with his staff, and guides it with feet and mouth.*"

This sandy plot is plain; guide, if thou canst,
This after me. I have writ my name,
Without the help of any hand at all.

[4.1.69–71]

Lavinia's inscription on the "sandy plot" indicates the truth of her
condition, identifying her rapists as the sons of Tamora. "There is
enough written on this earth/ . . . To arm the minds of infants to ex-
claims" (4.1.84–86). *In-fans,* unable to speak, disarmed by her mutila-
tion, Lavinia signs her deposition with a missing hand, a hand that is
both "bloody and invisible."

The literal ghosts, the portentous Senecan stalkers from the revenge
tradition, tend in Shakespeare's plays to be male and paternal. But as
the example of Lavinia suggests, there is another whole group of ghost
writers in his plays who are similarly under erasure, and these ghost
writers are women—women marginalized by their gender, by their
putative or real madness, or by their violation. The story of Delia
Bacon—overprotected by her brother, misled by a theology student
into thinking he would marry her, gaining authority as a seer and

prophetess from her rejection, and with it the license to go abroad and speak dangerous things, dying mad—this is the story of Ophelia. "Her speech is nothing," says a gentleman to Horatio and the queen,

> Yet the unshaped use of it doth move
> The hearers to collection; they yawn at it,
> And botch the words up fit to their own thoughts,
> Which as her winks and nods and gestures yield them,
> Indeed would make one think there might be thought,
> Though nothing sure, yet much unhappily.
>
> [*Hamlet* 4.5.7–13]

To this statement, itself a foreclosure of judgment ("her speech is nothing") Horatio adds an even more political warning: "'Twere good she were spoken with, for she may strew/Dangerous conjectures in ill-breeding minds" (4.5.14–15). Horatio's word "strew" predicts her flower giving, "a document in madness, thoughts and remembrance fitted," as Laertes will describe it (4.5.178–79). *Her* open grave, and not Old Hamlet's, will provide the scene for the final struggle. It is perhaps no accident that Claudius will shortly blame the whole mess on Hamlet ("he most violent author/Of his own just remove" (4.5.80–81]). The "shaped use" of Ophelia's speech can be licked into shape like a bear whelp by whoever assumes the authority of the dam.

Equally marginalized, equally erased, moving through the events of her play like a ghost, Cassandra is dismissed by her brothers as "our mad sister" (*T&C* 2.2.98), but the design toward which she moves, the story she tells, is the story of the Trojan War. Cassandra's authority is such that she speaks truth and is not believed—and this is also the case with Ophelia and indeed with Lady Macbeth. Lady Macbeth's sleepwalking places her physically in exactly the condition of present absence, marginal stance, and legible erasure we have come to expect of such ghosts. Indeed, perhaps the most threatening female authority of all in the plays is also the most effaced—Sycorax, Caliban's mother, predecessor magician to Prospero, whose name is evoked as the justification for his authority and authorship on the island—and who never appears in the play. Like Claribel, who would be the next heir to Naples but is half a world away in Tunis, Sycorax exists beyond the play's margins, and only Miranda remains as another figure of female self-erasure in the present, eagerly accepting her father's tutelage in the Elizabethan World Picture.

Thus, again and again, the plays themselves can be seen to dramatize questions raised in the authorship controversy: Who wrote this? Did someone else have a hand in it? Is the apparent author the real author? Is the official version to be trusted? Or are there suppressed stories, hidden messages, other signatures?

I will end with an example that can serve as a cautionary tale, warning us that all decipherings of the truth of the authorship question—including this one—run the risk of being too clever by half. For the phenomenon of life imitating art has never been more amply demonstrated than in the proliferation of questers after the Shakespeare cipher. Their great model and predecessor, the most ingenious cryptographer of them all, is Malvolio, who opens Maria's forged letter to discover not only ciphers and codes but an anagram as well.

> Why, this is evident to any formal capacity, there is no obstruction in this. And the end—what should that alphabetical position portend? If I could make that resemble something in me! Softly! M. O. A. I.—...M.—Malvolio; M.—why, that begins my name.... M.—but then there is no consonancy in the sequel that suffers under probation. A should follow, but O does.... M. O. A. I. This simulation is not as the former; and yet, to crush this a little, it would bow to me, for every one of these letters is in my name.

Mrs. Windle, Dr. Owen, and Ignatius Donnelly are pale shadows of this strong precursor. But if his narcissistic reconstruction of the text is a warning, it is a warning that *every* Shakespearean interpreter should heed before beginning excavation in the river Wye.

NOTES

1. *The Riverside Shakespeare,* ed. G. Blakemore Evans (Boston: Houghton Mifflin, 1974), 1684. All citations from the play are to this edition.

2. James G. McManaway, *The Authorship of Shakespeare* (Washington, D.C.: Folger Shakespeare Library, 1962), 12.

3. Ibid., 12–13.

4. Ibid., 29.

5. Ibid., 19.

6. Charlton Ogburn, Jr., *The Mysterious William Shakespeare: The Myth and the Reality* (New York: Dodd, Mead, 1984), 145.

7. William F. Friedman and Elizabeth S. Friedman, *The Shakespearean Ciphers Examined* (Cambridge: Cambridge University Press, 1957), 7, 181.

8. Ibid., 1.

9. Ibid., 5.

10. Michel Foucault, *Language, Counter-Memory, Practice,* ed. and trans. Donald F. Bouchard (Ithaca: Cornell University Press 1977), 125.

11. Frank W. Wadsworth, *The Poacher from Stratford* (Berkeley & Los Angeles: University of California Press, 1958), 52. Wadsworth's book gives a good overview of the controversy.

12. Ibid., 45.

13. *Harvard Magazine,* January 1975.

14. Ibid., April 1975.

15. Ibid.

16. John H. Stotsenburg, *An Impartial Study of the Shakespeare Title* (Louisville, Ky., 1904), 174.

17. S. Schoenbaum, *Shakespeare's Lives* (Oxford: Clarendon Press, 1970), 612.

18. Georg Brandes, *William Shakespeare: A Critical Study* (New York: Macmillan, 1909), 87. Cited in Ogburn, *The Mysterious William Shakespeare,* 153.

19. Wadsworth, *The Poacher,* 89.

20. Mark Twain, "Is Shakespeare Dead?" in *What Is Man? and Other Essays* (New York: Harper & Brothers, 1917), 324.

21. Ralph Waldo Emerson to William Emerson, 29 May 1849, in *The Letters of Ralph Waldo Emerson,* ed. Ralph L. Rusk (New York: Columbia University Press, 1939), 4, 149.

22. Horace Traubel, *Walt Whitman in Camden* (Boston: Small, Maynard, 1906), 136.

23. Walt Whitman, "November Boughs," in *Complete Poetry and Prose of Walt Whitman, as Prepared by Him for the Death Bed Edition* (New York: Pelligrini & Cudahy, 1948), 2:404.

24. Sir Charles Spencer Chaplin, *My Autobiography* (New York: Simon & Schuster, 1964), 364. Ogburn, *The Mysterious William Shakespeare,* 260.

25. Ralph Waldo Emerson, *Representative Men: Seven Lectures,* in *Complete Works of Ralph Waldo Emerson* (Boston: Houghton Mifflin, 1876), 4.208.

26. Ibid., 212.

27. James to Hunt, 26 August 1903, in *The Letters of Henry James,* ed. Percy Lubbock (New York: Scribner, 1920), 1:424.

28. Henry James, "The Birthplace," in his *Selected Short Stories* (New York: Rinehart, 1955), 246–47.

29. Ibid., 238.

30. Ibid., 256.

31. Twain, "Is Shakespeare Dead?" 372.

32. Ralph Waldo Emerson, *The Journals and Miscellaneous Notebooks of Ralph Waldo Emerson,* ed. Ralph H. Orth and Alfred R. Ferguson (Cambridge, Mass.: Harvard University Press, Belknap Press, 1971), 9:184.

33. Dickens to Sandys, 13 June 1847, in *Complete Writings of Charles Dickens,* ed. "by his sister-in-law" (Boston: Charles E. Lauriat, 1923).

34. Samuel Taylor Coleridge, *Biographia Literaria* (1817), chap. 15.

35. John Keats to George and Thomas Keats, 21 December 1817, in *The Selected Letters of John Keats,* ed. Lionel Trilling (Garden City, N.Y.: Doubleday Anchor Books, 1956), 103.

36. John Keats to George and Georgiana Keats, 14 February–3 May 1819, ibid., 229.

37. John Dryden, "An Essay on Dramatic Poesy," in *The Works of John Dryden,* Notes and Life by Sir Walter Scott; revised by George Saintsbury (Edinburgh: William Patterson, 1882–83), 15:344.

38. Foucault, *Language, Counter-Memory, Practice,* 130.

39. "Shakespeare," in *The Poems of Matthew Arnold,* ed. Kenneth Allott (London: Longmans, Green & Co., 1965), 48–50.

40. Allott (48) cites Arnold's letter to Arthur Hugh Clough (undated, late December 1847): "I keep saying, Shakespeare, Shakespeare, you are as obscure as life is."

41. Foucault, *Language, Counter-Memory, Practice,* 116.

42. Ibid., 117.

43. Nichols Rowe, "Some Account of the Life, & c., of Mr. William Shakespeare," in *The Works of Mr. William Shakespeare in Six Volumes.* vi (London: Jacob Tonson, 1709), 1.vi.

44. William Oldys (c. 1743–61), quoted by E. K. Chambers, *William Shakespeare: A Study of Facts and Problems* (Oxford: Clarendon Press, 1930), 3:278.

45. Jacques Derrida, "Signature, Event, Context," in his *Margins of Philosophy,* trans. Alan Bass (Chicago: University of Chicago Press, 1982), 328.

46. T. S. Eliot, "Shakespeare and the Stoicism of Seneca," in his *Selected Essays* (New York: Harcourt, Brace & World, 1960), 67; M. C. Bradbrook, *Shakespeare and Elizabethan Poetry* (Harmondsworth: Penguin Books, 1964), 96; E. M. W. Tillyard, *Shakespeare's History Plays* (New York: Collier Books, 1962), 160. In a lecture on *Titus Andronicus* delivered at the Stratford, Ontario Shakespeare Festival some years ago, Richard Wheeler alluded to this peculiar tendency in *Titus* criticism.

Mary Nyquist

Gynesis, Genesis, Exegesis, and the Formation of Milton's Eve

I

A neologism coined by Alice Jardine, *gynesis* is used by her to suggest the ways in which various modernist projects—the putting in question of the self-identity of the *cogito,* the determinations of narrative and of representation—are associated with woman or with the space of the other as, figuratively, feminine. Jardine's recently published study, *Gynesis,* discusses modernism as a movement figuring forth the breakdown of Western culture's master discourses.[1] Yet Jardine asks, repeatedly, what modernism has to do with women as subjects and as writers; or what relation feminist discourses might have to those of modernism, predominantly male authored. Because the writings of James Joyce have been appropriated in such a wild welter of modernist ways by French female and male theorists alike, I would like to let a passage from *Ulysses* serve as an introduction to some of the issues and texts to be addressed here. In what is perhaps a deservedly neglected passage in the "Aeolus" episode of *Ulysses,* the irrepressible Lenehan remarks, "Our old ancient ancestors, as we read in the first chapter of Guinness', were partial to the running stream." The context, which develops an elaborate analogy between the lofty-minded Jewish and Irish mentalities as oppressed by the bloody-minded Roman and English, channels the Guinness' running stream into the sewers and water closets constructed by the Anglo-Roman "cloacal obsession."[2] The quip thereby becomes *Ulysses'* own kind of cloacal commentary on the second verse of the first chapter of Genesis: "And the earth was without form and void; and darkness was upon the face of the deep. And the Spirit of God moved upon the face of the waters."[3] The passage, in any case, does not merely rename the sacred book of origins; by disturbing the signifier *Genesis,* "Guinness's" opens the floodgates to irrelevant and irreverent associations that work to erode the notion of created, originary meaning. If "Guinness's" runs into the "running stream" and hence into the watery "deep" of Genesis, it does so in *Ulysses* by circling back to pick up the associations with the sea established in *its* first chapter. The sea, "Thalatta," "our mighty mother," "the snotgreen sea," becomes linked in Stephen's, and thus the reader's, mind with his own mother's dying waste vomited into a bowl, which, when a shadow moves over the face of the waters, makes the sea itself in Stephen's internal eye "a bowl of bitter waters."[4] As a kind of life-giving liquid, Guinness is, appropriately, a notoriously bitter drink. And perhaps for that reason, in the world of *Ulysses*, Guinness or porter is definitely a manly drink. Indeed, the ancient past that Lenehan here invokes would seem to be for men only, "our old ancient ancestors" being gendered by context if not by explicit authorial fiat.

Although the straight and narrow ways of biblical scholarship are not the ways of Jardine's "Gynesis" or of Joyce's "Guinness's," both ancient and modern commentaries on the opening chapters of Genesis are similarly preoccupied with questions of ancestry and of gender specification. Twentieth-century commentators regularly set the first three chapters of Genesis in the context of other Near Eastern creation and fall myths, the most important of which for the "P" or Priestly account of creation in Genesis 1.1 through 2.4a is *Enūma eliš*, the Sumero-Babylonian text that includes, although it does not feature, a story of creation. Designed to celebrate the god Marduk's primacy over rival gods, *Enūma eliš* has the form of a theogony that installs Marduk in the position of the maker of the ordered universe. Marduk assumes this role after defeating Tiamat, mother of all the gods and associated, at the epic's beginning, with the primeval salt waters. It is from her slaughtered body that Marduk fashions the universe; Tiamat—that is, the waters she represents—is divided in half to become first the sky and then the earth. Of the many points of similarity between this epic and the Priestly account of creation in Genesis, one of the more striking involves the way in which both connect the creation of the firmament with an act dividing the primeval watery chaos into terrestial and celestial waters (the Hebrew account in Genesis 1.6 has, "And God said, Let there be a firmament in the midst of the waters, and let it divide the waters from the waters").[5]

Biblical scholars disagree about the degree of relationship this Mesopotamian text has to the Priestly creation account. Conservative commentators are anxious to avoid any suggestion that *Enūma eliš* is a source on which Genesis, as a derivative or secondary text, actually depends. E. A. Speiser, on the other hand, permits Genesis an overtly allusive and systematically critical relationship with its Mesopotamian ancestor. Translating the opening verses of Genesis in an unorthodox but linguistically permissible manner, Speiser cites the syntactical structure of the opening lines of *Enūma eliš* as justification for opening Genesis with a dependent rather than an independent clause. The Anchor Bible thus has (instead of the conventional "In the beginning God created the heaven and the earth"), "When God set about to create heaven and earth," with the phrases regarding the formless waste, the abyss or deep, and the waters taking a parenthetical form and the main clause being, then, "God said, let there be light."[6] An important and obviously controversial consequence of this translation is that the chaotic or watery materials appear to coexist with the creator, a suggestion the entire Greco-Christian tradition would adamantly deny. Yet ultimately their possible coexistence in translation hardly matters at all, since modern editors and commentators including Speiser are completely agreed that any similarities *Enūma eliš* or any other Near Eastern creation myths might have to Genesis merely serve to underscore the Hebrew text's specificity, or rather the success with which it appears confidently to have established the absolute priority of its god over other gods, not worthy even of mention. This is especially true of the "abyss" or "deep," discussions of which strongly emphasize the total absence of conflict in the Hebrew creator-god's relationship to this chaotic space, associated, impersonally, with the "waters." Although the Hebrew Bible elsewhere alludes to an originary struggle, associated with creation, between Yahweh and a sea-monster (Psalm 74.12–17; Isaiah 27.1, 51.9; Job 26.13, 38.8–11), even the slightest trace of any *Chaoskampf* has disappeared from the Priestly account of creation. Although the Hebrew *tĕhōm*, commonly translated the "abyss" or "deep," is etymologically related to *Tiamat,* biblical scholars would have it that *tĕhōm* does not necessarily recall or evoke Marduk's mythological antagonist. If there is anything like an allusion here, it would seem simply to signify that the process of demythologization has, by the beginning of this text, always already occurred. Far from setting himself against a female antagonist, or even against a rebellious cosmic principle from whose ancestral body the universe is fashioned, the autonomous, ancestorless god of Genesis creates with his voice alone, his "Let there be" overshadowing the now neutered body of the deep.

In stressing the oppositional relationship of Genesis to Mesopotamian myth, even a conservative commentator such as Cassuto can inadvertently suggest, however, that the "deep" bears some faint, residual traces of its female character. Cassuto, who retains the orthodox translation of the opening verses, states of the "deep's" relation to the willful waters of ancient Eastern mythology: "The Torah, however, refrained from accepting any part of this tradition. In the Pentateuch, . . . *tĕhōm* denotes simply the primeval World-Ocean—a purely physical concept. It is matter and has no personality or autonomy; it had not existed from time immemorial but was created by the will of God, and was ready to receive whatever form its Maker would be pleased to fashion for it."[7] Here, in spite of his determination to expound the Hebrew text itself, Cassuto's language implicates itself in the Greek philosophical tradition, which has in one way or another informed commentaries on Genesis since Philo. Formless, dependent matter, which passively awaits and receives the form actively bestowed upon it by its maker, is, in this tradition, of course a feminine as opposed to a masculine principle. In Plato's *Timaeus,* one of the main texts used to assimilate Greek and Judeo-Christian traditions, the unformed chaos ordered by the Demiurge is unambiguously feminine. The "nurse" of material things in their changeability, Plato's *chōra* preexists the informing activity of the Demiurge.[8] Yet by concentrating on the masculine creator's form-giving activity, early Christian exegetes and apologists managed a reconciliation of compet-

ing systems, persuading themselves that Greek thought in its conception of a transcendent creator, master of matter, derived from Hebrew, its venerable ancestor.

Besides being written, in spite of itself, from this overdetermined
synthesis, the passage I have just cited from Cassuto's commentary reveals the logocentric and recuperative pressures that the discourse of
biblical exegesis seems relentlessly to exert on its practitioners. Yet
the demythologizing character of the Priestly creation account—a
character brought out by the comparative and critical methods used
by twentieth-century scholars—would seem almost designed to invite
such discourse. It is now generally agreed that the "P" creation
account is the product of a lengthy process of exegetical activity, a
process that produced from ancient mythical materials a text that
would seem to be doctrinally self-conscious. In its hieratic austerity
and formulaic self-consistency, the "P" account seems to have the kind
of textual self-identity that befits its own conception of a sovereign,
transcendent father-god. Recent feminist texts often suggest that the
"J" or "Yahwist" creation story in the second chapter of Genesis provides our culture's most influential paradigm for woman's relation to
discourse, for it is in that more lively, narrative account that Adam
names the creatures his divine father brings to him for that purpose
before Eve is even created.[9] But a postmodernist feminist analysis
might perhaps find in the "P" account an even more significant paradigm. For it is there that we find—or do not find—the absent or repressed maternal body, which has been unveiled by modern critical
methods but still assigned a place apart from the sacred text itself. And
the absence of this "old ancient ancestor" would seem to be the condition for a discourse associating the potency of the divine father's
word with a historically and theologically motivated mastery of
meaning, a mastery that seems easily to translate itself into more
speculatively logocentric discursive statements.

It is over and against some such view of dominant Western discourses as inherently phallogocentric that much postmodernist feminist counterdiscourse produces itself. In a text relevant to our discussion here, the Québecoise feminist writer Nicole Brossard seeks to

undo the work of the dominant patriarchal discourses by interrogating and talking with the mother. Subtitled *Le Chapitre Effrité* ("The Disintegrating Chapter"), Brossard's modernist text is titled, punningly, *L'Amèr* (joining the familier pun on *mère,* as in "mother," and *mer* as in "sea," with *amer,* "bitter," as well as with "l'amour").[10] In its course, the text seeks to take up arms against/be born from the engulfing and bitter waters of the patriarchal mother and to write the body of the mother-daughter-lover in embrace. (This text's mother, by the way, is busy writing and drinks beer.) Although it might be tempting to suggest that Brossard's self-consciously disunified text is set against the "P" creation account, her work only infrequently echoes the Genesis text. A number of recent feminist writers have, however, directly engaged Genesis or the Genesis traditions in order actively to rewrite or reproduce them: Judith Plaskow in her rewriting of the Lilith legend; Pamela White Hadas with *In Light of Genesis;* Ursula Le Guin in her recent *New Yorker* piece, a tale of Eve's liberatory undoing of Adam's discursive work; Monique Wittig's rewriting of the temptation story in *Les Guérillères;* and the Québecoise Louky Bersianik's fantastical rewriting of Genesis, a rewriting that playfully posits suppressed gynocentric accounts of the creation story.[11]

II

That these all present themselves as countertexts rather than commentaries is obviously significant. As a genre, the editorial or exegetical commentary on a biblical book or books is (among other things) strongly gendered. And commentaries on Genesis, whether on the opening chapters alone or on the entire book, are, as it were, legion, numbering hundreds if not thousands of texts. Elizabeth Cady Stanton's *Woman's Bible* represents what, so far as I know, is the first woman-authored contribution to this ancient and important genre.[12] In this pioneering and extremely controversial feminist Bible, selected passages from Old and New Testaments appear together with commentaries undisguisedly critical of misogynistic assumptions and biases, as well as of the sexist practices certain passages are used to defend.

Another, more recent, contribution—complexly related to that of Stanton, as I hope to show—is Phyllis Trible's rereading of the "J" or "Yahwist" creation and Fall stories in chapters 2 and 3 of Genesis. In "Depatriarchalizing in Biblical Interpretation," Trible specifically claims that she is rereading, not rewriting, the biblical text, which she regards as sacred and whose original meaning she seeks to explicate.[13] Her aims are thus generally those of her exegetical ancestors, even though her methods are those of an "immanent" (or in terms of literary-critical traditions, "New") criticism. Yet Trible's central argument is that it is the exegetical tradition itself that is responsible for the sexist meanings attributed to the first three chapters of Genesis; Genesis is innocent of these meanings, as the operation of "depatriarchalization" within Scripture itself shows, when it is permitted to by means of her exegesis. More specifically, Trible argues that the second chapter of Genesis tells the story not of the creation of a patriarchal Adam, from whom a secondary Eve is derived, but the story of the creation of generic and androgynous "man" (the Hebrew *hā'ādām* is ostensibly a generic term), to whom the sexually distinct woman and man are related as full equals. Although Trible notes that her reading coincides with an ancient rabbinical view, she insists that it "stands as documented from the text" (DBI 37–38n). In Trible's reading the man and woman are created simultaneously and as equals. Their simultaneous emergence is signaled, she argues, when Yahweh brings the newly fashioned partner to the previously undifferentiated *hā'ādām* or "man," who responds with the lyrically erotic utterance, "This is now bone of my bones and flesh of my flesh: she shall be called Woman, because she was taken out of Man" (Genesis 2.23).

As commentators regularly point out, the Hebrew plays verbally here with *îš* and *iššâ* ("man" and "woman"). With regard to this speech, which is of crucial importance to her argument, Trible makes three interrelated points. She states that *îš* is the first unambiguously gender-specific reference to a creature of masculine gender. Second, she asserts that "taken out of" or "from" this gender-specific "man" is to be understood in the sense of "differentiated from."[14] Third, she argues that this speech does not represent an act of ritual naming, giving the man supremacy over woman. *Woman* is here not a proper name but a common noun (DBI 38). It is only later, in the scene of divine judgment upon the fallen woman and man, that the man "called his wife's name Eve" (Genesis 3.20). Since *îš* and *iššâ* are thus originally differentiated from one another as equals, it follows for Trible that this later act of naming "faults the man for corrupting a relationship of mutuality and equality" and that the penalty for disobedience assigned Eve in Genesis 3.16, which includes the pronouncement that "thy desire shall be to thy husband, and he shall rule over thee," merely calls attention to the way the man and woman's mutual violation of the prohibition unnaturally disrupts the created, egalitarian order (DBI 41).

Since this particular judicially formulated text certainly has been used, historically, to authorize male supremacy, Trible's remark indicates that she is articulating ultimately a kind of neo-Protestantism, which believes it can rescue the text from the error-ridden interpretative accretions that are "alien" (her term) to it (DBI 40). My skepticism, here, does not extend to the claim that Genesis has been given influential misogynistic interpretations; or that iconographic, didactic, and literary traditions have used the creation and fall stories in Genesis in ways that perpetuate androcentric and phallocratic views. Genesis 3.6, "She took of the fruit thereof, and did eat, and gave also unto her husband with her: and he did eat," for example, would hardly seem to lead just in and of itself to the countless and widely influential representations of Eve as alluring temptress. Nor would 3.7, "And the eyes of them both were opened, and they knew that they were naked," give rise all on its own to Augustine's decidedly phallocentric view that their eyes were opened to the novel disobedience or movement of their bodily members—a view that is given a deeply ironic rerun in Beckett's *Krapp's Last Tape,* where the protagonist ends up quite literally replaying the moment of his antirecognition scene, the moment of his "Farewell to Love," when, bending over his lover, he finally gets her to open her eyes. "Let me in" he then says, their eyes thus both opened, the punt they lie in meanwhile drifting in among the reeds, which go down, sighing, so that the couple lie there "without moving," the waters meanwhile moving them "gently, up and down, and from side to side."[15]

In Trible's view, however, just as Yahweh, in spite of his traditionally masculine character, transcends gender specification, so does Genesis as a text transcend the various interpretations that have, historically, been given it. Yet Trible's argument is in several ways implicated in the very exegetical tradition she wishes to challenge. There is first the neat and fixed distinction between a created and a fallen order, a staple feature of Christian apologetics. Related is Trible's exploitation of the generic and gender-specific senses of *man,* a sign that, as we shall see, has operated throughout the history of commentaries on Genesis in an exceptionally slippery and motivated manner. Trible claims that *hā'ādām* or "man" is textually ambiguous (DBI 35). In a revised and expanded version of her essay, in which she removes some of the inconsistencies in her own linguistic practice, Trible carefully controls these supposed ambiguities, stating that the self-identical signifier, *hā'ādām,* passes through three semantic phases, referring first to a sexually undifferentiated earth creature (commentators regularly point out that the word *hā'ādām* is punningly related to the word for ground or earth *hā'ādāmâ*); then, after the simultaneous creation of sexually differentiated creatures, to the creature of male sex; and then, after the Fall, to an oppressive or false generic "man" who subsumes woman.[16]

I would like to argue that Trible's strategic exploitation of this malleable man results from the third feature of her discussion that assimilates it to the tradition she opposes, that is, her attempted reconciliation of the two historically distinct accounts of creation in Genesis, the "P" account in chapter 1, and the "J" in chapter 2. The desire to relate or unify these two accounts—that is, to master the differences between them—is a constant of the exegetical tradition; and just as constantly it is motivated by an interest in the representation of sexual difference.

For centuries the two accounts were of course assumed to be

authored, at least indirectly, by Moses. Since the late nineteenth century, however, the documentary view has had virtual hegemony, which has meant that "P" and "J" are regarded as separate texts, compiled in different historical periods.[17] "J," which occupies second place, is now regarded as the older of the two. It is also thought to be more primitive in the sense that it is much more comfortable than "P" with its use of mythic materials. Indeed, "J's" creator, who makes man from the dust of the ground and woman from a rib, would seem to be in the relation of Lévi-Strauss's *bricoleur* to "P's" scientist. Writing on "J" alone, but with a view to reconciling "J" with "P," Trible hopes to reconcile feminist and theological interests. This project, difficult and challenging enough, is made even more so by "J's" well-established character as a text that is more openly masculinist. Since Theodore Reik's study, it has been possible to point to the resemblances between Hesiod's account in his *Theogony* of Athena's birth from Zeus's head and "J's" narrative of Eve's birth from Adam's side.[18] Although the aggressively conflictual and power-oriented character of Zeus's symbolic appropriation of female reproductive activity as represented in the *Theogony* is absent from the Genesis story, it is nevertheless possible to read "J's" narrative as participating, like the *Theogony,* in a systematic transvaluation of symbols associated with the earth mother or goddess.

In any event, it is without question "J's" creation story, not "P's," that has proved so useful in the oppression of women. As Elizabeth Cady Stanton has summed it up: "The canon and civil law; church and state; priests and legislators; all political parties and religious denominations have alike taught that woman was made after man, of man, and for man, an inferior being, subject to man. Creeds, codes, Scriptures and statutes, are all based on this idea. The fashions, forms, ceremonies and customs of society, church ordinances and discipline all grow out of this idea" (*WB* 7). There is no question but that the purpose of Trible's rereading of "J's" creation story is also to challenge not merely this idea, but also the social practices it has been used to justify. Stanton's challenge, however, is based on a complete rejection of "J's" story of the creation of the sexes, which she contrasts with the Priestly account found in verses 26–28 of the first chapter of Genesis, where the possible equivalence of the sexes is suggested by verse 27's ceremonial, "So God created man [*hā'ādām*] in his own image, in the image of God created he him; male and female created he them." Stanton opens her commentary on Genesis with an enthusiastic endorsement of the egalitarian sentiments she finds in these verses, stating, "Here is the sacred historian's first account of the advent of woman; a simultaneous creation of both sexes, in the image of God" (*WB* 14). And she concludes, roundly, that "all those theories based on the assumption that man was prior to the creation, have no foundation in Scripture" (*WB* 15). In a neo-Protestantism that in spite of differences is in some ways the foremother of Trible's, *The Woman's Bible* regards "J's" account as basically unauthentic, the product of some "wily writer" who could not tolerate the egalitarian message of the first chapter (*WB* 21). Far from trying to reconcile the two accounts, Stanton and her coeditors use the documentary hypothesis to defrock the offending "J." As *Woman's Bible* commentator Ellen Battelle Dietrick puts it, in a prudently undogmatic spirit: "Now as it is manifest that both of these stories cannot be true; intelligent women, who feel bound to give the preference to either, may decide according to their own judgement of which is more worthy of an intelligent woman's acceptance. Paul's rule is a good one in this dilemma: 'Prove all things: hold fast to that which is good'" (*WB* 18).

Trible cites Stanton's remark that, in "J's" account, Eve's creation is "a mere afterthought" but does so in refuting the view that the Yahwist's account makes woman "a second, subordinate, inferior sex" (DBI 35). Trible does not ever state that she is committed to reconciling the two texts. Yet I would argue that her entire thesis is motivated by the desire to neutralize the discrepancy between the "P" and "J" accounts by assimilating "J" to "P," which is assumed to recognize the equality of the sexes and therefore to provide the meaning of the two creation accounts taken together as one.[19] Because "P" suggests the possibility of a symmetrical, nonhierarchical relationship between male and female, "J" is said to tell the story of the creation of a sexually undifferentiated creature who becomes "sexed" only with the creation of woman.

As this discussion indicates, whether choosing intelligently between "P" or "J" or mastering the discrepancies between them, commentators seem necessarily involved in an implicit or explicit privileging of one text over the other. I would like to go on to suggest, further, that this privileging frequently relies on one of the most basic and well-articulated principles of phallogocentric thought: that to come first in order of succession is to be first and therefore best. Whether in philosophical, theological, or legal contexts—that is, in the cases, respectively, of first principles, first causes, or firstborn sons—priority in the order of temporal succession is often associated with some kind of privilege. Or to put this more circumspectly, when it comes to paired or coupled items, that which is temporally later is also, frequently, regarded as being secondary in the sense of derivative or inferior. This principle might possibly be at work, very unobtrusively, when, in telling of the fourth day's work of creation in verse 16, "P" mentions the "greater" before the "lesser" light; if so, the example is not without significance, since the couple *sun/moon* plays such a well-recognized role in our culture's gender-coded symbolism. The principle is in any case conspicuously and productively at work in 1 Timothy 2.11–14, the text that forbids women positions of authority within the church. "Let the woman learn in silence with all subjection. But I suffer not a woman to teach, nor to usurp authority over the man, but to be in silence. For Adam was first formed, then Eve. And Adam was not deceived, but the woman being deceived was in the transgression." Note that the principle that chronological priority brings with it ontological or socioeconomic privilege does not permit the temptation narrative in the third chapter of Genesis to be summed up with the perfectly accurate "For Eve was first to transgress, then Adam"; to preserve man's superiority, 1 Timothy gets rid of the language of temporal order, using, in its place, a simple contrast between being and not being deceived.

When it comes to articulating a relationship between "P" and "J," commentators have frequently appealed, indirectly, to this same principle. As we have seen, Stanton rejects the scriptural authority of "J's" secondary and inferior account of a secondary and inferior woman but refers to verses 26–28 of the Priestly version as the "sacred historian's first account." Although formulated from within a more consistently historical-critical perspective, Robert Alter's view of "J's" relation to "P" is implicitly developed along similar lines. Alter suggests that the redactor of Genesis gave pride of place to "P's" account of the creation of man and woman as equals because he believed it to represent the ideal state of affairs the deity brought into being. Since he also, however, recognized the fact of sexual inequality in the world in which he lived, "J's" more sexist account was appended, the resulting "tension of views" being the purpose of the redaction.[20] Another prominent contemporary biblical scholar, Brevard Childs, defends the unity of the two accounts in a different but related manner, appealing once again to a principle that is implicitly hierarchical. Though not especially interested in the representation of sexual difference, Childs argues against the view that the two accounts have simply been "juxtaposed" as "parallel creation stories," proposing instead that, as a result of canonical shaping, "J's" account of the creation is subordinated to "P's," which is prior, an ordering he illustrates by stating, "What now follows proceeds from the creation in the analogy of a son to his father."[21]

One could object, here, that there are other ways of regarding items temporally ordered. And indeed, the order of creation in "P's" creation account has often been thought to suggest the possibility of an alternative valorization. For commentators have with remarkable unanimity understood the creation of "man" last, on the sixth day, to signify that "man" there appears as the end or *telos* of creation. In other instances, when this alternative valorization is referred to items paired or coupled (rather than to a succession of things as in "P"), it reveals what Derrida has called the logic of supplementarity at work, since the temporally later term then becomes the superior, being both more perfect than and necessary to its predecessor. Within a Christian framework, the manifold dynamics of this logic are most clearly at work in hermeneutical reflections on the relations of the New to the Old Testament. But as I will later on be able to demonstrate, when discussing another influential reading, namely John Milton's, this logic has also played a part in the history of exegetical attempts to unify the two different accounts of creation in Genesis.

Intended to counter the view that Eve is a derivative creature because created second, Trible's "Depatriarchalizing" at one point appears to enlist the alternative, teleological principle in this cause. "But the last may be first, as both the biblical theologian and the literary critic know. Thus the Yahwist account moves to its climax, not its decline, in the creation of woman. She is not an afterthought; she is the culmination. Genesis 1 itself supports this interpretation, for there male and female are indeed the last and truly the crown of all creatures" (DBI 35–36). If woman were likewise the crown of man's creation, being then a necessary supplement, she would in a sense be his superior, as in Genesis 1 "man" is said to have "dominion" over the rest of creation. But Trible cannot pursue this line of reasoning, whose claims would exceed by an embarrassing degree those she is interested in making. Instead she interprets the New Testament dictum, "The last shall be first, and the first last" to illustrate yet another principle, that of nonhierarchical equivalence, which in her view the Yahwist conveys by the literary device of *inclusio* or of "ring composition." This, at any rate, would seem to be the meaning of the statement immediately following the passage just cited. "In Hebrew literature the central concerns of a unit often appear at the beginning and the end as an *inclusio* device. Genesis 2 evinces this structure. The creation of man first and of woman last constitutes a ring composition whereby the two creatures are parallel. In no way does the order disparage woman" (DBI 36).

In this passage "man" is obviously being used in a gender-specific sense, and the formal parallelism between the creation of "man" in Genesis 2.7 and "woman" in 2.22 is being given the meaning of ordained equality. Taken on its own, it would suggest that Trible is employing a formalist argument to empty of hierarchical value the temporal ordering of the creation of the two sexes. But as I have indicated, Trible's central thesis is that the two sexes were created simultaneously, not successively. The order does not disparage woman because Trible gets the Yahwist to tell the story not of woman's creation after man, but instead of a sexually undifferentiated creature's becoming, simultaneously, both male and female. In a more representative statement of her thesis, Trible sums this narrative up with, "Hence the first act in Genesis 2 is the creation of androgyny (2.7) and the last is the creation of sexuality (2.23)" (DBI 37). The contradiction between these two passages is of considerable significance and deserves some attention. As I earlier suggested, Trible's thesis neutralizes the differences between "P" and "J" by getting "J" to tell in narrative form "P's" supposed account of the simultaneous creation of male and female as equals. In the latter of the two passages I have quoted, "androgyny" is made to perform a similar neutralization with regard to sexual difference. Implicitly, then, both "P" and "androgyny" are being privileged. That in terms of Trible's narrative order, the androgynous or gender-free earth creature appears first therefore cannot be regarded as a neutral fact, balancing the later emergence of two creatures who happen to be sexually differentiated. For the firstness or, in her terms, "primacy" of androgyny is what in Trible's argument alone determines that the later act of sexual differentiation signifies—as if in and of itself—an original equality of the sexes.

Trible's discussion can remain blind to its own inconsistencies, and to its complicity with the tradition it seeks to challenge, precisely because it so consistently attempts the neutralization of hierarchical oppositions. What her depatriarchalizing reading of the Yahwist's account seeks and finds is the absence of sexual difference, the forgetting of subordination and domination. We are asked to believe in the existence of an undifferentiated earth creature to whom Yahweh brings a creature the text unequivocally refers to as "woman (*'iššâ*)" (Genesis 2.22). Trible rejects her earlier use of the view that "man" was originally androgynous on the ground that the term *androgyny* assumes sexual difference.[22] Yet it is still difficult to know why, particularly in a text produced by a patriarchal culture, a truly ungendered earth creature would avow a gender upon discovering his female partner if such an *hā'ādām* had not already acted his gendered part in the story. By privileging the absence of sexual difference over difference, Trible's discussion accepts the phallogocentric view that sexuality, associated with woman (as the contradiction noted above indicates) is secondary to an ideal state prior to gender; that sexual difference itself is difference from a self-identical norm, a norm that, historically, has always been implicitly masculine. Androgyny, whether named or not, would therefore seem to function in Trible's discussion as it often, if not always, does (and as the order of its constituent parts, with *andro* preceding *gyn,* would indicate), that is, in a covertly masculinist manner.

III

I have dwelt at such length on Trible's revisionary rereading in part because it has been so widely influential. Among feminist theologians it would seem to have established a new orthodoxy. It has also been circulated more popularly in the highly successful book *Words and Women,* which expounds Trible's reading more fully than I have done here, stating, "when the language of the story is examined outside the traditional confines of patriarchal interpretation, the evidence of full equality is inescapable."[23] In what one might think would be an even more secular context, it has more recently been given credence in an issue of *Poetics Today* devoted to "The Female Body in Western Culture: Semiotic Perspectives." There, in an essay by semiotician Mieke Bal, Trible's reading is taken to be the accepted meaning of the ancient text, which Bal further defends from its sexist detractors.[24]

The story Bal tells is essentially the same as Trible's, though it is also more completely and self-consistently elaborated. She, too, begins with a sexually undifferentiated earth creature, *hā'ādām.* And she renarrates Genesis 2.21 and 22 in accordance with Trible's thesis that gender specification occurs when *'iššâ* is differentiated from *'îš.* "A deep sleep makes the earth creature unconscious. It almost returns it into *hā'ādāmâ.* This sleep is the death of the undifferentiated earth creature. It will emerge from it differentiated" (SSS 26). Like Trible, Bal plays, briefly, with the notion of female superiority. Referring to the order of creation in the "Priestly" account, where humanity is the "climax" of the creation, she suggests that in the Yahwist's account "woman" is a more sophisticated and perfect creation than the earlier undifferentiated *hā'ādām* (SSS 27). Bal follows Trible's practice by interpolating her reading into the passage she cites, in this instance into Genesis 2.22. "And Jahweh God built the rib which he took from/ [undifferentiated] *hā'ādām* into woman [*iššâ*]." Commenting on this passage, she states: "Of the two words, *îš* and *iššâ*, which in this text indicate sexually differentiated beings, *iššâ*, woman, appears first. It is *iššâ* who changes the meaning of *hā'ādām* from earth being into earth man. In this semiotic sense, the woman was formed first, then the man (contra 'Paul')" (SSS 27).

But Bal shares with Trible a desire to resist this line of thought and to emphasize instead whatever will be suggestive of symmetry, balance, mutuality, equality. She therefore goes on to point out that it is the man (now dubbed "*hā'ādām* the Second") who first speaks and who, in speaking of *îš* and *iššâ*, bestows upon woman her sexual identity while assuming his own. Traces of the formal balance Trible associated with ring composition can be found in Bal's concluding remarks on the Yahwist's narrative of sexual differentiation as process. "If the woman is differentiated first, the man is the first to recognize sexual difference. I contend that this distribution of semiotic roles implies a dialectic equivalence of sign and subject which mutually constitute each other. Man and woman, then, were created at the same time" (SSS 30).

In this passage, Bal uses the principle of balanced, nonhierarchical equivalence as if it were logically equivalent to simultaneity. As I indicated earlier, the belief that the Yahwist's story has man and woman created together, at the same time, is complexly dependent both on the notion of an originary androgyny and on the view that the Priestly account affirms the simultaneous creation of the two sexes. Bal agrees with Trible that the terms *androgynous* or *bisexual* do not properly apply to the undifferentiated earth creature. But she finds "androgyny" being "explicitly attributed to the being named *hāʾādām*" in Genesis 5.1-2, a text I will cite here since we will be returning to it in a moment. "This is the book of the generations of Adam. In the day that God created man, in the likeness of God made he him; Male and female created he them; and blessed them, and called their name Adam, in the day when they were created." This text is part of the Priestly work, which in Genesis 1.26-27 also, for Bal, implies a conception of androgyny (SSS 25). In Bal's argument the determination to unify the two creation accounts takes an ingenious form, no doubt the by-product of her complete confidence that the reading Trible has installed is actually yielded by the text "as it stands" (SSS 30). Far from contradicting what she calls the Priestly "'equal rights' version," the Yahwist's story in Bal's view "provides a specified narration of what events are included in the idea that 'God created them male and female'" (SSS 30). That they cohere in this way is not, however, an accident, for Bal argues that the Yahwist's historically earlier account was given an accurate reading by the authors of "P," who merely "completed retrospectively" "J's" narrative of an earth creature who became, at one and the same time, male and female (SSS 30 n. 9).

It should by now be clear that the reading posited by Trible and Bal is profoundly ahistorical, fully justifying the sentimental and logocentric conclusion expressed in *Words and Women* that the biblical recorder of "that early human effort to understand the nature and meaning of existence speaks across the millenniums of patriarchy."[25] It assumes that the exegete has, by an effort of will, positioned herself outside the confines of patriarchal interpretation; and that the text bears no significant traces of the society that produced it. As a corrective to the latter view, I would now like briefly to discuss an important essay that situates its exegesis of Genesis 1.27b, "male and female created he them," in a historicized understanding of the Priestly creation account and of the larger Priestly work.[26]

Phyllis Bird's construction of this statement's textual and historical contexts is so painstakingly developed that it is difficult to summarize concisely. But put very simply, Bird's thesis is that the words of sexual distinction in verse 27, "male and female created he them," do not refer back to the preceding clause, "in the image of God created he him," as if to explain its meaning, but instead prepare the way for the words of blessing that follow in verse 28. Bird argues that the parallelism of the two statements, far from suggesting a relation of equivalence, aims at drawing a distinction between the sense in which *hā'ādām* resembles God from the sense in which, as creature, and therefore unlike God, *hā'ādām* is characterized by sexual distinction.

To substantiate this reading, Bird, like other commentators, distinguishes the words of announcement (the *Wortbericht*) in verse 26 from the execution report (the *Tatbericht*) in verse 27. Situating the *Wortbericht*'s crucial phrase, "in the image of God" (*selem 'ĕlōhîm*), in the context of the royal ideology of the ancient Near East, Bird then goes on to suggest that verse 28, which opens with the blessing of fertility, may have a polemical intention. By emphatically and repeatedly drawing attention to the way the deity bestows the means and power of reproduction upon every species, the Priestly account subverts the raison d'être of any fertility cult, making redundant all other gods but this one. But for the sake of the very omnipotence thereby asserted, the theme of fertility has to be kept distinct from the theme of dominion, associated with creation in the divine image. The blessing of fertility, which presupposes a creature characterized by sexual differentiation, must therefore be introduced as a separate theme with precisely this presupposition. It is this introductory purpose that is served by the statement concluding the *Tatbericht* in verse 27, "male and female created he them."

On the basis of this analysis, Bird argues that the word of sexual distinction in verse 27 is of radically more limited significance than is commonly held. It does not pertain directly to the image, to *hā'ādām*'s relation to the deity, or to the subject of dominion. Nor, more importantly, is it of relevance to the social constitution of the sexes in relation to each other. The word refers solely to the biological pair, male and female. Bird points out that *zākār* and *nĕqēbâ* (male and female) are biological terms, unlike the Yahwist's *îš* and *iššâ* in Genesis

2.22–24, though the practice of harmonizing the two accounts has operated to obscure this difference, even at the level of translation (MF 146–50).

Bird does not only argue, very persuasively, for the sharply delimited significance of "male and female created he them." She also says firmly of the generic *hā'ādām* in both "P" and "J" that "the representative and determining image of the species was certainly male" (MF 151). In my discussion of Bal, I quoted the first two verses of the fifth chapter of Genesis, where certain features of "P's" creation account are recapitulated; in the third, transitional, verse, not mentioned by Bal, *hā'ādām* for the first time becomes the proper name, Adam. "And Adam lived an hundred and thirty years, and begat a son in his own likeness, after his image; and called his name Seth." Eve is conspicuously absent here, though she receives her proper name in the third chapter of Genesis. As Bird points out, the *hā'ādām* who becomes Adam is continued not in Noah and his wife but in Noah and his sons (MF 151 n. 55). Although in her article Bird expresses concerns that are distinctly theological, she does not hesitate to draw out clearly the implications of her argument. One obvious consequence is the vanishing into thin air of that worthy ancient ancestor, "P" the early "equal-rights theologian" (MF 156). Another is the coming into focus of the continuity of Genesis 1 with the rest of the Priestly work, "in which," as she puts it, "the genealogies that form the essential link between creation and the establishment of the cult know only male names (unlike the older "family" stories incorporated into this lineal framework); in which the cult which represents the culminating word or work of God has no place for women in its service; and in which circumcision is the essential sign of identity for members of the covenant people" (MF 156).

If one accepts Bird's thesis, the voice of the proandrogyny Yahwist speaking across the millennia of patriarchy becomes exceedingly faint, reduced, perhaps, to a muffled clearing of the throat. Yet it must be emphasized that Bird situates her analysis in a historically specific form of patriarchy. If one ignores this, it becomes far too easy to adopt the opposing or rather complementary view of Genesis as a text that inaugurates a transhistorically homogeneous patriarchal culture, continuous across the millennia. In the field of literary studies this particular assumption is often encountered, but it is most frequently and compellingly expressed in discussions of Milton's *Paradise Lost.* Several factors work to keep it alive. It is probably safe to say, first, that the Genesis creation and fall texts continue to circulate within this field of study largely by virtue of, as well as in relation to, *Paradise Lost.* Second, in spite of the existence of scholarly studies of the history of Genesis in its exegetical traditions, the view that the relationship of *Paradise Lost* to Genesis is basically direct or at least unproblematically mediated continues to flourish. And so, as a result, does an entire network of misogynistic or idealizing commonplaces and free-floating sexual stereotypes, relating, indifferently, to Genesis and to this institutionally privileged text by Milton, English literature's paradigmatic patriarch.

The notion of a timeless and ideologically uninflected "patriarchy" is of course vulnerable on many counts, not least of which is its capacity to neutralize the experience of oppression. I would therefore like to intervene in the field of Milton studies by attempting to situate historically Milton's own appropriation of the Genesis creation accounts. It is certainly not difficult to recognize Trible's reading as a product of its time. For the last decade and a half, the notion of an originary androgyny has had tremendous appeal, especially to mainstream or liberal feminism. Taken to represent an ideal yet attainable equality of the sexes, androgyny is often implicitly associated metaphorically with an ideal and egalitarian form of the marriage relation. A passionate interest in this very social relation, or rather, institution, makes itself felt throughout Milton's divorce tracts, in which his interpretation of the two creation accounts first appears. Milton's exegesis is, not surprisingly, representative of the kind of masculinist "mis"-reading that Trible seeks to overturn. Yet by emphasizing its historical specificity, I hope to show that it is so for reasons that cannot be universalized. I also want to suggest that, in spite of crucial differences, Milton's interpretation has interesting affiliations with those we have just discussed, including Bird's. Although both Trible and Bal would find Milton's views alien to the text as it stands, Milton is himself determined to rescue Genesis from the "mis"-interpretations that have been imposed on it. In doing so, his exegesis, like theirs, becomes the product of an ideologically overdetermined desire to unify the two different creation accounts in Genesis.

IV

Milton's own appropriation of these two texts, first in the divorce tracts and then in *Paradise Lost,* can best be appreciated by comparing earlier methods of reconciling the texts with those used by some of his Protestant contemporaries. Philo and many of the fourth-century Greek Church Fathers tended to use a Platonic schema in relating the two texts. According to Philo, for example, the first or "P" version reports the making of "an idea, or type or seal, an object of thought (only), incorporeal, neither male nor female, by nature incorruptible," while the second version tells of the creation of the corporeal body of man, and then of the creation of woman, whose presence puts an end to man's oneness and thereby associates itself with evil.[27] Using a modified Platonic schema less misogynistic than Philo's, Augustine regards the two accounts as a narrative telling the story of the graduated or two-staged generation of humankind. In Augustine's view, Genesis 1.27 ("So God created man in his own image") records the creation of the *rationes seminales* of the first parents, the simultaneous creation of "male and female" as *homo,* that is, as creatures of reason, in the image of god; Genesis 2.7–24, on the other hand, records the physical and temporal creation of Adam and Eve as distinct persons and as different sexes, hierarchically ordered.[28] It is not difficult to see that, given the Platonic bias of Augustine's interpretive framework, the first account, concerning the spiritual, comes first because it involves what is best.

By contrast, the Reformed method of reconciling these two texts is radically uni-leveled or this-worldly. For leading commentators such as Calvin and Pareus, the two accounts do not correspond to two stages in the creation of humankind, the intelligible and the sensible. Indeed, there are not in their view two accounts in this sense at all, but instead one story told in two different ways: once, in the first chapter of Genesis, in epitome, and then, in the second chapter, in a more elaborated or enlarged form. Simplifying matters considerably, and using terms introduced into the analysis of narrative by Gérard Genette, one could say that in the view articulated especially cogently by Calvin and then elaborated, aggressively, by Milton, the *story* consists of the creation in the image of God of a single being supposed to be representative of humankind, Adam, and then the creation of Eve; the *narrative discourse* distributes this story by presenting it first in a kind of abstract and then in a more detailed or amplified narrative fashion. More specifically, the first two statements of Genesis 1.27, "So God created man in his own image, in the image of God created he him," are thought to refer to the creation of the representative Adam, told in a more leisurely and graphic fashion as a creation involving the use of the dust of the ground in the second chapter; while the concluding "male and female created he them'" is taken to refer to the creation from this Adam of his meet help, Eve.

The model implicitly at work for the Reformers would seem to be provided by Renaissance rhetoric; the relation posited between the two texts is ostensibly one of equivalence, with the Yahwist's *amplificatio* merely stating in other words the meaning of the Priestly *propositio*. The language that commentators use to characterize the relation is accordingly neutral and seemingly objective. Echoing similar statements by Paraeus, Milton, for example, writes of the second chapter's narrative of Eve's creation for Adam: "This second chapter is granted to be a commentary on the first, and these verses granted to be an exposition of that former verse, 'Male and female created he them.'"[29] A closer and more critical examination, however, reveals attitudes not quite so disinterested, not quite, as it were, so hermeneutically sealed. For it appears that the second chapter has the status of a commentary in part because of the gaps, ambiguities, or troublesome suggestions to be found in the first. Commenting on the blessing of fertility in Genesis 1.28, for example, Calvin says that it is given to the human couple after they have been joined in "wed-locke," although this event is not narrated until the following chapter.

> Therefore let us note, to whom God speaketh when he commaundeth them to growe, and to whome he appointeth his blessing. He hath not given libertie to men and women, that they may fall into wandering lusts without exception and shame: but beginning at holie and chaste wedlocke, he commeth to generation. For this also is worthie to be noted, that Moses briefly toucheth here those things which afterward he handleth more largely: and that he so disdordereth the historie, that neverthelesse it may appear what was done first or last.[30]

The interpretation Calvin's exegesis wants to preempt is one that understands the "male and female" in the verse immediately preceding the blessing in a merely sexual sense, without reference to the institution of marriage. Assuming as axiomatic that the second chapter of Genesis sets forth the instituting of marriage, Calvin can also assume that, in spite of appearances, the words of blessing in chapter one come after, and therefore have meaning only with reference to, the divine instituting of marriage related in chapter two. As this example suggests, for Protestant commentators who adopt this basic schema, insofar as the rhetorically amplified second version is capable of interpreting and completing the account that comes before it, it is the last creation account that tends to take precedence over the first.

If the Protestant exegetes Milton cites in his divorce tracts find the meaning of "male and female created he them" in the narrative of the creation of a help meet for Adam, it is of course also because that narrative is read ideologically, as proving that marriage, far from being what in their view the Roman Church would have it, a remedy prescribed for the spiritually weak, is divinely instituted, indeed recommended. That woman was created solely or even primarily for the purposes of procreation is the low-minded or "crabbed" (Milton's adjective) opinion that the Protestant doctrine of marriage sees itself called to overturn.[31] Emphasizing, eloquently, the psychological or personal needs sanctioned by the deity's words instituting marriage ("It is not good that the man should be alone" [Genesis 2.18]), the Reformers enable an emerging bourgeois culture to produce what has the appearance at least of an egalitarian view of the marital relation. The very phrase *meet for him* is said by Calvin to suggest in the Hebrew *kĕneged* the quality of being "like or answerable unto" [*quia illi respondeat*] the man and to vividly indicate that likeness of a psychological dimension is what marriage as an institution is based on,[32] a view Milton endorses when he takes the untranslatably expressive Hebrew "originall" to signify *"another self, a second self, a very self itself"* (*T* 600), and which he has Adam's divine interlocutor voice in book 8 of *Paradise Lost,* when Adam is promised "Thy likeness, thy fit help, thy other self,/Thy wish, exactly to thy heart's desire" (ll.450–51).[33]

As has often been pointed out, in the divorce tracts Milton raises to unprecedented and undreamt of heights this early-modern tendency to spiritualize and idealize the marriage bond. The extent to which he relies upon an implicit privileging of "J" over "P" (indeed, over the other texts he treats, as well) in order to do so has not been commented upon, however. Milton's advocacy of a more liberalized interpretation of the grounds for divorce proceeds by countering the mean-spirited misinterpretations of scripture promulgated by scholastics and canonists.[34] On its more constructive front, it seeks to harmonize different and radically conflicting scriptural texts. The most urgent and taxing exegetical feat Milton has to perform is the reconciliation of Matthew 19.3–11, where it appears that remarriage after divorce is forbidden on grounds other than "fornication," and Deuteronomy 24.1–2, read by Milton as sanctioning divorce for reasons of what we would now call incompatibility. *Tetrachordon,* the tract in which Milton's skills as exegete are most on display, announces in its very title his determination to establish unity and sameness in the place of seeming difference and contradiction. Meaning "four-stringed," and thus referring to the four-toned Greek scale, *Tetrachordon* attempts to harmonize what on the title page are referred to as the "foure chief places in Scripture, which treat of Mariage, or nullities in Mariage." The first text given on the title page is "Gen. 1.27.28 compar'd and *explain'd by* Gen. 2.18.23.24" (*T* 577).[35]

The explaining of Genesis 1 *by* Genesis 2 is of multifronted strategic importance to Milton's polemical attack on existing English divorce laws, which do not properly recognize the spiritual nature of marriage. It is possible that, like Calvin in the passage cited above, Milton might have been aware that the Hebrew translated "male and female" could suggest sexual difference conceived biologically. Calvin, however, can read the words instituting marriage back into the phrase *male and female*, getting this phrase itself to signify the creation of a wedded union narrated more completely in the second chapter.

> When he addeth streight after, that God created them male and female, he commended unto us the matrimoniall state, whereby the societie of mankinde is mainteined. For this forme of speach, *God created man, male and female created he them*, is as much in effect, as if he had said, that the man is half a man, and that for this cause woman was joyned to him for a mate, that they two might be one: even as he more plainly declareth in the seconde Chapter.[36]

By contrast, Milton tends to want to exploit rhetorically the sexual connotations of "male and female," partly as a means of articulating the divorce tracts' central, and most tirelessly and energetically worded argument, which is that neither sexual union in and of itself nor procreation is the primary end of marriage as originally constituted. Commenting directly on "male and female created he them" in *Tetrachordon*, Milton states that it has reference to "the right, and lawfulnes of the mariage bed." When, like Calvin in the passage just cited, Milton relates this text to its immediate context, he claims that sexual union is an "inferior" end to that implied by the earlier "So God made man in his image, in the image of god made he him" (Milton's detailed exegesis of which I will examine later) (*T* 592). As this suggests, a bipolar and hierarchical ordering of the spiritual and physical dimensions of experience structures many of Milton's exegetical moves in these tracts. The following commentary on "male and female" is fairly representative and illustrates, in addition, the important role played by "J":

> He that said *Male and female created he them*, immediately before that said also in the same verse, *In the Image of God created he him*, and redoubl'd it, that our thoughts might not be so full of dregs as to urge this poor con-

sideration of *male and female,* without remembring the nobelnes of that former repetition; lest when God sends a wise eye to examin our triviall glosses, they be found extremly to creep upon the ground: especially since they confesse that what here concerns mariage is but a brief touch, only preparative to the institution which follows more expressely in the next Chapter. (*T* 592)

That the words *male and female* have a distinctly sexual signification for Milton is evident in several passages. In *The Doctrine and Discipline of Divorce,* for example, Milton makes it known that he is prepared to meet up with two kinds of opponent: those enslaved to "custom and the letter of the Text" and those "whose grosse and vulgar apprehensions conceit but low of matrimoniall purposes, and in the work of male and female think they have all."[37] Yet the aim of Milton's argument, carried out by means of a privileging of "J" over "P," is to reduce these two kinds of opposition to one. For the mind that does not creep upon the ground ought to be properly impressed with the fact that in Genesis 2.18 God himself speaks, revealing in no uncertain terms what the end of marriage is. "And the Lord said, it is not good that man should be alone; I will make him a help meet for him." Expounding the true meaning of the earlier verse, "Male and female created he them," this verse declares "by the explicit words of God himselfe" that male and female is none other "than a fit help, and meet society" (*T* 594). Milton is willing to put this even more strongly. It is not just that we have here the words of God himself, expounding the meaning of an earlier text. God here actually explains *himself.* "For God does not heer precisely say, I make a female to this male, as he did briefly before, but expounding himselfe heer on purpos, he saith, because it is not good for man to be alone, I make him therefore a meet help" (*T* 595).

Like Calvin and other commentators, Milton is confident that the second chapter of Genesis both expounds the first and makes the true order of events apparent. The blessing of fertility, which therefore comes after the instituting of marriage, shows by coming last that it refers to an inferior end. Similarly, by appearing after the words instituting marriage, as well as after the creation of Eve, Adam's speech in Genesis 2.24 ("Therefore shall a man leave his father and his mother, and shall cleave unto his wife, and they shall be one flesh") indicates that becoming one flesh is subordinated to becoming meet helps. Milton on several occasions appeals to this presumed chronological order, casting it into an opposition between spirit and flesh. Its strategic importance for his polemic against the special status given adultery and impotence or frigidity (and thus the body) by the existing laws is evident in the following:

> For although God in the first ordaining of marriage, taught us to what end he did it, in words expresly implying the apt and cheerfull conversation of man with woman, to comfort and refresh him against the evill of solitary life, not mentioning the purpose of generation till afterwards, as being but a secondary end in dignity, though not in necessitie; yet now, if any two be but once handed in the Church, and have tasted in any sort the nuptiall bed, let them finde themselves never so mistak'n in their dispositions through any error, concealment, or misadventure, that through their different tempers, thoughts, and constitutions, they can neither be to one another a remedy against lonelines, nor live in any union or contentment all their dayes, yet they shall, so they be but found suitably weapon'd to the lest possibilite of sensuall enjoyment, be made, spight of *antipathy* to fadge together, and combine as they may to their unspeakable wearisomnes & despaire of all sociable delight in the ordinance which God establisht to that very end. (*DDD* 234–36)

Or again, in the well-known passage in which it is affirmed that "a meet and happy conversation is the chiefest and the noblest end of mariage," Milton alludes to this putative order when stating, "And indeed it is a greater blessing from God, more worthy so excellent a creature as man is, and a higher end to honour and sanctifie the league of mariage, whenas the solace and satisfaction of the minde is regarded and provided for before the sensitive pleasing of the body" (*DDD* 246). So integral to his argument is this ordering that Milton can exploit polemically the word *preposterous* in its Latinate sense of an absurd putting before of what comes after. "How vain therefore is it and how preposterous in the Canon Law to have made such careful provision against the impediment of carnall performance, and to have had no care about the unconversing inability of minde, so defective to the purest and most sacred end of matrimony" (*DDD* 248).

If we set this exegetical practice briefly against Trible's, we can now see that her reading and Milton's are significantly alike in subtly but unmistakably valorizing a state that transcends sexual difference as vulgarly understood. In Trible's case this state is prior to sexual differentiation itself, while in Milton's it is distinct from nearly everything commonly associated with sexuality. Yet whereas Trible makes use of a spiritualized interpretation of "male and female created he them" to produce the egalitarian version of "J's" narrative, Milton finds in that very narrative a spiritualized interpretation of the more lowly and bodily "male and female." Indeed, "J's" narrative, understood as instituting a relationship primarily and rapturously spiritual or psychological, provides the very basis for the phrases and passages emphasizing mutuality to be found throughout the divorce tracts. The above citations give some indication of the eloquence with which Milton can celebrate the pleasures of a heterosexual union that is ideally—that is, on the spiritual plane intended by its divine institutor—fitting or meet. And there are numerous other moments in these works where, without rhetorical flourish, mutuality is clearly asserted or implied. The woman and man of the marriage relation can, for example, be referred to as "helps meete for each other" (*DDD* 276). Or it can be stated that nothing that concerns marriage should be subordinated to "the glory of God and the main good of either party" (*T* 650). On a more practical level, and of direct relevance to the legal reforms he is proposing, is the statement Milton offers of his position when opening the first chapter of *The Doctrine and Discipline of Divorce*: "*That indisposition, unfitnes, or contrariety of mind, arising from a cause in nature unchangable, hindring and ever likely to hinder the main benefits of conjugall society, which are solace and peace, is a greater reason of divorce than naturall frigidity, especially if there be no children, and that there be mutuall consent*" (*DDD* 242). The explicit reference to "mutual consent" here is matched or perhaps even deliberately introduced by the opening words of the subtitle appearing in both the first and second editions of this work: *Restor'd to the Good of Both Sexes, From the bondage of Canon Law, and other mistakes. . . .*

Much as the dominant discourse of the academy would like to celebrate this praiseworthy attention to mutuality, however, there are very few passages of any length in the divorce tracts that can be dressed up for the occasion. Milton refers to what he regards as ineffectual attempts "to save the *Phaenomenon* of our Saviours answer to the Pharises" (*DDD* 243). I would suggest that the phenomenon of Milton's enlightened Christian humanism can most effectually be saved if the challenge presented by the divorce tracts is simply ignored, or if they are read with a high degree of selectivity. For over and over again, throughout the tracts, this laudable mutuality loses its balance, teetering precariously on the brink of pure abstraction. And the reason it does so is that it stands on the ground of a lonely Adam who is not in any sense either ungendered or generic. It becomes clear, finally, that the concluding phrase of Milton's position statement—"and that there be mutual consent"—is not expected to stand up in a court of law. In the penultimate chapter of the second edition of *The Doctrine and Discipline of Divorce*, Milton states his view "that the absolute and final hindring of divorce cannot belong to any civil or earthly power, against the will and consent of both parties, *or of the husband alone*" (*DDD* 344; emphasis mine.) Even if this could, improbably, be attributed to a moment's forgetfulness on the part of an author busy revising and enlarging his original, it still would not be able to pass itself off as an instance of simple self-contradiction. For, as I hope briefly to demonstrate, this particular assertion is also the self-consistent outcome of the deeply patriarchal assumptions at work in Milton's articulation of a radically bourgeois view of marriage.

To a certain extent, the precariousness of mutuality's stance is the result of the intensely subjectivist and idealist foundation it is given. Commenting on "It is better to marry than to burne" (1 Corinthians 7.9), Milton argues that the burning referred to here is not a mere physical burning, which might be allayed by diet and a strict regime, but the very "rationall burning that mariage is to remedy." The desire for "conjugall fellowship" is "an intelligible burning, not in Paradise to be resisted." This desire itself is "properly call'd love," an act of naming on Milton's part that in and of itself suggests something of the

ideality of which mutuality must partake (*DDD* 250–52). And this
ideality is stabilized, rhetorically, when over and over again Milton
relies on a form of syllogistic reasoning to advance his polemic. The
argument this reasoning produces goes basically like this: since marriage was divinely instituted to remedy a rational burning, a woman
and man who find that their joining together does not satisfy this desire are not really married. Logically, they don't even need to divorce
since, in the only sense that really matters, "God never joyn'd them"
(*DDD* 277).

Yet there is obviously more to it than this. The divorce tracts are
now generally taken to represent a critical moment in the development of Milton's views on Scripture and on natural law.[38] Yet the
"law" that gets itself produced in these tracts is the fundamentally ex-
tralegal interiority of the bourgeois subject, constituted on the basis
of "the faultles proprieties of nature" (*DDD* 237). In their articulation
of a radically interiorized view of the marriage relationship, the
divorce tracts reveal the emergence of a new form of subjectivity. Yet
I would argue that they also reveal the dependency of this emergence
on the securely masculinist position of the author. The discourse of
the divorce tracts would be unthinkable without the traditions of
commentary relating to law, philosophy, and theology, besides the
related discourses of courtly and neo-Platonic love, all of which were
available almost exclusively to men and also assumed an almost exclusively androcentric perspective. But even more significant are the
social practices and assumptions of the patriarchal society in which
Milton lives, since they permit him to argue that one of the advantages of the reforms he is proposing would be that the business of
divorce would be restored rightfully to the "maister of family" (*DDD*
353).[39]

Time and again, the language of the tracts passes through the use
of plural forms potentially inclusive of both sexes only to come to
rest with a nongenerically masculine *he*, as it does very clearly in the
following passage, where it is argued—in some desperation, it would
appear—that an unhappy marriage might endanger life:

The Canon Law and Divines consent, that if either party be found contriving against the others life, they may be sever'd by divorce. . . .The same may be said touching those persons who beeing of a pensive nature and cours of life, have summ'd up all their solace in that free and lightsom conversation which God & man intends in mariage: whereof when they see themselves depriv'd by meeting an unsociable consort, they ofttimes resent one anothers mistake so deeply, that long it is not ere grief end one of them. When therfore this danger is foreseen that the life is in perill by living together, what matter is it whether helples greef, or wilfull practice be the cause? This is certain that the preservation of life is more worth then the compulsory keeping of mariage; and it is no lesse then cruelty to force a man to remain in that state as the solace of his life, which he and his friends know will be either the undoing or the disheartning of his life. . . . [N]othing more inviolable then vows made to God, yet we read in *Numbers*, that if a wife had made such a vow, the meer will and authority of her husband might break it; how much more may he break the error of his own bonds with an unfit and mistak'n wife, to the saving of his welfare, his life, yea his faith and vertue from the hazard of over-strong temptations; for if man be Lord of the Sabbath, to the curing of a Fevor, can he be lesse then Lord of mariage in such important causes as these? (*DDD* 273–74)

Here, the ostensibly generic "man" of the concluding statement receives his gender long before we come upon him, consolidating along the way his solidarity with the law devaluing women's speech.

Even more significant, however, are the ideological assumptions of that little "how much more." As the discussion up to this point has indicated, insofar as the story of Eve's creation from Adam's rib is thought to articulate the Protestant doctrine of marriage, it is not her creation *after* Adam per se that is so significant, but her creation *for* him, as a remedy of his loneliness. As we have seen, this exegesis produces a historically unprecedented emphasis on the satisfaction of psychological needs as the very "end" for which marriage was ordained. Yet it also places an equally unprecedented emphasis on Adam as the "person" whose desire is primarily in question. The egalitarian sentiments apparently expressed, sporadically, throughout the divorce tracts do not in any way obscure Eve's secondary status as a "gift" from one patriarch to another. Created for Adam, Eve is, as Milton's Adam puts it in *Paradise Lost*, "Heav'n's last best gift" (5.19).

The author Milton's solidarity with this Adam is not just evident here and there, in the occasional passage. It is the very principle structuring and motivating the arguments deployed in the divorce tracts, and is one with the privileging of "J" over "P" instituted by Protestant commentators. The man who puts away his wife "with the full suffrage and applause of his conscience" is "claiming by faith and fulnes of perswasion the rights and promises of Gods institution" (*T* 670). And these are rights and promises that simply do not apply to the woman, since it is not she for whom this institution was ordained. More than once Milton has to refute the view that the Deuteronomic text seeks to protect wives from the abuses of their husbands' power to dismiss them without cause, a view held by Calvin, several other Protestant commentators, and modern historians as well.[40] In one passage where he does so, he again makes use of the punning "preposterous," though with an important difference from the passage cited earlier. "For certainly if man be liable to injuries in mariage, as well as woman, and man be the worthier person, it were a preposterous law to respect only the less worthy; her whom God made for mariage, and not him at all for whom mariage was made" (*T* 627). In another he introduces his rebuttal with the summary exclamation, "Palpably uxorious!" (*DDD* 324). Perhaps the unacknowledged loneliness of mutuality can best be illustrated by the following pithily worded statement: "But all ingenuous men will see that the dignity and blessing of marriage is plac't rather in the mutual enjoyment of that which the wanting soul needfully seeks, then of that which the plenteous body would jollily give away" (*DDD* 252). "Mutual enjoyment" does here seem to be a real and concretely imagined value, but only if we do not notice that the opposition between spirit and body is being carried by the parallelism between the "wanting soul," paradigmatically Adam's, and the "plenteous body," which has no choice but to be jollily masculine.

Yet Eve is also, of course, created *from* Adam, as well as *for* him. And in Milton's view, as Adam's "likeness," she does not even have the status—to use Satan's description of "man" in *Paradise Lost*—of the Father's "latest," meaning most recent, "image" (4.567). For by unifying the two creation stories in the way Reformed principles permit

him to, Milton's exegesis makes possible the production of two ideologically charged and historically specific readings, contradictorily
related: on the one hand an interpretation of "male and female" that
psychologizes heterosexual union and dignifies marriage, and on the
other an explication of "created man in his image" that tends to re-
strict the meaning of "man" to an individual Adam, from whom and
for whom the female is then made. It is important to put this exactly,
for of course biblical commentators always claim that woman is also
in some sense made in the image of God. Yet Calvin, both in the passage cited above on "male and female created he them" and in the following, locates the generic sense of "man" in the first and gendered
man's representative status. Because the two accounts are one, the
generic "man" of the Priestly account is also the gendered Adam from
whom and for whom Eve was made. Commenting on Genesis 2.18,
"I will make him an help meet for him," Calvin responds to the question, Why isn't the plural form, "Let us make" used here, as it was
in the creation of "man"?

> Some think, that by this speach, the difference which is betweene both
> sexes is noted, and that so it is shewed, how much more excellent the man
> is, then the woman. But I like better of another interpretation, which dif-
> fereth somewhat, though it be not altogether contrarie: namely, that when
> in the person of man, mankinde was created, the comman worthinesse of
> the whole nature, was with one title generally adorned, where it is said, *Let
> us make man:* and that it was not needful to be repeated in the creating of
> the woman, which was nothing else but the addition and furniture of the
> man [*quae nihil aliud est quam viri accessio*]. It cannot be denied, but the
> woman also was created after the image of God, though in the seconde
> degree. Whereupon it followeth, that the same which was spoken in the
> creation of the man, perteineth to womankind.[41]

A more striking example of the supposed identity of the generic and
the gendered "man" could probably not be found. Yet so long as this
"man"—whether gendered, generic or somehow gendered-generic—is
temporally prior to woman, as he must be when the Yahwist's narrative is given prominence, then woman's relationship to the image
of God is necessarily secondary, derivative. Milton's stridently mas-

culinist "He for God only, she for God in him" obviously goes much further than Calvin in drawing out the phallocratic implications of this hermeneutical practice. Yet the notion that Eve is derived from an Adam who is created immediately in his Father's image is one that does not leap full-grown out of Milton's own lonely head.

Pursuing the logic of this exegesis with maddening precision, in his commentary on "in the image of God created he him," the intermediate statement of Genesis 1.27, Milton can state that "the woman is not primarily and immediately the image of God, but in reference to the man," on the grounds that, though the "Image of God" is common to them both, "had the Image of God been equally common to them both, it had no doubt bin said, In the image of God created he them" (*T* 589). Much has been made of the way Milton appears to qualify the verses he quotes from 1 Corinthians 11 on the subjection of wives to their husbands: "Not but that particular exceptions may have place, if she exceed her husband in prudence and dexterity, and he contentedly yeeld, for then a superior and more naturall law comes in, that the wiser should govern the lesse wise, whether male or female." Yet this text can be used to save the phenomenon of Milton's supposed egalitarianism only if its context is suppressed. For the passage that immediately follows indicates that Milton has qualified the famous Pauline dicta only to save the phenomenon of his own rationalism. It effectively empties of social or even rhetorical relevance any hypothetical exceptions to the divinely ordained masculine rule Milton associates both with 1 Corinthians 11 and with the text from Genesis on which he comments:

But that which far more easily and obediently follows from this verse, is that, seeing woman was purposely made for man, and he her head, it cannot stand before the breath of this divine utterance, that man the portraiture of God, joyning to himself for his intended good and solace an inferiour sexe, should so become her thrall, whose wilfulnes or inability to be a wife frustrates the occasionall end of her creation, but that he may acquitt himself to freedom by his naturall birthright, and that indeleble character of priority which God crown'd him with. If it be urg'd that sin hath lost him this, the answer is not far to seek, that from her the sin first proceeded, which keeps her justly in the same proportion still beneath. She is not to gain by being first in the transgression, that man should furder loose to her, because already he hath lost by her means. (*T* 589–90)

Among the many things worthy of notice in this passage, not least significant is the way Milton willingly exposes the motivated status of the notion of "priority" that the statement in 1 Timothy 2.13 on which he here implicitly comments would seem to wish to conceal. So securely, not to say complacently and outrageously, masculinist is Milton's discourse here—so confident that priority in the order of creation has priority over all other priorities—that it is asserted without any consciousness of inconsistency that Adam's being first ensures his spiritual and social superiority while Eve's being first keeps her rightly in her place.

It thus continues to matter that Adam was formed first, then Eve. Yet as has already been suggested, in the divorce tracts this "indeleble character of priority" is not associated directly with the order of creation but tends rather to be inscribed in the divine words instituting marriage, "It is not good that the man should be alone; I will make him an help meet for him" (Genesis 2.18). It is these words that Milton frequently refers to simply as "the institution." And as I have been arguing, the priority Milton gives this instituting of marriage is inscribed indelibly in every one of his major rhetorical and logical moves. In concluding this discussion of the divorce tracts, I would like to show how consistently or systematically this priority is for him associated with the deity's instituting words.

It has not yet been mentioned that Matthew 5.31, 32 and Matthew 19.3–11, which together constitute one of the four texts treated in *Tetrachordon,* and which appear unequivocally to forbid divorce except for fornication, are susceptible to Milton's polemical appropriation of them precisely because in chapter 19 Jesus is represented quoting from Genesis. The relevant verses, cited by Milton, are 3–6.

And the Pharises came unto [Jesus] tempting him and saying unto him, Is it lawful for a man to put away his wife for every cause? And he answered and said unto them, Have ye not read, that he which made them at the beginning made them male and female, And said, For this cause shall a man

leave father and mother, and shall cleave to his wife: and they twain shall
be one flesh? Wherefore they are no more twain, but one flesh. What therefore God hath joined together, let not man put asunder.

The two texts cited here are the now familiar "male and female created he them" (Genesis 1.27) and "Therefore shall a man leave his
father and his mother, and shall cleave unto his wife: and they shall
be one flesh" (Genesis 2.24). Milton's strategy in commenting on the
verses from Matthew is to subvert their literal and accepted meaning
by referring the citations back to the divine words of institution,
which, he points out, significantly are *not* quoted. He does this by
arguing that Jesus' intention is to refer us back to these instituting
words, which alone are of doctrinal efficacy, and which the tempting
Pharisees, his immediate interlocutors, are not worthy of being
taught.

> If heere then being tempted, hee desire to bee the shorter, and the darker
> in his conference, and omit to cite that from the second of *Genesis*, which
> all Divines confesse is a commentary to what he cites out of the first, the
> *making of them Male and Female;* what are we to doe, but to search the insti-
> tution our selves; and we shall finde there his owne authority giving other
> manner of reasons why such firme union is to bee in matrimony, without
> which reasons their being male and female can be no cause of joyning them
> unseparably. (*T* 649)

That Milton is here relying entirely on "J's" priority over "P" is evident from his stating, later on, that to truly understand "what right
there may be, in ill accidents, to divorce, wee must repaire thither
where God professes to teach his servants by the prime institution,
and not where we see him intending to dazle sophisters: We must not
read *hee made them Male and Female* & not understand he made them
more intendedly *a meet helpe* to remove the evill of being *alone.* We
must take both these together, and then we may inferre compleatly
as from the whole cause why a man shall cleave to his wife, and they
twaine shall be one flesh" (*T* 650).

  With this, Milton gets the instituting words to govern the manner
in which the Son's citations are disseminated. In framing what Milton
regards as "his prudent ambiguities and concealments," Jesus cites

Adam's words as well (*T* 650). Yet this presents no problem to the exegesis, precisely because Milton has already determined that Adam's speech also has meaning only with reference to the words of divine institution. As we saw earlier, both Trible and Bal find their central concerns articulated in Adam's first speech, "This is now bone of my bones and flesh of my flesh; she shall be called Woman, because she was taken out of Man. Therefore shall a man leave his father and his mother, and shall cleave unto his wife: and they shall be one flesh" [Genesis 2.23–24]). Pointing out that this is the first human utterance to appear in Genesis, they both read it as a lyrical utterance, a spontaneous love poem spoken by the just-gendered Adam to the creature who has just been differentiated from him. By contrast, Milton finds Adam here expounding his maker's words. Apprehending "at first sight the true fitnes of that consort which God provided him," Adam "therefore spake in reference to those words which God pronounc't before; as if he had said, this is she by whose meet help and society I shall no more be alone; this is she who was made my image, ev'n as I the Image of God; not so much in body, as in unity of mind and heart" (*T* 602). Those who think that Adam is in the first part of his speech formulating the doctrine of marriage's undissolvability are not only sadly mistaken but guilty of using "the mouth of our generall parent, the first time it opens, to an arrogant opposition, and correcting of Gods wiser ordinance" (*T* 603).

The next part of Adam's speech (verse 24), which opens with "therefore," shows *by* opening with "therefore" that Adam confines the implications of his utterance only to "what God spake concerning the inward essence of Mariage in his institution" (*T* 603). The Father's words are the "soul" of Adam's and must be taken into Adam's if Adam's are properly to be understood. Adam's words about becoming one flesh, if they pertain to the dissolvability of marriages in the fallen world at all, do so only to the extent that they "presuppose the joyning causes" (*T* 605). This curious phrase refers to the "causes" which truly, that is, in accordance with the promise of the instituting words, join a man and woman in marriage.[42] But so determined is Milton to limit the application of Adam's speech that the phrase might also seem to refer to the causes joining Adam's speech to the words of divine institution. Adam's "therefore" makes undissolvability conditional upon the presence of the "form" of marriage promised in the instituting words (*T* 608). Indeed, as this brief summary suggests, Milton's exegesis gets "our old ancient ancestor" to sound much more like a preoccupied theologian or lawyer than a joyous young lover. Milton concludes, however, by attributing this treatiselike quality to the author Moses, not Adam. Conceding that "it be not for the Majesty of Scripture to humble her self in artificial *theorems,* and definitions, and *Corollaries,* like a professor in the Schools," he argues that this makes it all the more significant that Moses "condescends in this place to such a methodical and School-like way of defining, and consequencing, as in no place of the whole law more" (*T* 613–14). We have here, I think, another joining of causes: by incorporating a little treatise into Adam's speech, Moses eases the burden of trying to respect the authority of Scripture for Milton, whose treatise is—well, yes—a treatise, but certainly not the first.

V

One of the questions concerning *Paradise Lost* that this discussion of the divorce tracts has, I hope, made it possible to address is, Why does Milton's Eve tell the story of her earliest experiences first, in book 4? Why, if Adam was formed first, then Eve, does Adam tell *his* story to Raphael *last,* in book 8? An adequate response to this question would require a full-scale analysis of the ways in which *Paradise Lost* articulates a putative sequential order of events or story with the narrative discourse that distributes the story. As a genre, epic is of course expected to develop complicated relations between a presumed chronological and a narrative ordering of events. But *Paradise Lost* would seem to use both retrospective and prospective narratives in a more systematic and motivated manner than does any of its predecessors, in part because it is so highly conscious of the problematical process of its consumption. I would like to argue here that

Paradise Lost's narrative distribution of Adam's and Eve's first experiences is not just complexly but ideologically motivated, and that the
import of this motivation can best be grasped by an analysis aware
of the historically specific features of Milton's exegetical practice in
the divorce tracts.

This practice is crucially important to *Paradise Lost*'s own telling of
the Genesis creation stories. In the case of the passage it most obviously informs, Raphael's account of the creation of "man" on the
sixth day of creation in book 7, certain features are intelligible only
in the light of this historically specific context. If commenting on this
passage at all, critics have tended to suggest that Raphael gives something like a heavenly, as compared with Adam's later more earthly,
account of creation. J. M. Evans, for example, says that Raphael's narration is like the Priestly document in portraying creation "from
above" and that Adam's is like the Yahwist's in presenting it "from
below."[43] This does not, however, even begin to do justice to the intricately plotted relations of the "P" and "J" accounts in the following:

> Let us make now Man in our image, Man
> In our similitude, and let them rule
> Over the Fish and Fowl of Sea and Air,
> Beast of the Field, and over all the Earth,
> And every creeping thing that creeps the ground.
> This said, he form'd thee, *Adam,* thee, O Man
> Dust of the ground, and in thy nostrils breath'd
> The breath of Life; in his own Image hee
> Created thee, in the Image of God
> Express, and thou becam'st a living Soul.
> Male he created thee, but thy consort
> Female for Race; then bless'd Mankind, and said,
> Be fruitful, multiply, and fill the Earth,
> Subdue it, and throughout Dominion hold
> Over Fish of the Sea, and Fowl of the Air,
> And every living thing that moves on the Earth.
> Wherever thus created, for no place
> Is yet distinct by name, thence, as thou know'st
> He brought thee into this delicious Grove,
> This Garden, planted with the Trees of God,
> Delectable both to behold and taste;

And freely all thir pleasant fruit for food
Gave thee, all sorts are here that all th' Earth yields,
Variety without end; but of the Tree
Which tasted works knowledge of Good and Evil,
Thou may'st not; in the day thou eat'st, thou di'st;
Death is the penalty impos'd, beware,
And govern well thy appetite, lest sin
Surprise thee, and her black attendant Death.
Here finish'd hee, and all that he had made
View'd, and behold all was entirely good;
So Ev'n and Morn accomplish'd the Sixt day.

[7.519–50]

The first thing to be noticed is the way in which "P" and "J" are carefully spliced together in this account, creating a single and apparently seamlessly unified narrative of creation. Genesis 1.26–28 is given in what is virtually its entirety. But the principal acts of Genesis 2.7–17 are also related: Yahweh's making of "man" from the dust of the ground (2.7), his taking of this man into the garden of Eden (2.15), and his giving of the prohibition (2.16, 17). One could argue that even Milton's "artistry" here hasn't received its proper due, since this splicing economically makes from two heterogeneous accounts a single one that is both intellectually and aesthetically coherent.

Yet it does more, far more, than this. For the first and most important thing Raphael's account achieves is the removal of any trace of ambiguity—the residual generic dust, as it were—from the Priestly account of the creation of *hā'ādām* or "man" in the image of God. This it does by a set of speech-acts unambiguously identifying this "man" with Raphael's interlocutor, Adam. The direct address in "he form'd thee, *Adam*, thee O Man/Dust of the ground" has what amounts to a deictic function, joining the representative "Man" to Raphael's gendered and embodied listener, who is specifically and repeatedly addressed here, while Eve (yet an auditor) very pointedly is not. It is clearly significant that these very lines effect the joining of the Priestly and Yahwist accounts. By placing "thee O Man/Dust of the ground" in apposition to the named "Adam," it is suggested that this "Adam" actually *is hā'ādām* or representative man and the punning *hā'ădāmâ,* "ground," an identity that only the joining of the two accounts reveals. To convey this identity, Milton ingeniously invents a *Tatbericht* or execution report that picks up details of the Yahwist's account—creation from the dust of the ground and the imparting of the breath of life—for inclusion in the official *Tatbericht* of Genesis 1.27: "in his own Image hee/Created thee, in the Image of God/Express, and thou becam'st a living Soul."

The impression this joining creates is that the two accounts have always already been one in narrating the creation of Adam. The same cannot be said of Raphael's account of the creation of Eve, however. The statement immediately following, "Male he created thee, but thy consort/Female for Race" (7.529–30) is also of course part of this *Tatbericht.* But in contrast (I would like to say something like "in striking contrast," yet it has not really been noticed) to the ingenious joining that takes place for the sake of Adam, this is all Raphael has to say about Eve's creation.[44] Outside of this meager "but thy consort/Female for Race," Raphael's account does not otherwise even allude to the creation of Eve, although, as we have seen, other details of the narrative in the second chapter are included in it. Indeed, if we examine the matter more closely, it appears that the Yahwist's account is made use of only up to and including Genesis 2.17 (narrating the giving of the prohibition) precisely because Genesis 2.18 inaugurates the story of the creation of a help meet for Adam. This narrative would thus seem deliberately to be excised from Raphael's account. Or to put it another way, in the case of the creation of Eve, no attempt whatsoever has been made to join the two creation accounts in this, the epic's own telling of the Genesis creation stories.

In Raphael's account, then, the blessing of fertility follows directly upon the words of sexual distinction, which, with the explicit reference to "Race" or generation, here signify (as in Bird's historicized reading of their appearance in "P") sexual differentiation conceived biologically. But if we return to the exegetical problematic discussed earlier, it becomes clear that Milton could have interpolated the entire "J" narrative into this account, concluding it with the words of blessing coming after the "marriage" of Adam and Eve. Not only would the true succession of events thereby have become apparent, but the true significance of "male and female" would also have been revealed. Why doesn't this happen? Why doesn't this account attempt even a modest joining of "male and female" with the story of Eve's creation? Why, in Raphael's account, do the words of sexual differentiation come to represent or to take the place of the narrative of Eve's creation?

The answer obviously cannot be the one Milton provided to explain Jesus' use of this very passage: that the most vulgar and bodily text is cited to convince and dazzle his sophistical auditors, the Pharisees. For Raphael here recites the "original" text in what presents itself as a version of its "original" form to auditors who are themselves to exemplify the higher forms of wedded bliss in its "original" perfection. If we look only to Raphael's account, these questions would seem not to have an answer. But of course the story of Eve's creation is not excised from *Paradise Lost* altogether, which is, presumably, why readers have not protested its absence here. It is told later, by another teller, Adam. The Yahwist's narrative of Eve's creation is not told until Adam himself tells it to Raphael in book 8, where it comes to amplify and complete Raphael's brief and wholly inadequate "Male he created thee, but thy consort/Female for Race." What this means, among other things, is that Adam's story has exactly the same relation to Raphael's as, in the divorce tracts and in Protestant commentaries, the second chapter of Genesis has to the first: it is an exposition or commentary upon it, revealing its true import.

Yet this second telling can have this status only because Adam is its teller. As our discussion indicated, Milton's argument in the divorce tracts rests on a radical privileging of "J" over "P" in the specific form of a privileging of the words of divine institution in Genesis 2.18. Had Milton interpolated the story of Eve's creation into Raphael's creation account, he would have had to record these words in the form of indirect speech (as he does the words of prohibition in lines 542–47) or else to have reproduced both the creator's speech and Adam's. In either case, the instituting words would have been displaced from their centers of authority. By transferring the entire narrative to

Adam and by interpolating a dramatic colloquy into this narrative, *Paradise Lost* ensures the coincidence of narrator and auditor of the instituting words, of narrator and of the first man's instituting response. By dramatizing this commentary, this necessary supplement to Raphael's account, in the form of a colloquy narrated by Adam, *Paradise Lost* in this way makes sure that the doctrine of marriage is both produced and understood by the person for whom it is ordained, just as in the divorce tracts it is the privileged male voice, Milton's, that expounds the true doctrine of divorce.

As the divorce tracts never tire of insisting, the true doctrine of marriage relates only to the satisfaction of that which the wanting soul needfully seeks. In *Paradise Lost* this doctrine is coauthored by Adam and the "Presence Divine," who work it out together. It is also communicated, formally, by the extraordinary emphasis placed on Adam's subjectivity, on his actual experience of desire. As Milton has masterminded the exchange, the divine instituting words come *after* Adam has been got to express his longing for a fitting companion (8.444–51), so that this longing has the kind of priority that befits the first man. Yet this longing is also very clearly a rational burning. With its strong filiations to the disputation, the very form of the colloquy establishes that this desire is rational, and that merely reproductive ends are certainly not what Adam has in mind. Although procreation is referred to, it is presented as a kind of necessary consequence of the conjunction of male and female, but for that very reason as a subordinate end. Adam's language cleverly associates it with a prior lack, a prior and psychological defect inherent in his being the first and only man.

> Thou in thyself art perfet, and in thee
> Is no deficience found; not so is Man,
> But in degree, the cause of his desire
> By conversation with his like to help,
> Or solace his defects. No need that thou
> Shouldst propagate, already infinite;
> And through all numbers absolute, though One;
> But Man by number is to manifest
> His single imperfection, and beget

    Like of his life, his Image multipli'd,
    In unity defective, which requires
    Collateral love, and dearest amity.

                                                    [8.415–25]

The way Milton's Adam responds to the deity's formal presentation
to him of his bride, Eve, is just as motivated. The Genesis 2.23–24
speech is cited, but only after it has been introduced in a way that
joins it explicitly to the causes implicit in the deity's instituting words.

    This turn hath made amends; thou hast fulfill'd
    Thy words, Creator bounteous and benign,
    Giver of all things fair, but fairest this
    Of all thy gifts, nor enviest. I now see
    Bone of my Bone, Flesh of my Flesh, my Self
    Before me; Woman is her Name, of Man
    Extracted; for this cause he shall forgo
    Father and Mother, and to his Wife adhere;
    And they shall be one Flesh, one Heart, one Soul.

                                                    [8.491–99]

This speech is presented as a species of spontaneous lyrical utterance
("I overjoy'd could not forbear aloud" [l.489]) and according to Adam
is "heard" by Eve. Yet it is obviously addressed not to her but to her
maker, who is thanked for the gift itself, but not until he has been
praised for having kept his word. Before letting Adam commit himself to the project of becoming one flesh with Eve, Milton has to
make it clear that Adam does so believing that the "Heav'nly Maker"
has done what he has promised, that is, created a truly fit help. Just
as, in the divorce tracts, Milton joins Adam's words to those of the
paternal maker, the instituting words thus becoming the very soul of
Adam's "Flesh of my flesh."
    Not only the placement of Adam's narrative after Raphael's but also
its most salient formal features can thus be seen to be motivated ideologically, and to illustrate the causes joining the divorce tracts and
Paradise Lost. Before turning to Eve, I would like to summarize the
discussion so far by emphasizing that these causes are joined, and to
man's advantage, both when "P" and "J" are united and when they are

not. By joining "P" and "J" as it does, Raphael's account specifies the gendered Adam of *Paradise Lost* as the "man" who is made in the divine image. By disjoining them Raphael's account lets Adam himself tell the story of the creature made to satisfy his desire for an other self.

VI

We can now, more directly, take up the question, Why does heaven's last best gift tell her story first? One way of approaching this question might be to suggest that, in addition to the interests already discussed, the positioning of Adam's narrative after Raphael's and long after Eve's serves the interests of *Paradise Lost* as a text unfolding in the reader's linear experience of it. By delaying Adam's telling of Eve's creation until book 8, *Paradise Lost* is able to defer the revelation of the first man's subjectivity until the last possible moment, that is, until shortly before the presentation of the Fall in book 9. Adam's retrospective narrative in book 8 interiorizes him while producing the doctrine of marriage. But it also gives to his character the illusion of psychological depth that would seem to be the condition for his confession of uxoriousness to Raphael, which then permits the dramatic discourse of the separation scene.

It is also possible, though, that had Eve's narrative of her earliest experiences appeared where "naturally," in the order of creation, it should have, that is *after* Adam's, *Paradise Lost* might have risked allowing her to appear as the necessary and hence, in a certain sense, superior creature suggested by the logic of the supplement, undeniably set in motion by Adam's self-confessed "single imperfection." *Paradise Lost*'s narrative discourse would seem to want to subvert this logic by presenting Eve's narrative first. And it seems to want to subvert it further by placing immediately *after* Adam's narrative a confession in which Eve's completeness and superiority are made to seem an illusion to which Adam is, unaccountably, susceptible. In this part of Adam's dialogue with Raphael, the language of supplementarity as artificial exteriority seems curiously insistent: Eve has been given

"Too much of Ornament" (8.538); she is "Made so adorn for thy delight the more" (8.577), and so on.

Yet the logic of supplementarity may nevertheless be at work in the place of priority given Eve's narrative. For if Eve is created to satisfy the psychological needs of a lonely Adam, then it is necessary that *Paradise Lost*'s readers experience her from the first as expressing an intimately subjective sense of self. From the start she must be associated in a distinctive manner with the very interiority that Adam's need for an other self articulates. Or, to put this another way, Eve's subjectivity must be made available to the reader so that it can ground, as it were, the lonely Adam's articulated desire for another self. Appearing as it does in book 4, Eve's narrative lacks any immediately discernible connection with the Genesis creation accounts on which both Raphael and Adam draw. Its distance from Scripture as publicly acknowledged authority is matched by Eve the narrator's use of markedly lyrical, as opposed to disputational, forms. Set in juxtaposition to the rather barrenly disputational speech of Adam's that immediately precedes it in book 4, Eve's narrative creates a space that is strongly if only implicitly gendered, a space that is dilatory, erotic, and, significantly, almost quintessentially, "private."

In a recent essay, Christine Froula reads Eve's first speech thematically and semiallegorically, as telling the story of Eve's (or woman's) submission of her own personal experience and autonomy to the voices (the deity's, then Adam's) of patriarchal authority. As the very title of her essay—"When Eve Reads Milton"—indicates, Froula wants to find in Milton's Eve if not a protofeminist then a potential ally in contemporary academic feminism's struggle to interrogate the academic canon together with the cultural and political authority it represents. Milton's Eve can play the part of such an ally, however, only because for Froula the privacy of Eve's earliest experiences and the autonomy she thereby initially seems to possess are equivalent to a potentially empowering freedom from patriarchal rule.[45] Given the liberal assumptions of the feminism it espouses, Froula's argument obviously does not want to submit the category of personal experience to ideological analysis.

In attempting to give it such an analysis, I would like to suggest that Eve's speech plays a pivotal role, historically and culturally, in the construction of the kind of female subjectivity required by a new economy's progressive sentimentalization of the private sphere. It is possible to suggest this in part because the subjective experiences Eve relates are represented as having taken place before any knowledge of or commitment to Adam. That is, they are represented as taking place in a sphere that has the defining features of the "private" in an emerging capitalist economy: a sphere that appears to be autonomous and self-sustaining even though not "productive" and, in so appearing, is the very home of the subject. In book 8 Adam recalls having virtually thought his creator into existence and having come up with the idea of Eve in a dialogue with his fellow patriarch. By contrast, Eve recalls inhabiting a space she believed to be uninhabited, autonomous, hers—but for the "Shape within the wat'ry gleam." It is, however, precisely because this belief is evidently *false* that it is possible to see this space as analogous to the "private" sphere, which is of course constituted by and interconnected with the "public" world outside it. Illusory as this autonomy is, inhabiting a world appearing to be her own would nevertheless seem to be the condition of the subjectivity Eve here reveals.

Editors and critics frequently point out that in desiring an other self, Adam uses language associated with friendship. In valorizing the psychological needs marriage fulfills, Protestantism often appeals to the model of friendship, which in its classical formulations is a relationship best practiced by men who are equals. A transvaluation of this relationship would seem to occur in comments such as the following from *Tetrachordon*, on the all-important "It is not good for man to be alone":

And heer *alone* is meant alone without woman; otherwise *Adam* had the company of God himself, and Angels to convers with; all creatures to delight him seriously, or to make him sport. God could have created him out of the same mould a thousand friends and brother *Adams* to have bin his consorts, yet for all this till *Eve* was giv'n him, God reckn'd him to be alone. (*T* 595)

A seldom cited passage from *Colasterion* helps explain what otherwise remains rather obscure: why is woman alone capable of satisfying this need? Once again attacking the crabbedness and body-mindedness of Augustine, Milton states:

> Nor was it half so wisely spokn, as some deem, though *Austin* spake it, that if God had intended other then copulation in Mariage, he would for *Adam* have created a freind, rather than a wife, to convers with; and our own writers blame him for this opinion; for which and the like passages, concerning mariage, hee might bee justly taxt of rusticity in these affairs. For this cannot but bee with ease conceave'd, that there is one society of grave freindship, and another amiable and attractive society of conjugal love, besides the deed of procreation, which of it selfe soon cloies, and is despis'd, unless it bee cherisht and re-incited with a pleasing conversation.[46]

Yet this is perhaps only the most explicit moment at which friendship between men gets differentiated from the meet and happy conversation of husband and wife. Elsewhere Milton can associate the marriage relationship with the need man has for "sometime slackning the cords of intense thought and labour" (*T* 596). In a passage already cited, he can refer to the seeking of "solace in that free and lightsome conversation which God & man intends in marriage." It should go without saying that man can have this need for companionship remedied, can intend to enjoy "lightsome conversation" as opposed to "grave friendship," only if woman is constituted as less grave, more attractive, more lightsome, and more amiable than her male counterpart; and if she is associated with a world apart.

It has long been a commonplace of commentaries on *Paradise Lost* that a network of contrasts are articulated between Eve's narration of her earliest experiences and Adam's, the contrasts all illustrating the hierarchically ordered nature of their differences. Thus Adam, like Eve, awakens on a bed of flowers ("the flow'ry herb" in Adam's case). But whereas Eve is soon lying prone gazing into waters, Adam gets up to begin a skyward leaping about, demonstrating moments later a capacity for abstract thought that opposes itself to Eve's image and illusion-bound reflections; and so forth. Yet it has not been clearly enough recognized that while shadowing forth these bipolar opposi-

tions, Eve's narrative is supposed to rationalize the mutuality or inter-
subjective basis of their love. For by means of the Narcissus myth,
Paradise Lost is able to represent her experiencing a desire equivalent
or complementary to the lonely Adam's desire for an other self.

It is not hard to see that Adam's own desire for an other self has
a strong "narcissistic" component. Yet Adam's retrospective narrative
shows this narcissism being sparked, sanctioned, and then satisfied by
his creator. By contrast, though in book 4 Eve recalls experiencing a
desire for an other self, this desire is clearly and unambiguously constituted by illusion, both in the sense of specular illusion and in the
sense of error. Neo-Platonic readings of the Narcissus myth find in
it a reflection of the "fall" of spirit into matter. Milton transforms this
tragic tale into one with a comic resolution by instructing Eve in the
superiority of spirit or, more exactly, in the superiority of "manly
grace and wisdom" over her "beauty."[47] But because this happily ending little *Bildungsroman* also involves a movement from illusion to
reality, Eve is made to come to prefer not only "manly wisdom and
grace" as attributes of Adam but also, and much more importantly,
Adam as embodiment of the reality principle itself: he whose image
she really is, as opposed to the specular image in which her desire
originated.

To become available for the mutuality the doctrine of wedded love
requires, Eve's desire therefore must in effect lose its identity, while
yet somehow offering itself up for correction and reorientation. As
has often been noted, Eve's fate diverges from that of Narcissus at the
moment when the divine voice intervenes to call her away from her
delightful play with her reflection in the "waters." We have seen that
in book 8 Adam's desire for an other self is sanctioned by the divine
presence's rendering of "It is not good that the man should be alone;
I will make him an help meet for him." When the divine voice speaks
to Eve, it is to ask that she redirect the desire she too experiences for
an other self:

> What thou seest,
> What there thou seest fair Creature is thyself,
> With thee it came and goes: but follow me,

And I will bring thee where no shadow stays
Thy coming, and thy soft imbraces, hee
Whose image thou art, him thou shalt enjoy
Inseparably thine, to him shalt bear
Multitudes like thyself, and thence be call'd
Mother of human Race.

[8.467–75]

Unlike the instituting words spoken to Adam in book 8, these have
no basis in the Yahwist creation account. Yet they are clearly invented to accompany the only part of that account that Milton has
to work with here, the brief "and brought her unto the man" (Genesis
2.22), which in Genesis immediately precedes Adam's words of recognition. Marked inescapably by literary invention and uttered by a
presence that is invisible to Eve, the voice's words have a curiously
secondary or derivative status, at least compared with those spoken
to Adam. They seem indeed, fittingly, to be a kind of echo of the
divine voice. In the context of allegorical readings of the Narcissus
story, this suggestion appears less fanciful, for the figure of Echo in
Ovid's tale has been made to signify the effect the divine breath or
voice can have on the human soul. In this reading, Echo gets identified with the Hebrew *bat kol* or "the daughter of the divine voice."[48]
It might be that in *Paradise Lost* this is the only kind of divine utterance the derived and secondary Eve has ears to hear. (In book 9's
temptation scene, Eve refers to the prohibition as "Sole Daughter of
his voice" [653].)

The voice Eve hears can be related to Echo in another way as well.
Insofar as it effects a separation of Eve from her physical image, this
word in a way echoes what Milton calls the creator's originary "di-
vorcing command" by which "the world first rose out of Chaos"
(*DDD* 273). But the separation of Eve from her image is not the only
divorce effected here. Before this intervention the "Smooth Lake"
into which Eve peers seems to her "another Sky," as if the waters on
the face of the earth and the heavens were for her indistinguishable
or continuous. The divine voice could therefore much more precisely
be said to recapitulate or echo the paternal Word's original division of

the waters in Genesis 1.6–7. Before describing her watery mirror and her other self, Eve mentions "a murmuring sound / Of waters issu'd from a Cave"—murmurs, waters, and cave all being associated symbolically with maternality, as critics have pointed out. When the paternal Word intervenes, Eve's specular autoeroticism seems to become, paradoxically, even more her own, in part because it no longer simply reflects that of Ovid's Narcissus. And when Eve responds to the verbal intervention by rejecting not only his advice but also Adam, "hee / Whose image" she is, preferring the "smooth wat'ry image," an analogical relationship gets established between female autoeroticism and the mother-daughter dyad. But—and the difference is of crucial importance—this implicit and mere analogy is based on specular reflection and error alone.

In Milton's recasting of Ovid's tale of Narcissus, then, Eve's illusion is not only permitted but destined to pass away. What this means is that, grounded in illusion, her desire for an other self has from the outset been appropriated by a patriarchal order. The serene confidence with which this appropriation is accomplished can perhaps best be appreciated if, initially, we set this passage in *Paradise Lost* against the *Oresteia*. In "The Dynamics of Misogyny: Myth and Mythmaking in the 'Oresteia,'" Froma Zeitlin argues that the *Oresteia* deploys the myth of matriarchy ideologically, placing it in the service of an attempt to account for and justify the present and ideally permanent patriarchal order of things.[49] It does so by means of what she calls an "Amazon complex," which projects from a woman's (or women's) rejection of subordination the establishment of an order ruled so irrationally and so dangerously by women that it virtually cries out to give way to its opposite, an order ruled by men. Zeitlin's analysis shows the dynamics of this complex at work on a number of dramatic and rhetorical levels. But the dynamics can perhaps be seen most clearly in the progressive devaluation and attenuation of the mother-daughter dyad, potentially the most threatening social unit to an insecure patriarchal order since it contentedly excludes the male. In the *Agamemnon*, Clytemnestra's desire to avenge herself on her daughter Iphigenia's death is progressively conflated with her illegitimate desire for rule, which is in turn made to seem almost indistinguishable from her adulterous sexual desire. The mother-daughter bond is thereby loosened and undone, with the result that in the *Choephoroi* Electra is her mother's antagonist and the relationship of mother and son has assumed center stage. Furthermore, as Zeitlin points out, in the *Choephoroi* Clytemnestra's illicit sexuality is made to express itself as maternal hostility. The process of devaluation and resubjection reaches its culmination in the famous trial scene in the *Eumenides,* where the notoriously male-identified Athena decides with Apollo that paternity is the only unassailable ground of generation and social continuity.

As it gets articulated by the *Oresteia,* the establishment of patriarchal rule occurs through a process that is openly conflictual and agonistic. Slightly closer to home, and in a more muted and playful manner, the conflictual dynamics of the Amazon complex can also be seen at work in Shakespeare's *A Midsummer Night's Dream.* The displaced presence of this complex is announced at the very beginning of the play by Theseus, who boasts his victory over Hippolyta, former Amazon. But that the *agon* is yet to be endured is what the action unfolds. Two speeches that do much to convey the poignancy of the drama's conflictual dynamics are of special relevance to our discussion here. First, there is Titania's speech in 2.1, in which Titania recalls a dreamlike experience of female-only procreation and parenting as a means of defending her present desire to protect from male intrusion the (now surrogate) mother-child bond. The second, also delivered in the midst of open hostility and discord, is Helena's impassioned plea to Hermia, in which she begs her to recall their earlier "union in partition," their "ancient love" (3.2.198–219). Both speeches project into the past a time and place of undisturbed union between women, a union associated in one case with pregnancy, in the other with childhood. Like Eve's speech in book 4 they are delicately sketched and relatively brief retrospective narratives, and like hers they use a lyricism associating itself, through imagery, with pastoral.

But these very similarities help to measure the historical distance between Shakespeare's drama and *Paradise Lost* and the greater security of the patriarchal order that the further development of bourgeois society seems to have established. The presence of the Amazon complex in *A Midsummer Night's Dream* is possibly related to the cultural presence of that problematically gendered monarch, Elizabeth.[50] Yet its complete absence from *Paradise Lost* obviously cannot be accounted for simply by the passing of her reign. In its very choice of subject, Milton's epic seems to testify to the progressive privatization and sentimentalization of the domestic sphere.[51] That this privatization and sentimentalization make possible the construction of a different female subjectivity is nowhere clearer than in Eve's first speech, where the very absence of *agon* can make itself felt only if other texts, other commentaries, are drawn in. *Paradise Lost* is in this sense uncannily like the Priestly account of creation, whose strategic and preemptive assertion of its monotheistic god's supremacy can be grasped only by the process of textual and historical reconstruction. Although in *Paradise Lost* "chaos" is at times a disturbingly real presence,[52] the official creation account is introduced with a statement by the Father to the Son that completely absorbs the "deep" into Milton's monism.

> My overshadowing Spirit and might with thee
> I send along, ride forth, and bid the Deep
> Within appointed bounds be Heav'n and Earth,
> Boundless the Deep, because I am who fill
> Infinitude, nor vacuous the space.
>
> [7.165–69]

Earlier, we saw that Marduk's combat with the watery sea-mother Tiamat can be resuscitated for a reading of the opening verses of Genesis only with the help of scholarship and on the basis of an almost drowned etymological connection. This passage in *Paradise Lost* would seem to hope that the scene of open conflict remain forever beyond recall. So, too, would the moment in Eve's retrospective narration in which the divine voice echoes the words originally dividing the waters from the waters, words that in their derived context separate Eve from the self that is only falsely, illusorily (m)other.

VII

In concluding, I would like to suggest, both tentatively and speculatively, that the absence of anything resembling the operations of an Amazon complex in *Paradise Lost* is related to the presence in Milton's works of what we would now confidently call an Oedipal complex. Quite commonly, when neat symmetries are perceived or constructed between psychoanalytical thought, whether Freudian or Lacanian, and Milton's, they are taken somehow to validate psychoanalytic paradigms or, in the case of Kerrigan's recent study, to validate a psychic structure whose congruent shapes are Freudian psychoanalysis and Miltonic Christianity.[53] I would like to suggest something quite different, however, which is that the exegetical practice informing both the divorce tracts and *Paradise Lost* is part of a network of discursive practices mediating and enabling the emergence of a new economic order. And that it is these practices that become the conditions of possibility for Freud's psychoanalytical discourse. Could this be established persuasively, there would of course be no point in trying to reverse the terms of the relationship by arguing the genesis of Freud's ideas in Milton. But it is significant, nevertheless, that *Paradise Lost* was one of Freud's favorite texts.[54] And that Havelock Ellis could draw attention to the importance of the very passage from *Paradise Lost* we have been examining in his brief history of the development of the psychoanalytic concept "Narcissism," a concept that, as his essay and Freud's both indicate, is associated primarily with femininity or women.[55] In any event, Freud's introductory essay, "On Narcissism," has startlingly close affinities with some of the structures and motivated turns I have been pursuing here. In that essay Freud plots for the first time the divergent and oppositional libidinal choices of the two sexes. Men, he claims, tend toward overvaluation of the loved object, while women tend toward self-love or "narcissism." While not denying the "narcissistic" component in the male's overvaluation of the loved object (often, and of course to his distress, this choice inevitably being the narcissistic woman), Freud quite obviously seems to find in this overvaluation a sign of man's superiority. He also hastens

to add that he has no tendentious desire to depreciate women in char-
acterizing their erotic choices as narcissistic.[56]

As these "observations" develop, they get attached to theories
emphasizing the differences between the lines of development under-
gone by the two sexes. Assuming the Oedipal complex and its desired
resolution as his norm, the asymmetry Freud becomes most interested in is the developing woman's skewed relation to both complex
and resolution. Many years ago Cleanth Brooks mentioned that Eve's
speech in book 4 recalled Freud's observations on the comparative difficulty the female has in the transition to adult heterosexuality.[57] If
we return to Eve's speech, it would indeed seem to represent that difficulty, and with a curiously marked emphasis on the importance of the
transition's success that seems in many ways similar to Freud's. But
it does so in a context in which female desire is so constituted as to
situate the process of transition within competing representational
media, within which is almost a kind of hall of voices and mirrors.[58]

This takes us to the very last feature of Eve's storytelling to be considered here. As has been suggested, Protestant exegetes consider
Adam's declaration in Genesis 2.24, "This is now bone of my bones
and flesh of my flesh," to be part of the first wedding ceremony. A
version of this ceremonial utterance appears in Adam's narrative and
(highly abridged) in Eve's. In Genesis, this declaration follows "and
brought her unto the man," a verse that is translated into action in
both of *Paradise Lost*'s accounts. Calvin, when commenting on this
phrase, views the action from Adam's point of view, as involving the
exchange of a gift. "For seeing Adam tooke not a wife to him selfe
at his owne will: but tooke her whome the Lord offered and ap-
pointed unto him: hereof the holinesse of matrimonie doeth the
better appeare, because we know that God is the authour thereof."[59]
Yet Milton is not alone in seeing this moment from Eve's point of
view as well as from Adam's, for Diodati, commenting on "And
brought her unto him," says, "As a mediator, to cause her voluntarily
to espouse her self to Adam and to confirm and sanctify that conjunction."[60] In *Paradise Lost,* the story Eve tells stresses with remarkable persistence the difficulty and the importance of Eve's "vol-

untarily" espousing herself to Adam. This entire discussion of the relation between *Paradise Lost*'s retrospective creation narratives and the divorce tracts can therefore be put in the following, summary terms. If in book 8's recollected colloquy Adam is revealed articulating the doctrine of marriage, in book 4's recollected self-mirroring Eve is portrayed enacting its discipline. Or, to formulate this somewhat differently, by associating Eve with the vicissitudes of courtship and marriage, and by emphasizing her voluntary submission both to the paternal voice and to her "author" and bridegroom, Adam, *Paradise Lost* can *first* present the practice, for which Adam *then,* at the epic's leisure, supplies the theory. In doing so, *Paradise Lost* manages to establish a paradigm for the heroines of the genre Milton's epic is said to usher in. In the Yahwist's Genesis, Adam may have been formed first, then Eve. But Milton's Eve tells her story first because the domestic sphere with which her subjectivity associates itself will soon be in need of novels whose heroines are represented learning, in struggles whose conclusions are almost always implicit in the way they begin, the value of submitting desire to the paternal law.

NOTES

This essay has benefited from the encouragement and comments offered by Derek Attridge, Eleanor Cook, Margaret Ferguson, Patricia Parker, Karen Widdicombe, and Margaret Williamson.

1. Alice Jardine, *Gynesis: Configurations of Woman and Modernity* (Ithaca: Cornell University Press, 1985).

2. James Joyce, *Ulysses* (Harmondsworth: Penguin Books, 1968), 132, 133.

3. Unless otherwise specified, biblical references are to the King James Bible.

4. Joyce, *Ulysses,* 15.

5. See James B. Pritchard, ed., *Ancient Near Eastern Texts Relating to the Old Testament,* 2d ed. (Princeton: Princeton University Press, 1955), 60–72. Alexander Heidel discusses the parallels in *The Babylonian Genesis: The Story of Creation* (1942; reprint, Chicago: University of Chicago Press, 1951), 82–140.

6. E. A. Speiser, *Genesis. The Anchor Bible* (Garden City, N.Y.: Doubleday, 1964), 3, 8–13. Among the many other twentieth-century editions or commentaries consulted, the following are of most relevance to the discussion here: Robert Davidson, ed.,

Genesis 1-11. The Cambridge Bible Commentary (Cambridge: Cambridge University Press, 1973); Bruce Vawter, *On Genesis: A New Reading* (London: G. Chapman, 1977); and Claus Westermann, *Genesis 1-11: A Commentary,* trans. John J. Scullion, S.J. (London: SPCK, 1984).

7. Umberto Cassuto, *A Commentary on the Book of Genesis,* pt. 1, trans. Israel Abrahams (Jerusalem: Magnes Press, Hebrew University, 1961), 24.

8. Plato, *Timaeus,* 30A, 50D, 52Dff. Frank E. Robbins discusses the importance of Greek philosophy to the commentary tradition in *The Hexaemeral Literature: A Study of the Greek and Latin Commentaries on Genesis* (Chicago: University of Chicago Press, 1912).

9. See, for example, Mary Daly, *Beyond God the Father: Toward a Philosophy of Women's Liberation* (Boston: Beacon, 1973), 8.

10. Nicole Brossard, *L'Amèr: Ou le Chapitre Effrité* (Montreal: Les Editions Quinze, 1977).

11. Judith Plaskow, "Epilogue: The Coming of Lilith," in *Religion and Sexism,* ed. Rosemary Ruether (New York: Touchstone Books, 1974), 341-43; Pamela White Hadas, *In Light of Genesis* (Philadelphia: Jewish Publication Society of America, 1980); Ursula Le Guin, "She Unnames Them," *The New Yorker,* 21 January 1985, 27; Monique Wittig, *Les Guérillères* (Paris: Les Editions de Minuit, 1969); Louky Bersianik, *L'Euguélionne* (Paris: Hachette, 1978).

12. Elizabeth Cady Stanton, *The Woman's Bible,* ed. Dale Spender (1895-98; reprint, Edinburgh: Polygon, 1985). References to this edition will appear parenthetically in the text as *WB*.

13. Phyllis Trible, "Depatriarchalizing in Biblical Interpretation," *Journal of the American Academy of Religion* 16 (1973): 30-48. Subsequent references will appear parenthetically in the text as DBI.

14. This is a point made much more clearly in the later, revised version of this argument in Phyllis Trible, *God and the Rhetoric of Sexuality* (Philadelphia: Fortress Press, 1978), 100-101. Because it has been so influential, I shall continue to make reference to Trible's earlier essay.

15. Samuel Beckett, *Krapp's Last Tape and Embers* (1959; reprint, London: Faber & Faber, 1983), 17, 19-20. In "Textual Overlapping and Dalilah's Harlot-lap," in *Literary Theory/Renaissance Texts,* ed. Patricia Parker and David Quint (Baltimore: Johns Hopkins University Press, 1986), 341-72, I examine a passage in Milton's *Paradise Lost* that has itself been given a misogynistic misreading along these lines. The issues discussed in this essay will be given more extensive and fully documented treatment in a study of Milton, discourse, and gender to be published by Cornell University Press.

16. Trible, *Rhetoric,* 98.

17. For a history of modern critical approaches and a survey of some of the debates, see Brevard S. Childs, *Introduction to the Old Testament as Scripture* (London: SCM Press, 1979), 112-35.

18. Theodor Reik, *The Creation of Woman: A Psychoanalytic Inquiry into the Myth of Eve* (New York: George Braziller, 1960), 128-31.

19. In "Depatriarchalizing," Trible states that in Genesis 1.27 "God creates *'adham* as male and female in one act" (p. 35). The first chapter of *God and the Rhetoric of Sexuality* provides a reading of Genesis 1.26-28 that elaborates this view (pp. 1-30).

20. Robert Alter, *The Art of Biblical Narrative* (London: Allen & Unwin, 1981), 141-46.

21. Childs, *Introduction*, 150.

22. Trible, *Rhetoric*, 141; see also p. 18.

23. Casey Miller and Kate Swift, *Words and Women* (1976; reprint, Harmondsworth: Penguin Books, 1979), 34. Their exposition and endorsement is cited approvingly by several writers. See, for example, Adrienne Munich, "Notorious Signs, Feminist Criticism and Literary Tradition," in *Making a Difference: Feminist Literary Criticism,* ed. Gayle Greene and Coppélia Kahn (London: Methuen, 1985), 242.

24. Mieke Bal, "Sexuality, Sin, and Sorrow: The Emergence of the Female Character (A Reading of Genesis 1-3)," *Poetics Today* 6 (1985): 21-42. Subsequent references will appear parenthetically in the text as *SSS*.

25. Miller and Swift, *Words and Women*, 36.

26. Phyllis A. Bird, "'Male and Female He Created Them': Gen 1:27b in the Context of the Priestly Account of Creation," *Harvard Theological Review* 74 (1981): 129-59. Though an example of what she calls "text-critical" or "historical" exegesis, as opposed to "theological construction," Bird's essay is self-admittedly an intervention into the debate sparked in recent years by the feminist critique—including Trible's—of the theological and exegetical traditions. Subsequent references will appear parenthetically in the text as MF.

27. Philo, "On the Account of the World's Creation Given by Moses," secs. 46 and 53, in *Philo*, trans. F. H. Colson and G. H. Whitaker, Loeb Classical Library (London: Heineman, 1929), 107, 119-21. See also Richard A. Baer, Jr., *Philo's Use of the Categories Male and Female* (Leiden: E. J. Brill, 1970).

28. Augustin, *De Genesi ad Litteram*, trans. and ed. P. Agaësse and A. Solignac, in *Oeuvres de Saint Augustin* (Paris: Desclée De Brouwer, 1972), 6.3.4.446-48 and 6.5.7-9.452-56. For a discussion of these issues, see Kari Elizabeth Børreson, *Subordination et équivalence: Nature et rôle de la femme d'après Augustin et Thomas d'Aquin* (Oslo: Universitetslaget, 1968), 25-51.

29. John Milton, *Tetrachordon*, ed. Arnold Williams, in vol. 2 of *Complete Prose Works of John Milton*, ed. Ernest Sirluck (New Haven: Yale University Press, 1959), 594. Subsequent references to this edition of *Tetrachordon* will appear parenthetically in the text as *T*. See David Paraeus, *In Genesin Mosis Commentarius* (Frankfurt, 1609), 267, 293. This would seem to be related to the methods of embellishing discussed by Erasmus under "On Copia of Thought," *On Copia of Words and Things,* trans. Donald B. King and H. David Rex (Milwaukee: Marquette University Press, 1963), 43-55.

30. John Calvin, *A Commentarie of John Calvine, upon the first booke of Moses called Genesis,* trans. Thomas Tymme (London, 1578), 47.

31. Margo Todd argues for the importance of relating Protestant to humanist views in "Humanists, Puritans and the Spiritualized Household," *Church History* 49 (1980): 18–34. For a discussion of the distinctively Puritan development of this ideology, see William Haller and Malleville Haller, "The Puritan Art of Love," *Huntingdon Library Quarterly* 5 (1942): 235–72; William Haller, "Hail Wedded Love," *ELH* 13 (1946): 79–97. Two rather more recent studies concerned to situate Milton's views on marriage are John Halkett, *Milton and the Idea of Matrimony: A Study of the Divorce Tracts and "Paradise Lost"* (New Haven: Yale University Press, 1970), and James T. Johnson, *A Society Ordained by God: English Puritan Marriage Doctrine in the First Half of the Seventeenth Century* (Nashville: Abingdon Press, 1970).

32. Calvin, *Commentarie,* 74. Latin cited from *Mosis Libri V, cum Johannis Calvini Commentariis* (Genevae, 1563), 19.

33. Quotations from Milton's poetry are from John Milton, *Complete Poems and Major Prose,* ed. Merritt Y. Hughes (New York: Odyssey Press, 1957).

34. The political, legal, and social contexts for Milton's tracts are discussed by Chilton L. Powell, *English Domestic Relations, 1487–1653* (New York: Columbia University Press, 1971), 61–100; and by Ernest Sirluck, ed., *Complete Prose Works of John Milton,* 2:137–158. Milton's rhetorical strategies are examined by Keith W. Stavely, *The Politics of Milton's Prose Style* (New Haven: Yale University Press, 1975), 54–72, and by John M. Perlette, "Milton, Ascham, and the Rhetoric of the Divorce Controversy," *Milton Studies* 10 (1977): 195–215.

35. Emphasis mine. For a discussion of the title, see the preface by Arnold Williams, *Tetrachordon,* 571.

36. Calvin, *Commentarie,* 46.

37. John Milton, *The Doctrine and Discipline of Divorce,* ed. Lowell W. Coolidge, *Complete Prose Works of John Milton,* 2:240. Further references in the text will appear as *DDD.*

38. This is the view established by Arthur E. Barker in "Christian Liberty in Milton's Divorce Pamphlets," *MLR* 35 (1940): 153–61, and *Milton and the Puritan Dilemma, 1641–1660,* Department of English Studies and Texts, no. 1 (Toronto: University of Toronto Press, 1942), 63–74.

39. On this, see Gordon J. Schochet, *Patriarchalism in Political Thought: The Authoritarian Family and Political Attitudes Especially in Seventeenth Century England* (Oxford: Blackwell, 1975); Lawrence Stone, *The Family, Sex and Marriage in England 1500–1800* (London: Weidenfeld & Nicolson, 1977), 123–218; Ruth Perry, *Women, Letters, and the Novel* (New York: AMS Press, 1980), 27–62; and Jonathan Goldberg, *James I and the Politics of Literature* (Baltimore: Johns Hopkins University Press, 1983), 85–112.

40. R. Kenneth Kirby discusses the more liberal view Milton here opposes in "Milton's Biblical Hermeneutics in 'The Doctrine and Discipline of Divorce,'" *Milton Quarterly* 18 (1984): 117–24.

41. Calvin, *Commentarie*, 72; *Mosis Libri V*, 18.

42. Johnson discusses Milton's use of Ramist logic in Appendix B of *Society Ordained*, 199–208. Although I cannot develop this here, Milton manages to get Ramist method to join causes with his privileging of "J" over "P."

43. J. M. Evans, *"Paradise Lost" and the Genesis Tradition* (Oxford: Oxford University Press, 1968), 256.

44. If commented upon at all, the emphasis on procreation here is entirely naturalized so that it becomes an expression of Raphael's character or situation. Aers annotates these lines by suggesting that Raphael is revealing a typically "distorted view of sexuality" (*John Milton, "Paradise Lost": Books VII–VIII*, ed. David Aers and Mary Ann Radzinowicz, in *The Cambridge Milton for Schools and Colleges*, ed. J. B. Broadbent [Cambridge: Cambridge University Press, 1974], 99). Halkett points out that Raphael later (8.229–46) reveals that he was not present the day of Eve's creation (*Matrimony*, 111). But since both are supposed to take place on the same "Day," Raphael's absence obviously cannot explain the different treatment given Adam's creation and Eve's in his account. I would argue that such character- and situation-related effects are part and parcel of the ideologically motivated narrative distributions examined here.

45. Christine Froula, "When Eve Reads Milton: Undoing the Canonical Economy," *Critical Inquiry* 10 (1983): 321–47.

46. John Milton, *Colasterion*, ed. Lowell W. Coolidge, *Complete Prose Works of John Milton*, 2:739–40.

47. See Louise Vinge, *The Narcissus Theme in Western European Literature up to the Early Nineteenth Century* (Lund: Gleerups, 1967), 35–40, 224–26.

48. Henry Reynolds attributes this "Divine sense" of the Narcissus tales to *"Iamblicus"* and his "fellow-Cabalists" (*Mythomystes. To Which is annexed the Tale of Narcissus briefly mythologized* [1632; reprint, Menston, Yorks.: Scolar, 1972], 110).

49. Froma Zeitlin, "The Dynamics of Misogyny: Myth and Mythmaking in the 'Oresteia,'" *Arethusa* 11 (1978): 149–84.

50. For a reading that explores this possibility, see Louis Adrian Montrose, "'Shaping Fantasies': Figurations of Gender and Power in Elizabethan Culture," *Representations* 1 (1983): 61–93; in this rich, interdisciplinary study, Montrose argues that *A Midsummer Night's Dream* "naturalizes Amazonomachy in the vicissitudes of courtship" (68).

51. On the emergence of bourgeois interiority in the seventeenth century, see Francis Barker's suggestive and synthetic study, *The Tremulous Private Body: Essays on Subjection* (London: Methuen, 1984). For a sharp analysis of the ways in which, among the upper classes, the development of an affective domestic sphere served to reinforce patriarchalism, making possible, among other things, the deeply sexist political theories of Rousseau, Kant, and Hegel, see Susan Moller Okin, "Women and the Making of the Sentimental Family," *Philosophy and Public Affairs* 11 (1981): 65–88.

52. For a discussion of this effect, together with its unacceptability on the level of doctrinal statement, see Regina Schwarz, "Milton's Hostile Chaos: 'And the Sea was no More'" *ELH* 52 (1985): 337–74.

53. William Kerrigan, *The Sacred Complex: On the Psychogenesis of "Paradise Lost"* (Cambridge, Mass.: Harvard University Press, 1983). For a study that attempts a similar ideological and historical analysis of psychoanalytic discourse in relation to Milton, specifically with reference to "vocation," see John Guillory, "The Father's House: *Samson Agonistes* in Its Historical Moment," in *Re-Membering Milton*, ed. Margaret Ferguson and Mary Nyquist (forthcoming).

54. Ernest Jones, *Sigmund Freud: Life and Work* (London: Hogarth Press, 1957), 3:453.

55. Ellis states that Milton "represented Narcissus in that feminine shape to which in modern times his attitude has always seemed best fitted, and showed the first Mother of Mankind in the typical Narcissistic attitude of adolescence before she had met Adam" (*Studies in the Psychology of Sex* [Philadelphia: F. A. Davis, 1928], 7:349).

56. Sigmund Freud, "On Narcissism: An Introduction," *The Pelican Freud Library*, trans. James Strachey and ed. Angela Richards (Harmondsworth: Penguin Books, 1984), 11:82–83.

57. Cleanth Brooks says that to the student of Freud, Eve's psychology may seem "preternaturally" convincing ("Eve's Awakening," in *Essays in Honor of Walter Clyde Curry* [Nashville: Vanderbilt University Press, 1954], 285). He also remarks that Eve is "charmingly feminine withal" (283).

58. For an analysis of why, within the Freudian economy, this should be so, see Luce Irigaray, *Speculum de l'autre femme* (Paris: Les Editions de Minuit, 1974), 36–51.

59. Calvin, *Commentarie*, 76–77.

60. Annotation on Genesis 2.22 in John Diodati, *Pious and Learned Annotations upon the Holy Bible*, trans. [R.G.], 3d ed. (London, 1651).

The English Institute, 1985

The Program

Thursday, August 28, through Sunday, September 1, 1985

I. Engendering Victorian Poetics
   Directed by Carol Christ, University of California, Berkeley
   Thurs. 2 P.M.   "The Difference—made me bold": The Engendering of
                       Genre in Rossetti and Dickinson
                       Sandra M. Gilbert, Princeton University
   Fri. 9:30 A.M.   The Painted Shell: Idyllic Poetics in Tennyson's "The
                       Gardener's Daughter"
                       Herbert F. Tucker, Jr., University of Michigan
   Fri. 11 A.M.   The Victorian Poet and the Feminine Subject
                       Carol T. Christ, University of California, Berkeley

II. Dimensions of Afro-American Modernism: The Harlem Renaissance Before
    and After
    Directed by Houston A. Baker, Jr., University of Pennsylvania
    Thurs. 3:30 P.M.   The Mastery of Form/The De-formation of Mastery:
                       Reflections on Afro-American Modernism
                       Houston A. Baker, Jr., University of Pennsylvania
    Fri. 2 P.M.   Langston Hughes and Approaches to Modernism in the
                       Harlem Renaissance
                       Arnold Rampersad, Rutgers University
    Fri. 3:30 P.M.   "Ain't you never heard Malindy": Four Representative
                       Afro-American Modernists
                       Eleanor Traylor, Montgomery Community College

III. New Perspectives on Shakespeare
     Directed by Marjorie Garber, Harvard University
     Sat. 9:30 A.M.   Fantasies of Maternal Power in Shakespeare
                       Janet Adelman, University of California, Berkeley
     Sat. 11 A.M.   Brothers and Others, or the Art of Alienation
                       Steven Mullaney, Massachusetts Institute of Technology
     Sun. 9:30 A.M.   Shakespeare and the Cannibals
                       Stephen Orgel, The Johns Hopkins University
     Sun. 11 A.M.   Shakespeare's Ghost Writers
                       Marjorie Garber, Harvard University

IV. The Bible: Text and Ideology
   Directed by Herbert Schneidau, University of Arizona
      Sat. 2 P.M.   Social Revolution and Literary Genres
                           Norman K. Gottwald, New York Theological Seminary
      Sat. 3:30 P.M.   Gynesis and the Genesis Eve
                           Mary Nyquist, New College, University of Toronto
      Sun. 2 P.M.   The Experience behind the Text
                           George E. Mendenhall, University of Michigan
      Sun. 3:30 P.M.   Social History and Scriptural Force
                           Steven Knapp, University of California, Berkeley

Sponsoring Institutions

Columbia University, Princeton University, Yale University, University of Rochester, Claremont Graduate School, Rutgers University, Michigan State University, Northwestern University, Boston University, University of California, Berkeley, University of Connecticut, Harvard University, University of Pennsylvania, University of Virginia, Amherst College, Brandeis University, Cornell University, Dartmouth College, New York University, Smith College, The Johns Hopkins University, Washington University, State University of New York at Albany, Temple University, University of Alabama, Birmingham, University of California, San Diego, Boston College, Brigham Young University, University of California, Los Angeles, Massachusetts Institute of Technology, Wellesley College, Stanford University, Indiana University, Bloomington, Tufts University, University of Colorado, Wesleyan University, Fordham University, State University of New York at Buffalo, University of California, Irvine, University of Maryland, University of Miami, Emory University, University of Illinois at Chicago, University of California, Riverside, University of Tulsa, University of Southern California, Ohio State University, University of Massachusetts, Amherst, the New York Public Library, University of Minnesota, University of Arizona

Registrants, 1985

Janet Adelman, University of California, Berkeley; Maria Allentuck, City University of New York and Wolfson College, Oxford University; Jonathan Arac, University of Illinois at Chicago; N. S. Asbrige, Central Connecticut State University

Charlotte Pierce Baker, Germantown Friends School; Houston A. Baker, Jr., University of Pennsylvania; J. Robert Barth, S.J., University of Missouri, Columbia; James F. Beaton, Middlesex School; Jerome Beaty, Emory University; J. Scott Bentley, University of Oregon; Nancy M. Bentley, La Jolla School; Jerry M. Bernhard, Emmanuel College; Susan Bernstein, Brandeis University; Rufus Blanshard, University of Connecticut; Kenneth Bleeth, Connecticut College; Morton W. Bloomfield, Harvard University; Frank Brady, Graduate School of the City University of New York; Peter Brand, Buffalo and Erie County Public Library; Phyllis N. Braxton, Howard University; Susan H. Brisman, Vassar College; Fahamisha Patricia Brown, Boston College; Jane

Buchanan, Bentley College; John Burt, Brandeis University; Ronald Bush, California Institute of Technology

Janet B. Campbell, Tufts University; Mary Wilson Carpenter, Harvard University; Stanley Cavell, Harvard University; Carol Christ, University of California, Berkeley; Gail Coffler, Suffolk University; Ralph Cohen, University of Virginia; Robert A. Coles, Fordham University; Richard Conner, Northeastern University; Richard Corum, Dartmouth College; Michael Cowan, University of California, Santa Cruz; A. Dwight Culler, Yale University; Jonathan Culler, Cornell University

Robert Adams Day, City University of New York; Richard Dellamora, Trent University; Julia M. DiStefano, New Hampshire College; Heather Dubrow, Carleton College

Lee Edelman, Tufts University; Julie Ellison, University of Michigan; David Erdman, State University of New York at Stony Brook and New York Public Library; Virginia Erdman; Peter Erickson; Elizabeth Ermarth, University of Maryland, Baltimore County

Margaret Ferguson, Yale University; Mary Anne Ferguson, University of Massachusetts, Boston; William C. Fischer, State University of New York at Buffalo; Philip Fisher, Brandeis University; Michael Fried, The Johns Hopkins University; Bettina Friedl, University of Stuttgart; Herwig Friedl, University of Heidelberg; Margaretta Fulton, Harvard University Press

Marjorie Garber, Harvard University; Burdett Gardner; Blanche Gelfant, Dartmouth College; William P. Germano, Columbia University Press; Sandra Gilbert, Princeton University; Albert Gilman, Boston University; Irene C. Goldman, Boston University; Norman K. Gottwald, New York Theological Seminary; Edward Graham, State University of New York, Maritime College; Linda Gregerson, Boston University

G. G. Harpham, Brandeis University; Joseph Harris, Harvard University; Pauline Harrison, Southwestern College; Geoffrey Hartman, Yale University; Joan E. Hartman, College of Staten Island of the City University of New York; Standish Henning, University of Wisconsin; Neil Hertz, The Johns Hopkins University; Baruch Hockman, Hebrew University; Sally Hoffheimer, University of Cincinnati; Susan Horton, University of Massachusetts, Boston; Sue E. Houchins, Scripps College; Peter Hughes, University of Zürich

Mary Jacobus, Cornell University; Barbara Johnson, Harvard University; Richard Johnson, Mount Holyoke College; Gerhard Joseph, City University of New York, Lehman College and Graduate Center; Terri Brint Joseph, Chapman College

André Kaenel, University of Geneva; Claire Kahane, State University of New York at Buffalo; Coppélia Kahn, Wesleyan University; Jonathan Z. Kamholtz, University of Cincinnati; Judith A. Kates, Harvard University; Dorothy Kaufman, Clark University; Robert Keefe, University of Massachusetts, Amherst; Jim Keil, Brandeis University; Wyn Kelly; Arthur F. Kinney, University of Massachusetts, Amherst; Steven Knapp, University of California, Berkeley; Beth Kowaleski-Wallace, Tufts University

G. P. Lair, Delbarton School; Alan Levitan, Brandeis University; Barbara K. Lewalski, Harvard University; Lawrence Lipking, Northwestern University; Joseph Litwak, Bowdoin College; Joseph P. Lovering, Canisius College; Peter Lundman, State University of New York at Stony Brook

Heather McClave, Radcliffe College; Anita D. McClellan, Twayne Publishers, G. K. Hall & Co.; James McDonnell, Carleton College; Deborah McDowell, Colby College; Darrel Mansell, Dartmouth College; Donald C. Mell, University of Delaware; George E. Mendenhall, University of Michigan; Ronald C. Meyers, East Stroudsburg University; Steven Mullaney, Massachusetts Institute of Technology; Adrienne Munich, State University of New York at Stony Brook

John Nesselhop, Wells College; Ruth Nevo, Hebrew University; Eric Nicholson, Yale University; Mary Nyquist, New College, University of Toronto

Margaret O'Brien, Trinity College, Dublin; Michael J. K. O'Loughlin, State University of New York, College at Purchase; Stephen Orgel, Stanford University; Charles A. Owen, Jr., University of Connecticut

Barbara Packer, University of California, Los Angeles; Stanley R. Palumbo, George Washington University; Patricia Parker, University of Toronto; Reeve Parker, Cornell University; Annabel Patterson, University of Maryland; Benn L. Petty, Hong Kong Baptist College; Leslie Phillips, Lexington High School; A. W. Phinney, Harvard University; Marie Plasse, Boston University; David Porter, University of Massachusetts, Amherst; Janice Price, Methuen; John Price, Middlesex School; Audrey Ann Procaccini, Boston College; David Quint, Princeton University

Arnold Rampersad, Rutgers University; Gail T. Reimer, Wellesley College; Albert J. Rivero, Marquette University; Bruce Robbins, Rutgers University; Ruth Rosenberg, Kingsborough College of the City University of New York

Florence Sandler, University of Puget Sound; Elaine Scarry, University of Pennsylvania; Herbert Schneidau, University of Arizona; Sue Weaver Schopf, Harvard University; Regina Schwartz, University of Colorado; Eve Kosofsky Sedgwick, Amherst College; Marvel Shmiefsky, State University of New York at Buffalo; Elaine Showalter,

Princeton University; Maeera Schreiber, Brandeis University; William Sievert, Pace University; Bennet Simon, Harvard Medical School; Susan Sutton Smith, State University of New York, College at Oneonta; Janice Sokoloff, Temple University; Ian Sowton, York University; Sandra Spielvogel, Paramus Catholic Girls High School; Susan Staves, Brandeis University; Holly Stevens; Margaret Storch, Bentley College; Mihoko Suzuki, University of Miami

Junko Tajima, University of the Sacred Heart; Mihoko Takeda, Nagoya Junior College; Yuichi Takeda, Aichi Gakuin University; John S. Tanner, Brigham Young University; Claudia Tate, Howard University; Irene Taylor, Massachusetts Institute of Technology; Nathaniel Teich, University of Oregon; Deborah A. Thomas, Villanova University; John Tobin, University of Massachusetts, Boston; Claudine Torchin, Brandeis University; Eleanor Traylor, Montgomery Community College; Mindele Anne Treib, Cambridge University; Herbert F. Tucker, University of Michigan; Lewis A. Turlish, Bates College

Helen Vendler, Boston University and Harvard University

Melissa Walker, Mercer University; James D. Wallace, Boston College; Alexander Welsh, University of California, Los Angeles; Joseph Westlund, Northeastern University; Carolyn Williams, Boston University; Joshua Wilner, City College of the City University of New York; Judith Wilt, Boston College; Susanne Wofford, Yale University

Ruth Bernard Yeazell, University of California, Los Angeles; Bruce W. Young, Brigham Young University